The Natural World of the California Indians

California Natural History Guides: 46

The Natural World of the California Indians

**Robert F. Heizer
and
Albert B. Elsasser**

UNIVERSITY OF CALIFORNIA PRESS
Berkeley Los Angeles London

California Natural History Guides
Arthur C. Smith, General Editor

Advisory Editorial Committee:
Raymond F. Dasmann
Mary Lee Jefferds
A. Starker Leopold
Robert Ornduff
Robert C. Stebbins

University of California Press
Berkeley and Los Angeles, California
University of California Press, Ltd.
London, England

© 1980, by The Regents of the University of California

Library of Congress Cataloging in Publication Data

Heizer, Robert Fleming, 1915—
  The natural world of the California Indians.

  (California natural history guides; 46)
  Includes bibliographical references and index.
  1. Indians of North America—California.
I. Elsasser, Albert B., joint author. II. Title.
III. Series.
E78.C15H433   979.4'004'97   79-65092
ISBN 0-520-03895-9
ISBN 0-520-03896-7 pbk.
1 2 3 4 5 6 7 8 9

CONTENTS

1. TRIBES, LANGUAGES, AND TERRITORIES

No one knows when humans first entered what is now North America. Archaeologists and geologists believe that from about 11,500 to 12,000 years ago man could cross from northeast Asia to northwest America on dry land, and that an ice-free corridor was open to the southeast, along which humans could cross Canada and enter the ice-free region of North America, which lay at about the present border between the United States and Canada.

As the new migrants from Asia moved southeast into the North American continent they found it easy to make a living by hunting. Animals of numerous kinds were abundant and unafraid of man, who was a new kind of predator. Still living on the continent were remnants of the large Pleistocene animals (megafauna), such as the elephant, the mastodon, and the giant bison, which the humans also hunted. The humans must have advanced and dispersed fairly rapidly, for by 10,000 years ago they had explored North America and South America as far south as Tierra del Fuego.

For California, the oldest definite evidence of man dates from 9000 to 10,000 years ago, despite some claims of greater age. By that time the North American continent must have been reasonably well explored and perhaps large parts of it settled.

As people gradually filled the continent, they divided and separated into groups that chose different areas to settle and adjusted their modes of living to accord with the plants, animals, and climates particular to those areas. The California of today represented the westernmost limit of settlement, and judging from the number of languages and tribes present when the whites first appeared in the sixteenth century, a dense network of tribes and tribelets speaking a wide variety of tongues were in full occupation of the entire area of the state.

The various environments (valley, foothill, high mountains, coast, and desert) each produced particular kinds of food. The Indian inhabitants tended to concentrate their food-securing energies on one or two fairly stable or assured food sources, such as salmon in northwestern California, acorns in the central part of the state, and wild seed crops and small game in the southern region. Despite some concentration on highly productive food resources, a host of supplementary foods (fish, large and small mammals, insects, seeds, roots, and so on) were exploited, not only to round out the diet but also to introduce some variation in the fare.

Of the great variety of peoples (over a hundred main tribal or subtribal groups) and their ways of dealing with their natural environment, almost nothing now remains. However, through the work of ethnologists who interviewed Indians and published the details of their cultures, we possess a relatively full and accurate understanding of these vanished cultures and the people who developed them.

The native peoples of California have been more intensively studied than those of any area of similar extent in the world. There are a number of reasons. The Spanish-Mexican occupation (1769-1846) of the state was limited to the coast south of San Francisco. The impact of the Gold Rush and the following settlement caused severe reduction in Indian numbers, but by the 1870s, when systematic examination of the Indian languages and cultures began, there were still many survivors who had reached adulthood before they saw their first white man. In 1900, some fifty years after the Gold Rush, many Indians were living on reservations in Southern California, and there were pockets of survivors scattered throughout the state, many of them single families or even single individuals, living in out-of-the-way spots where they would not be noticed. In addition, substantial numbers of the Pomo, Miwok, Maidu, Yurok, and Hupa tribes had weathered the storm.

From these remnants, ranging from single last survivors to substantial tribal groups and numbering altogether not over 20,000, a small and devoted band of ethnological researchers derived the knowledge we now have of the civilization that had occupied California for the preceding 10,000 years. These researchers were historians in the fullest sense of the word because they salvaged information about the people who lived in California for perhaps 200 times as long as the area has been under American statehood. Anthropology, the study of man, and its special branch, ethnology, the study of ethnic groups, had developed into sciences by the year 1900, so that trained researchers could study the culture of the California Indians with an understanding that had not been possible for the eastern Indians.

Through the energy and leadership of one anthropologist, Alfred L. Kroeber, who was associated with the University of California from 1901 to 1960, a huge accumulation of descriptions of native Californian cultures was published and provides a testimonial record of scores of now-vanished native societies.

Ethnological research completed up to 1923 made it possible to draw a map showing the names and territorial boundaries of all the California tribes. The tribal map (fig. 1) that appears here is a simplified version of the one drawn by Kroeber at that time. By the word "tribe" we mean a group of people that has a name, speaks one language (and dialects of it), and occupies a definite territory. Large tribes holding extensive areas and feeling a political unity were rare in California. The Yokuts of the San Joaquin Valley and the Yuman tribes of the Colorado River fell within this definition. Elsewhere in the state the so-called tribelet organization prevailed. A tribelet is one of a series of small groups that shared a language with their neighbors, but each had its own local name and territory (fig. 2). Tribelets contained from 100 to 500 persons and had from a few to a score of villages, one of which (usually the largest) was the tribelet capital because it was where the chief resided. Chiefs

FIGURE 1 (left) The topography of California. (above) Tribes of California drawn by A. L. Kroeber. (From R. F. Heizer, *Languages, Territories, and Names of California Indian Tribes*, 1966)

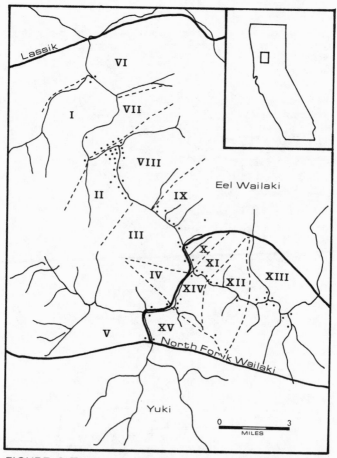

FIGURE 2 Two examples of tribelet territories: The Eel Wailaki and the North Fork Wailaki of Humboldt County. Villages are shown by dots, and tribelets by Roman numbers. Note how villages were sited along streams. The back country was used for hunting and gathering.

in California had little formal power, but were wise and experienced men whose advice was listened to, especially when it was supported by a majority of the old men, who constituted an informal council group. Chieftainship was customarily a hereditary position, with a chief's son usually succeeding him.

In this book we shall speak of the Indians and their cultures in the past tense. For the most part we shall describe the people, how they lived, and what they manufactured, and in some cases what they thought, before the whites destroyed the traditional aboriginal way of life. The old tribes are gone, but some of their descendants still live, preserve the tribal name, and often regulate their affairs through a tribal council on a reservation. Many other Native Americans than those of California origin now live in the state—perhaps 40,000—but of these we shall say little. Our main concern here is with the California Indians as they were, when they were the only human inhabitants within the present borders of the state.

Physically, the Indians of California were much like other American Indians. They varied in stature and included tribes that were among the tallest on the continent (the Mohave, averaging 67.7 inches or 171 cm.) and the shortest (the Yuki, averaging 61.8 inches or 157 cm.). They also varied in headform, noseform and faceform (the proportion of length to breadth). Three major physical types are recognized: (1) Yuki (short statured, low-faced, narrow-headed, and broad-nosed); (2) Western Mono (medium-statured, high-faced, narrow-headed, and medium-nosed); and (3) Californian (high-faced and broad-headed, with variable stature and noseform).

TRIBAL TERRITORIES

In California today prominent features of the terrain, such as rivers or lesser streams, tend to be boundary markers. The Indians had another way of defining borders: they used the drainages of streams, rather than the streams themselves. Watershed ridges, therefore, were the usual boundary lines, and ordinarily both banks of a watercourse belonged to the same people. A quotation from Kroeber illustrates this:

As seen on the map the distribution of the Yuki seems irregular. This is not because their location ran counter to natural topography but because it followed it. Their country lies wholly in the Coast Range mountains, which in this region are not, on the whole, very high, but are much broken. They contain some valleys but the surface of the land is endlessly rugged. The Yuki habitat is, however, not defined, except incidentally, by limiting mountains and ranges, but is given in block by the drainage of such-and-such streams. The native did not think, like a modern civilized man, of his people owning an area circumscribed by a definite line. This would have been viewing the land through a map, whether drawn or mental; and such an attitude was foreign to his habit.

Despite Kroeber's statement that the Indians did not view the land through a map, some Native Californians were able to visualize territory in terms of a map. For example, in 1850 J. Goldsborough Bruff, an Easterner on his way to the newly discovered gold region, described one of these native maps:

The old savage then took a pair of macheres [large flat leathers to throw over the saddle] and sprinkled sand over them, drew a model map of the country there, and beyond it, some distance. He heaped up sand to form buttes and ranges of mountains, and with a straw drew streams, lakes, and trails; then adjusted it to correspond with the cardinal points, and explained it. He pointed to the sun and by signs made them understand the number of days travel from one point to another.

Another such map was described in 1849 by a gold seeker at Lassen's Meadows:

While at the Meadows I met a friendly and intelligent Indian who made for me a map in the sand, a topographical map of the route over the Sierra Nevadas. The sand was piled up to indicate mountains and with his fingers he creased the heap to show the canyons and water courses. To indicate wood and timber he stuck in springs of sage, and spears of grass where grass was to be found, and made signs to inform us where the Indians were friendly or dangerous. It was really an ingenious affair and he was well acquainted with the country.

Such simple "sand maps" were frequently observed by early white travelers who were crossing territory unknown to them and were asking Indians for directions. It is probably no accident that these records were made in the desert areas where Indians moved about a great deal, sometimes over long distances, and were well acquainted with a large terrain. Among the more settled tribes of California, who traveled only within their own restricted territory, such

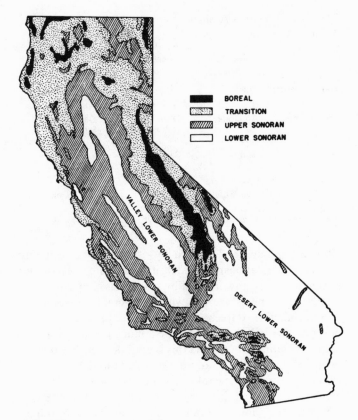

BOREAL
TRANSITION
UPPER SONORAN
LOWER SONORAN

VALLEY LOWER SONORAN

DESERT LOWER SONORAN

FIGURE 3 Life zones of California.

maps would have been unnecessary. In short, the way of life
in different environments led to different concepts and
practices.

California Indians had a strong tendency to stake out
their tribal territory so as to cover several life zones (fig. 3).
Life zones are areas characterized by a combination of
elevation, rainfall, climate, and certain plants and animals.
(In recent years biologists have tended to give the life zone
concept less importance than it had earlier because they
have learned that more than one single environmental
factor—temperature—is reflected in life zone demarcations.

TABLE 1. Resources Available to the Interior Miwok in Three Different Life Zones

Item	Lower Sonoran (valley)	Upper Sonoran (foothill)	Transition (mountain)
House coverings	Tule	Digger Pine bark	Yellow Pine bark
Pine nuts		Digger Pine	Sugar Pine
Food animals	Antelope Elk Rabbit	Deer Rabbit	Deer Squirrel
Fish	Salmon	Salmon	Trout
Birds	Ducks Geese	Valley Quail	Mountain Quail Pigeons
Acorns	Valley Oak	Blue Oak Live Oak	Black Oak
Vegetal foods	Grass seeds	Buckeye	Bulbs

"Biotic communities," defined by other factors, including soil moisture, atmospheric density, altitude, and species competition, are now favored by naturalists. Life zones and biotic communities are not wholly different, however.)

By being able to freely hunt and gather in more than one life zone, the Indians could secure a much greater variety of plant and animal foods, and this is doubtless the reason why many of the tribes arranged their territorial domains to include portions of several zones. For example, the Interior Miwok, who lived in the lower portions of the Sierra Nevada, were able to draw upon a variety of resources available in several life zones (see table 1 and fig. 4).

LANGUAGE FAMILIES IN CALIFORNIA

The most effective way to classify California tribes is by their language family, or stock. These families can be compared to the Indo-European language family, in which English and German are closely related, but to which also belong the Latin or Romance tongues, such as French, Spanish, Rumanian, and Italian. In North America there were a number of language stocks whose speakers were widely, often discontinuously, distributed. Many, but not all, had representatives in California. The California lin-

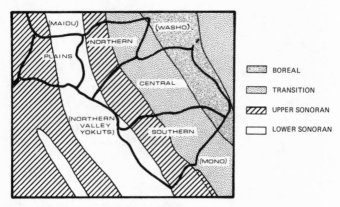

FIGURE 4 Interior Miwok dialects and life zones. Neighboring tribes are shown in parentheses.

guistic families were the Algonkian, the Athabascan, the Penutian, the Hokan, the Uto-Aztekan, and the Yukian. The tribes belonging to these language stocks are given below and shown in fig. 5.

Algonkian Tribes

The Yurok tribe (see fig. 1) occupied about fifty small villages along the lower course of the Klamath River and the seacoast from Little River and Trinidad Bay in the south to some miles above the mouth of the Klamath River. Their total population was probably about 3100. In terms of present-day political divisions, the Yurok ranged over northern Humboldt and southern Del Norte counties.

The Wiyot were a coastal tribe, southern neighbors of the Yurok, and were the second of the two Algonkian-speaking peoples of California. Their territory, measuring a mere 35 by 15 miles, centered at Humboldt Bay where the modern city of Eureka now stands. Their village sites were mainly located on freshwater streams near tidewater. The name Wiyot is a native one, referring to the southern portion of their territory along the lower course of the Eel River. Their former population is estimated at 3300.

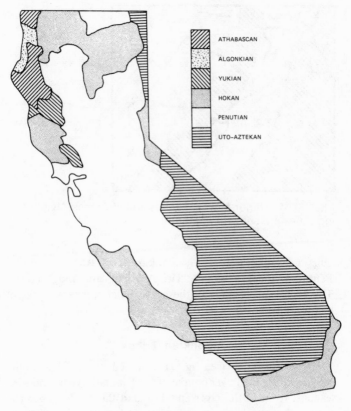

ATHABASCAN

ALGONKIAN

YUKIAN

HOKAN

PENUTIAN

UTO-AZTEKAN

FIGURE 5 Language families of native California.

Athabascan Tribes

The Tolowa were the northwesternmost people of California. Their territory comprised the northern half of Del Norte County and extended somewhat further along the lower Oregon coast. Their main cultural connections seem to have been with the Yurok, their southern neighbors. Their population probably did not exceed 2500 persons.

The Hupa group consisted of three tribes, the Hupa,

Whilkut, and Chilula, who formed a trio of adjoining and linguistically similar peoples. Of the three, the Hupa were the most important and populous (2000 persons). Their territory was the lower Trinity River, and their main settlements lay nested within Hoopa Valley. In most respects but speech the Hupa and the Yurok were culturally similar. The Chilula (not shown on map) held lower Redwood Creek but not its mouth; they were a small nation of 800 people occupying eighteen known villages. The Whilkut held upper Redwood Creek and the lower Mad River except its mouth. Little is known about them, since they passed from sight as a nation in the struggles against white encroachment beginning in the 1850s. Kroeber estimated their numbers at about 500.

The southern Athabascan tribes were the Mattole, Nongatl, Sinkyone, Lassik, Wailaki, and Kato. The Mattole, who held Cape Mendocino and the drainages of the Bear and Mattole rivers of southern Humboldt County, were never numerous or powerful. Their language was one of the most distinctive dialects of Athabascan. The Nongatl, their neighbors, were the northernmost members of five tribes whose closely related languages formed a linguistic subunit. These tribes are now virtually all gone, small groups who failed to survive the impact of the whites. The Sinkyone held the south fork of the Eel River and, in their intermediate position between the Klamath River and Central California tribes, shared in the distinctive cultures of both. The Lassik and Wailaki of the upper Eel River may have numbered about 1400 and 2800, respectively, in pre-Caucasian times. The Kato, southernmost of the Athabascan group, lived on the upper courses of the south fork of the Eel River and represented a salient driven deep into the Yuki territory that surrounded them on three sides. Their villages, of which about fifty are known, lay mainly in the small, open Coast Range valleys where now are situated the towns of Branscomb and Laytonville of northern Mendocino County. Total population of the six tribes is calculated to have been about 14,000.

Penutian Tribes

The Penutian linguistic stock, which included five tribal languages of Central California and the Modoc of Northeastern California, was spread widely throughout western North America. Its members lived scattered from northern British Columbia, Washington, Oregon, and California to southern Mexico.

The Wintun held the favored area of the west side of the Sacramento Valley from the east bank of the river to the crest of the Coast Range and were the most populous group in the northern part of the state. Their numbers are estimated at about 26,000, and their villages ran to well over a hundred. Within this territory were at least three recognizable dialects, or variants, of Wintun speech: Wintu in the north (in southern Shasta County); Central Wintun (in Glenn and Tehama counties); and Southern Wintun, or Patwin (in Colusa, Yolo, and Solano counties and the southern tip of Napa County). The Wintun occupied two different environments, which resulted in somewhat different types of cultural adjustment and therefore outlook on life: the valley plain, on the one hand, and the hill tracts that bordered the lowlands to the north and west, on the other. As a vigorous and wealthy people, their influence was felt by their neighbors, who numbered at least ten different tribes.

Four separate Miwok groups lived in Central California, two (the Coast and Lake Miwok) west of the Sacramento Valley and the others (the Plains and Sierra Miwok) in the delta region and on the east side of the valley and in the adjacent Sierran slopes. The cultures of the mountain, plains, lake, and coastal Miwok were rather different as a result of their adaptation over a long period of time (perhaps several thousand years) to local environmental conditions. The Miwok are the best example of the adaptability of culture among groups who once, as is made clear by their sharing of one language, constituted a single people.

The Coast Miwok, who held southern Sonoma County and all of Marin County, probably numbered about 3000 in former times. To them belongs the distinction of being the rightful owners of the north shore of the Golden Gate, and they are the tribe with whom Sir Francis Drake spent five weeks in the summer of 1579.

The Lake Miwok, who lived in the Clear Lake basin in lower Lake County, were neighbored by three peoples, the Pomo, the Wappo, and the Patwin, of alien speech. Former numbers of Lake Miwok probably did not exceed 500.

Of the Interior Miwok, the Sierra Miwok were concentrated in the lower foothills of the Sierra Nevada of Amador, Tuolumne, and Mariposa counties. A lesser division, the Plains (or Valley) Miwok, held the Cosumnes-Mokelumne river area where it flowed into and across the delta plain near Lodi. From the Cosumnes River in the north to Fresno in the south, and eastward to the crest of the Sierra Nevada, was the main Miwok area. Yosemite Valley on the upper Merced River was owned by the Miwok. Their territory lay in the gold region, the so-called Southern Mines, and of their former numbers of about 9000 only a few survivors of mixed blood remain today. The Spanish missions and the Gold Rush were effective factors in their elimination. The Miwok suffix *umni* or *amne*, meaning "place of," has been preserved in such modern names as Tuolumne and Mokelumne. The name Miwok itself comes from *miwu*, "person."

The Maidu held the high Sierras, the foothill tracts, and the valley plain north of the Interior Miwok. This is the drainage of the Feather and American rivers and includes the following counties: Eldorado, Placer, Nevada, Yuba, Butte, Plumas, and the southern half of Lassen. Three distinguishable Maidu dialects were spoken: northwestern, or Concow; northeastern; and southern, this last often referred to as Nisenan or Nishinam. Estimates of the former numbers of the Maidu vary from 4000 to 9000.

Yokuts land was the San Joaquin Valley floor from the mouth of the San Joaquin River south to Tehachapi Pass, the lower Sierran foothills south of Fresno River, and the lower Kern and Kings river lands in the southern valley. In this area, which extended about 250 miles in length and was nowhere over 100 miles in breadth, there lived about fifty distinct tribes, each with its own name, dialect, and territory. Among them were twelve major language groups. The dry west side of the San Joaquin Valley in ancient times, even as today, offered less advantage to settlement, and the great bulk of population was concentrated in the better-watered eastern valley margin. Dialect diversification followed topography, and among the valley tribes a Yokuts from the Stockton area could be understood by one from Bakersfield or Merced, their speech being common to the lowlands. The foothill dialects were spoken in a long stretch of diversified terrain, and their differences appear to have been greater than among the valley tongues. Ease or difficulty of ethnic contact, time of separation from the original Yokuts language group, and topography all enter into the explanation of these linguistic divergences. One instance of speech migration was shown by a trio of adjoining Yokuts-speaking tribes (Tuhohi, Hometwoli, and Tulamni) of the Buena Vista region near Bakersfield, whose idiom was of the distant foothill type even though they occupied the flat valley floor and had a culture like that of their immediate neighbors. The name Yokuts comes from *yokoch*, "people" or "person." They were called Tulareños, "people of the tule marshes," by the Spanish, who drew them into the coastal missions south of San Francisco Bay. Originally this great valley-foothill Penutian group numbered about 70,000 persons.

The name Costanoan comes from a Spanish word meaning "people of the coast." With the exception of the small Coast branch of the Miwok, they were the only Penutian tribe to dwell along the ocean shore. Their territory extended from the southern shores of San Francisco Bay south to Point Sur, and from the ocean coast inland to the crest of the Coast Range. Seven dialectic divisions are known, each clustering around one of the seven Franciscan missions founded in their territory. Their numbers were estimated at about 7000, but as with most such census figures, the computation was made from one-half to one and a half centuries after the native populations had experienced their first encounters with the whites.

The lands of the Modoc included Lower Klamath Lake and Tule Lake in Siskiyou County, and Lost River in Modoc County. They held Butte Creek to the west, land to the east as far as the divide between Goose Lake and Lost River, and the country to the south as far as the Pit River watershed. In Modoc territory lay the famed Glass Mountain with its great obsidian outcrops from which most of the northern California tribes made their arrowpoints. The former numbers of the Modoc have been estimated at 600 to 700, of whom half lived in Oregon.

Hokan Tribes

Languages of this family were widely distributed in California. Tribes speaking Hokan languages included the Karok and the Shasta in northern California and southern Oregon; Achomawi and Atsugewi (at times called the Pit River tribe) of the southern Modoc plateau and Pit River; the Yana with four dialects, the southernmost of which (Yahi) was the group from which the famous Ishi came; the Chimariko, a small tribe of the middle course of the Trinity River; the Pomo, who spoke seven languages, which were mutually unintelligible, and whose homeland centered on Clear Lake in Lake County and the surrounding Coast Ranges and extended to the Pacific shore; the Washo, whose original territory included Lake Tahoe; the Esselen, whose lands lay just south of Point Sur and about whom we know very little because they were early drawn into the missions of San Antonio and San Carlos (Carmel) and suffered near extinction; the Salinan, who lived in the Coast Ranges and on the coast south of the Esselen and whose language was divided into three dialects; and the Chumash, who spoke at least eight languages and whose territory lay from San Luis Obispo southward to Malibu on the coast. The Chumash also occupied the offshore islands of Santa Cruz, Santa Rosa, and San Miguel. South of the Chumash there were no Hokan speakers until one reached the Diegueño on the coast around Mission San Diego; the Kamia of

Imperial Valley; and still further east the Colorado River tribes named Yuma, Halchidhoma, and Mohave.

The Hokan tribes appear to have been ancient inhabitants of the state, to judge by the internal diversity of their speech forms and by their scattered distribution. Demographers calculate these tribal populations: Shasta, 600; Achomawi and Atsugewi, 3000; Yana and Yahi, 1850; Chimariko, 500; Pomo (seven divisions), 21,000; Washo, 500; Esselen, 500; Salinan, 3000; Chumash, 13,650; Diegueño, 3000; Yuma, 2500; Halchidhoma, 1000; and Mohave, 3000.

Uto-Aztekan Tribes

In California, speakers of this language family have been classified by linguists as follows:

Takic:	Luiseño and Juaneño
	Cupeño
	Cahuilla
	Gabrielino and Fernandeño
	Serrano
Numic:	Monache and Northern Paiute
	Panamint Shoshone
	Kawaiisu and Chemehuevi
Tübatulabalic:	Tübatulabal

Uto-Aztekan tribes occupied about one-third of the state, though it was for the most part the arid areas where people had to scratch hard for a living. The Uto-Aztekan family is represented to the southeast by the Hopi of Arizona and far to the south by the Aztec, or Nahuatl, people of central Mexico.

Members of the Takic branch in California included the Luiseño and the Juaneño, who were named by the Spanish from their proximity or attachment to the missions of San Luis Rey and San Juan Capistrano. The Cupeño were a small tribe centered at Warner Springs in San Diego County. The Cahuilla, still surviving today in some numbers, were an interior tribe whose lands did not reach westward to the ocean shore. Palm Springs is in Cahuilla territory. The Gabrielino, named from their residence at

Mission San Gabriel, spoke at least three languages. In the ancient past they had colonized and occupied the offshore islands of Catalina and San Clemente. The Fernandeño of the valley and mission of San Fernando and the little-known people of the island of San Nicolas spoke related tongues. The Serrano peoples held a large interior area, mainly desert, of Southern California. Speakers of the Serrano language included the Kitanemuk of the Tejon region, the Vanyume, and the Serrano proper.

The Numic branch included the Monache, or Western Mono, who were neighbors of the Yokuts in the southern Sierran slopes. They appear to have been recent migrants from the Great Basin area who had moved westward over the crest of the Sierra within the last thousand years. Their close linguistic relatives, living along the Nevada-California border east of the Sierra, were the Mono Paiute and the Owens Valley Paiute. To the south were the Panamint Shoshone, whose territory included Death Valley. Still farther south were the Kawaiisu, a tribe small in numbers but with large land holdings, and the Chemehuevi, or Southern Paiute.

The Tübatulabal were related Uto-Aztekan people who were distinctive linguistically from the Takic and Numic subgroups. They held the steep-canyoned drainage of the Kern River.

Tribal populations are estimated by ethnologists and demographers as follows: Luiseño, 4000; Juaneño, 1000; Cupeño, 500; Cahuilla, more than 2500; Gabrielino and Fernandeño, 5000; Serrano, Vanyume, and Kitanemuk, 3500; Monache, 2000; Paiute of Owens Valley and Mono Lake, 1000; Panamint Shoshone, 500; Kawaiisu and Cheme-huevi, 1500; and Tübatulabal, 500.

Yukian Tribes

The Yukian language family is the only one found exclusively in California. This language has been repeatedly analyzed and compared with other languages but has failed to demonstrate undoubted relationship to any other known tongue. Accordingly, Yukian ranks as an independent stock.

Moreover, Yukian speakers were of an unusual and distinctive physical type. The Yuki were extremely long-headed and short-statured, and in this combination of anatomical features they were unique in California. Although some Yukian-speaking peoples (such as the Wappo) were of the usual Central California physical type (taller and broader-headed than the Yuki type), and a few groups (such as the Kato) who did not speak the Yukian language possessed the unique long-headed and short-statured features, the original combination of distinctive speech and physical type is undoubted. Shifts of language or populations account for the exceptions. The Yuki probably represent the only living tribe that may be called with reason the original California Indian, all others (whose speech relatives lie outside the state) being later comers from the north, the east, or the south.

Yuki territory, almost wholly in northern Mendocino County, was hemmed in between that of foreigners, the small Athabascan tribes to the north, the Pomo to the south, and the Wintun to the east. Three dialectic divisions with the rank of subtribes are called Coast Yuki, Huchnom, and Yuki proper (fig. 6). The Yuki proper held the largest area, which was the drainage of the Eel River above the mouth of the North Fork except for the lower course of the South Eel, held by the Huchnom. Round Valley seems to have been a settlement center of the Yuki proper. The name Yuki comes from the Wintun and means "stranger" and "enemy," these words having quite different meanings in English but having the same meaning to California Indians. The Yuki proper may once have numbered 6800, but of these only a handful of mixed descendants remain today after contact with Caucasians for slightly more than a hundred years.

The Huchnom occupied the drainage of the South Eel River from Hullville nearly to the mouth. It is characteristic of California Indians in general to occupy a stream drainage rather than a stretch of territory where stream courses themselves serve as boundary lines. A map showing California counties will demonstrate the importance of

FIGURE 6 Yuki territory. (From R.F. Heizer, *Languages, Territories, and Names of California Indian Tribes, 1966)*

rivers as modern boundary lines. Such divisions would seem arbitrary to an Indian, since he is accustomed to thinking of his terrain in terms of natural topographic areas. The word Huchnom is a Yukian word meaning "mountain people." Their former population probably did not exceed 2000.

The Coast Yuki held the ocean front for about 20 miles from Cleone in the south to a little above Rockport. Inland their territory narrowed down and was joined to that of the Huchnom by a thin strip only 5 or 6 miles wide. The Yukian groups thus formed an international barrier between the Athabascans and the Pomo. The Coast Yuki may have numbered 750 in pre-Caucasian times.

The Yukian-speaking Wappo tribe, which received its name from an Americanization of the Spanish *guapo*, "brave" or "handsome," occupied what is now Napa County and the adjoining eastern part of Sonoma County and southern Lake County. Their territory consisted of low Coast Range mountains with settlements in the valleys. Of these, Napa Valley was the largest. Lack of geographical barriers, and their intermediate position between the Pomo to the west and the Southern Wintun (Patwin) to the east, allowed the Wappo to act as middlemen in the trade of coastal shells for beads and ornaments with interior groups. Their former strength is conjectural, but may have reached 1000.

In this kaleidoscope of major tribes, numbering about sixty, there are many unfamiliar names. How were tribes named? Some appellations were bestowed by the Spanish to groups brought into missions: Diegueño (Mission San Diego de Alcalá), Juaneño (San Juan Capistrano), Luiseño (San Luis Rey), Gabrielino (San Gabriel), Fernandeño (San Fernando). Others were named by the Spanish from their location: Serranos (mountaineers), Costanos (coast-dwellers). Salinan, as a tribal term, comes from the Spanish name of the river and valley they occupied: Salinas, "saline."

Other names have become current largely through accident or chance. Many, perhaps most, tribal names are labels that were attached to them by a neighboring tribe. Thus, Tolowa comes from *ni-tolowa*, a Yurok word meaning "I speak Athabascan of the Tolowa variety." Hupa is from Hupo, the Yurok name for the valley the Hupa occupy. Chilula is from Yurok *Tsulu-la*, "people of Tsulu" (the Bald Hills). Wailaki is a Wintun word meaning "north language." Karok is from the Karok word meaning "upstream," as distinguished from the powerful Yurok people who lived downstream on the Klamath River. Chimariko is from that language, *chimar*, "person." Washo is a variant of a word in this language, *washiu*, "people." The tribal name Pomo derives from a suffix added to the name of the principal village of a tribelet. Esselen is a village name that became affixed to the tribe as a whole.

The Indians of California were, of course, only a segment of the Indians of North America and a smaller portion of the native peoples of the New World. California tribes, except for those that farmed along the Colorado River, were hunters, gatherers, and collectors living off the foods produced by nature. The tribes observed the dictum that one did not overhunt, and they regulated the salmon fishing by ritual in such a way as to guarantee the continuance of the supply of fish in future years.

It is not incorrect, we believe, to view northwestern California salmon fishers or Sierra Miwok acorn collectors as food producers. The care taken by the Yurok and Karok tribes to avoid ritual contamination of the Klamath River and to accord the salmon a proper respect amounted, in the natives' view, to effective human intervention by preserving the natural habitat and encouraging the salmon to return each year to be caught. The Sierra Miwok carefully preserved the oak trees from which they annually gathered their staple food. They were mindful of destructive fires and breaking branches when they were engaged in the gathering process. Indians were involved in their own ways in what we now call natural resource management.

The California natives were labeled by the Gold Rush immigrants as "Diggers," a term intended to show how stupid and brutish were these people who knew no better than to dig up roots and bulbs to keep alive. That label was incorrect, as we know, but it helped create an attitude that the California Indians were weak, degraded, lazy, or cowardly savages who were better dead than alive. It was an accident of history that the tribes of the Great Plains, equipped with the white man's horse, cut such a dashing figure that they became epitomized as the noble savage, and that the California tribes came wrongly to be seen as the lowest order of humanity—mere Diggers.

Let us take the presumed physical or muscular weakness of the Indians. Records of the pressure in pounds exerted by the hand on a squeeze apparatus called a Collins dynamometer show that Indians of both sexes exerted stronger pressure with each hand than did "Old Americans" (native-born European whites who could trace American-born

TABLE 2. Comparison of Muscular Pressure Exerted by Indians and Europeans

	Squeeze pressure (lbs.)		
	Right hand	Left hand	Differences from Indian
Indian men	52	49	
Indian women	28	25	
"Old Americans," men	41.8	36.1	−10.2/−12.9
"Old Americans," women	23.2	19.4	−4.8/−5.6
Immigrants, men	38.1	36.3	−13.9/−12.7

ancestors back three generations on each side of the family). Indian men exceeded newly arrived European immigrant males employed as laborers in mines and factories. (See table 2, taken from a study by R. F. Heizer and C. Treanor.)

A further illustration of the physical power of at least some of the California Indians was their ability at long-distance running. Captain J. G. Bourke, a doctor in the U.S. Army, stationed at Fort Mohave in the 1890s, wrote about a Mohave runner named Panta-cha who ran 100 miles between sunrise and sunset and after a brief rest made the return trip, covering the whole 200 miles in 24 hours. Bourke also recorded details about a runner who went 21 miles in 3.5 hours (average speed, 6.0 miles per hour) and stated that this "was regarded as so commonplace a performance as to be worth but two dollars for the round trip."

THE INDIAN SETTLEMENT OF CALIFORNIA

In Indian times California was probably settled just as it was by whites after its discovery by Cabrillo in 1542. The population of California today is drawn from all corners of the earth. And so it was, in a slower and smaller way, in native times, when migrating contingents of people, speaking different languages and drawn from afar, moved westward, to come up finally against the shore of the Pacific, and settled down. What we see in this kaleidoscope of tribes is nothing more than the survivors of scores, or perhaps hundreds, of separate migrations of westward- or southward-migrating peoples.

It is calculated that at the time of the first Spanish settlement in 1769 there were about 310,000 Indians in California. With a land area of 155,650 square miles, the population density was thus about 1 person for each 2 square miles. Although this population is very low in terms of a modern population in excess of 22 million, for native North America before the white man came California was a densely occupied area—a favored area for settlement, as it is today. (In chapter 7 we shall examine the archaeological evidence for the Indians of the prehistoric period.)

Except for the Colorado River tribes, who placed a value on warfare, the California Indians were peaceable and unaggressive. This attitude goes far to explain why they submitted so readily to being brought into the missions and why, until they came to learn that it was all too often a mistake, they welcomed the strange white visitors in peace and friendship. Native Californians seem to have placed a value originally on trying to get along with their neighbors and to have learned, through practice, that a live-and-let-live attitude was a better guarantee of survival than one of aggression. California Indians evidently were separatists, and in the pre-white period there are no recorded political confederacies or leagues of tribes.

The tendency of California tribes to mind their own affairs, to defend their territorial boundaries jealously, and to take up arms against any territorial trespass by members of adjoining tribes may go far toward accounting for the linguistic differentiation we have noted. People who isolate themselves may develop speech peculiarities that will, over the course of centuries, lead to languages unintelligible to their neighbors. Linguists can detect these related languages and can often make informed guesses as to how long ago two groups of speakers separated.

In broad cultural terms the Indians of California share a great many features with most other American Indian societies. Among these are the hunting-collecting type of economy, no use of metals, a tribal organization, and common themes in folktales, myths, and the like.

There is no question but that in the time before the discovery of America by Columbus the California region was one of the most densely populated areas of the continent north of Mexico. The same is true today, when about 10 percent of the total population of the United States lives in California. Although we cannot be certain, it is probable that at the time of discovery most of the tribal populations were at or near maximum numbers. Maximum population for a tribal area was established by the smallest amount of food available during the leanest year within the lifetime of all members of the tribe at any time. Presumably the Indians themselves recognized that there was a danger in excess population and had devised and practiced various methods of population control to keep their numbers within the limits of the food which their habitat could supply. These included abortion, the drinking of plant infusions to prevent conception, and infanticide. Deformed infants were usually disposed of at birth, although some deformed persons lived for many years, as is evidenced in prehistoric cemeteries by the skeletons of hydrocephalic (large-headed) individuals and achondroplastic dwarfs (without normal cartilage development). Twins were almost everywhere considered abnormal, and one (or both) of such a pair was usually killed. Indians living under white law were generally reticent about discussing such matters, so our information is incomplete. But it appears that nearly all tribes did have certain cultural practices that served as population checks, and we can infer that these customs were aimed at reducing population pressure in societies where there was an absolute limit to the amount of year-round food available. If the Yurok had, through some genius born among them, devised a method of catching twice as many salmon in a year as the tribe had earlier secured, or if some Pomo genius had invented a new acorn-collecting device that would have made it possible for the tribe to gather twice as many acorns, there is little doubt that in a generation or two the tribal populations would have increased dramatically. These hypothetical examples allow us to speculate that, say, among the earliest Yurok, after they first occupied the salmon-rich Klamath River and invented or learned new fish-taking methods such as dip nets or weirs, the increased catch would have allowed an expansion of human numbers simply because there was more food to eat. Population numbers at any one time were probably determined in part by the efficiency of the entire food-securing apparatus.

Another measure of environmental productivity and the Indians' ability to utilize the available plants and animals is the density of population. By way of example, let us take tribal densities per square mile of territory in a west-to-east line running from the Yurok on the northwestern coast past the riverine Hupa and Karok, whose tribal lands adjoined on the east, and proceed further east to the Pit Rivers (Achomawi and Atsugewi) and the Modoc, who lived in the high, semidesert plateau beyond the range of salmon and oaks. The figures are Yurok, 4.66 persons per square mile; Hupa, 5.20; Karok, 2.42; Achomawi, 0.70; Atsugewi, 0.30; and Modoc, 0.30. Such population densities directly reflect the productiveness of the land in terms of available food resources. The richer the land, the more people, and vice versa.

A good idea of the variation in population numbers by area, taken from a 1976 study by S. F. Cook, is given in the following list:

Northwest Coast (Oregon line to San Francisco Bay)	70,400
Shasta, Achomawi, and Modoc	9,600
Sacramento Valley	76,100
San Joaquin Valley	83,800
Northern coastal Mission area	26,000
Central coastal Mission area	18,500
Southern coastal Mission area	20,000
Desert Uto-Aztekans of Mohave and Colorado deserts and Owens Valley	5,600
Total	310,000

2. REGIONAL LIFEWAYS

Anthropologists find it convenient to think of California Indian cultures in terms of areas where a particular kind or style of culture was characteristic to the extent that it can be distinguished from other such areas.

The map (fig. 7) shows the distribution of the six main culture areas of aboriginal California as they were defined by A. L. Kroeber. Although culture areas can be geographically delineated, they are more than mere geographic areas, for in each one there lived a series of tribes that shared among themselves a way of life distinctively different from that prevailing in the neighboring culture areas. The features that set off one culture area from another were often direct reflections of the potentiality of the environment and the ways in which people learned to utilize it. An area with numerous salmon streams would hold populations that had developed a number of devices (harpoons, nets, traps, weirs) for catching fish. An area that did not contain salmon streams and was rich in oak trees would lack much fishing gear and have a material culture that emphasized appliances and techniques for collecting, storing, and preparing acorns for food. Such differences in the economic base and the activities surrounding the securing of food helped to shape the whole pattern of life. Where there was food the year round that could be gathered and stored, habitation was permanent. In less productive areas the village group would have to move to different areas at particular times of the year to find the food necessary for survival.

Terrain, climate, available water, plants, and animals had direct effects on the human population. Different patterns of settlement (compact towns, dispersed villages with only a

NW = Northwest

NE = Northeast

C = Central

GB = Great Basin

S = Southern

CR = Colorado River

FIGURE 7 Culture areas of California.

few houses in each) and population numbers that varied in response to the amount and kinds of food available were therefore direct adjustments to the natural environment by the human population. Today we are much less dependent for food upon the immediate California environment in which we live. We can buy almost any fresh vegetables we desire in a supermarket that draws its produce from all over the United States and at times from other countries. We can insulate our houses in cold mountainous regions and install air conditioning in areas that would otherwise be uncomfortable to live in. The California Indian, who did not possess such amenities, was satisfied with a comparatively limited variety in his diet, and alternately shivered or was too hot, according to the season.

Culture provides the anthropologist with a ready means of pointing out regional differences in tools, dress, food-gathering methods, and house types, which can be used to identify the several culture areas within the state. Beyond the material are the nonmaterial aspects of culture. California Indian religions, for example, varied from simple shamanism, in which a man or a woman became a curing doctor because he or she had secured in a dream some supernatural sanction or "power" to cure the sick, to highly complex and organized cult religions in which many people participated and for which there were officials and a complex mythology underlying the cult. How did these practices come about? Nobody knows, because their origin lies far back in time—hundreds and in some cases perhaps even thousands of years—and there is no longer any way to discover that unwritten history.

Six culture areas have been agreed upon by researchers for native California: Northwestern, Northeastern, Central, Great Basin, Southern, and Colorado River.

NORTHWESTERN CALIFORNIA

Participating in the Northwestern culture were the Tolowa, Shasta, Karok, Yurok, Hupa, and Wiyot tribes and the Wailaki group south of the Hupa. The Yurok were the "hearth" tribe in which the climax development was reached. The Northwestern subculture was distinctive in many ways. Ecologically, it was closely adapted to the rain-forest environment, with its settlements situated along river banks and the ocean coast at stream mouths, lagoons, or bays. The dugout canoe was the most important means of travel, routes being along rivers and the ocean shore. There were trails for foot travel, and these were used to visit neighboring villages; but the canoe remained the best means for traveling any distance and for crossing the Klamath River, which over much of its course is wide, fast-flowing, and deep.

FIGURE 8 Indian villiage, Trinidad Bay, Humboldt County, from a drawing by J.G. Bruff, 1850 (Courtesy of the Huntington Library, San Marino, California)

The primary construction and craft material was wood, especially the soft, straight-grained Coast Redwood (*Sequoia sempervirens*). Trees were felled by controlled burning at the base and were split into planks with long elk-antler wedges pounded with bell-shaped stone mauls. A mussel-shell adze blade lashed to a curved stone handle was used to smooth rough spots on planks and to excavate the interior of the big, shallow-draft, redwood canoes. Northwestern houses were rectangular, gabled structures (fig. 8) with roofs and walls made of planks, especially of redwood where it was available, but most often otherwise of cedar. Basketry, in a wide variety of shapes adapted to special uses (for example, mush-cooking baskets, acorn-storage baskets, hats, and cradles), was made only with the twined technique (figs. 9 and 10). Coiling, so common in Central and Southern California, was here not employed as a basket-making technique.

FIGURE 9 Beach fishing with basketry "nets," Mendocino County. (From *Harper's Monthly*, August, 1861)

FIGURE 10 Schematic examples of techniques of twined basketry (left), and coiled basketry (right). In twining, the wefts or "moving elements," are shown twined around the vertical warps, or stationary elements. In coiling, the weft stitches are shown interlocking with one another around the horizontal warp rods (After A. B. Elsasser, in *Handbook of North American Indians*, 1978)

FIGURE 11 The White Deerskin Dance in Hupa Valley, an important part of the World Renewal ceremony. (Photograph by A. W. Ericson, ca. 1900)

The main ritual observed was the World Renewal ceremony (fig. 11), held once a year in a large town where the richest men provided free food for the guests, who came from villages as distant as 50 miles. The purpose of the World Renewal ceremony was to prevent the occurrence in the coming year of disasters, such as earthquakes, failure of the salmon runs, failure of the acorn crop, floods, hurricanes, and the like. Such disruptive events may have happened in the ancient past, and the ceremony was developed as a means of pacifying the supernatural spirits and thus averting a repetition. World Renewal rites were, therefore, basically ecological in their purpose. The power of nature to injure man was believed to threaten the stability of the world in its normal operations, and the rituals acknowledged that threat and were intended to ward off any impulse on the part of the powers of nature to act in ways detrimental to human life. Despite man's best efforts to prevent floods or the failure of the salmon run or the acorn crop, these calamities occasionally occurred, and one Indian explanation for man's lack of success in preventing them was that the prescribed rituals had been performed incorrectly. Because human welfare was at stake, the ceremonies were performed with the utmost solemnity and attention to proper detail so that nature would not be offended by mistakes made by the ritualists.

The Northwestern tribes had no chiefs as such. Their place was taken by men of wealth who, with their kinsmen, exercised what authority was required in a village simply because they were rich and therefore influential. The emphasis on possessions and property of all kinds probably encouraged among the Northwestern tribes a greater development of the idea of private ownership of food resources, which included oak groves, salmon-fishing pools on the river, deer-snaring spots, sea stacks where mussels grew, and stretches of ocean beach to which a man had particular rights, such as the ownership of dead whales cast ashore and surf-fish netting.

In 1920 the anthropologist T. T. Waterman made a study of the Yurok and encountered one man who held the exclusive rights to hunt, fish, and gather food at certain designated spots. Other persons who gathered food at any of these places without the permission of the owner were subject to a heavy fine. What is interesting about this one man's exclusive rights, as shown on the map (fig. 12), is how extensive they were, both in number and in geographical extent. There was clearly more available at these spots in the way of fish, acorns, and deer than one person and his immediate family could hope to gather, and it is safe to assume that the owner extended hunting and gathering privileges to friends. Whether he charged a fee is not known; if he did not, it is most probable that what he got for his generosity was loyalty and support from his friends, a reputation for being generous, and a name that commanded respect. This instance must have been unusual, since there

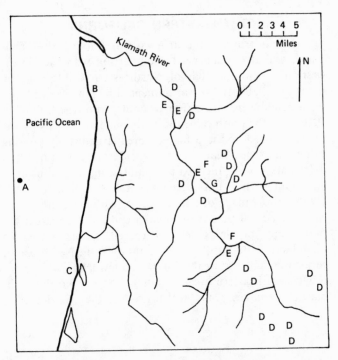

FIGURE 12 Property and exclusive rights of one Yurok Indian. (After T. T. Waterman, *Yurok Geography*, 1920)

would scarcely have been enough of such resource areas in Yurok territory to have been apportioned to, say, fifty such rich men. A possible explanation of the example just given is that, with the reduction of the Yurok population after 1850, the person to whom Waterman talked had inherited many rights from relatives who had died, so that possibly there came to be concentrated in this one person's possession what had been the total of a dozen men's property rights in earlier times. The Yurok obviously were keen on property and property rights. Their most sought-after money was *Dentalium* shell, a seashell they obtained from the north through trade.

NORTHEASTERN CALIFORNIA

The main tribes of this area were the Modoc, the Acho-mawi, and the Atsugewi. In comparison with the North-western subculture, that of Northeastern California was much less elaborate. It was influenced by practices diffused from neighboring areas. For example, from the Columbia Plateau to the north came the method of sweating by means of steam produced in a hide-covered structure by pouring water on stones heated in an outside fire (fig. 13). Skull deformation was practiced by compressing the forehead of an infant with a flat piece of wood or a tight binding. Clothing was made of tanned leather with cut fringes. The canoe, made of pine with squared ends, was apparently a poor copy of the gracefully carved canoes in whose manufacture the Yurok excelled, although the Northeastern canoe was fully serviceable on the shallow lakes of the area.

The Northeastern area is poorer than the Northwest in natural resources. Oaks, which produce the prized acorns,

FIGURE 13 Atsugewi sweathouse frame at Big Valley, Pit River region. (Photograph C. H. Merriam, ca. 1925)

are abundant in the western half of the area, and the salmon run up the Klamath River as far as Fall River. Where acorns and salmon could be gathered or fished, they were. Where they were lacking, the inhabitants of the eastern half of the region had to substitute whatever was available: deer, rabbits, grass seeds, or roots. Rabbits were hunted by numbers of people driving the animals into a low net set on sticks driven into the ground in a semicircle, where the animals were clubbed to death. This practice was apparently learned from the Great Basin peoples living to the east. Along the Pit River, deer were taken in pits that were dug out and covered with a layer of branches, a hunting practice that annoyed early white fur-trappers, who lost horses in them—a loss that gave rise to the name of the river. The aquatic yellow Indian Pond Lily (*Nuphar polysepalum*), which grows in shallow lakes in the area, produced nutritious seeds. A bearing season of only a few weeks and the slow and tedious process of grinding off the hard seed hulls combined to limit the importance of this food resource.

The Klamath Indians of southern Oregon raided the Modoc, the Achomawi, and the Atsugewi for captives, who were taken north to the great Indian market at The Dalles on the Columbia River and sold as slaves. It is not known whether this was an ancient practice or one that became common after the coming of the whites and the use of horses.

CENTRAL CALIFORNIA

The tribes exhibiting this style of native culture were the five Penutian nations (Costanoan, Miwok, Wintun, Maidu, and Yokuts), four of the Hokan nations (Yana, Pomo, Esselen, and Salinan), and one Uto-Aztekan nation (Monache). The environment of Central California varies considerably, ranging from the ocean shore eastward over the Coast Ranges, across the interior valley, and into the western slopes of the Sierra Nevada. As a result of different environmental adjustments, the population numbers of the tribes were variable. North of Monterey the salmon in Indian times ran the rivers that empty into the ocean, including the great Sacramento and San Joaquin rivers and their tributaries, which flow down from the Sierra. Everywhere in the area oaks were abundant, so that most tribes ate both salmon and acorns. Deer, elk, antelope, and rabbits were common, as were waterfowl, so there was no real food shortage. Ethnographers early in the century were often told that the Wild Oat (*Avena fatua*), which grows luxuriantly over most of the area, was a valued food, and that it had "always grown here." But the Indian words for *Avena* were often derived from the Spanish—words such as *arroz* (rice) or *semilla* (seed) or even *avena* (oats)—or from a Costanoan word, *honusmin* (grass seed), which occurred also among the Yokuts tribes. Botanists now know that *Avena* is an Old World plant, which must have been introduced by Europeans to the New World, but until they were certain of this the Indian statement that the plant had always been there had to be considered. Wild Oat probably was introduced with wheat seed brought to the Franciscan missions and soon spread from the mission fields. Numerous other weeds were introduced by the Spanish as escapees from the mission fields. Many were of no use to the Indians living away from the missions, but some did produce edible seeds. Among these are wild ryes (*Elymus* spp.) and other rye grasses (*Lolium* spp.).

The greatest variety in forms and weaves of basketry in the state is recorded for the Pomo. This tribe also produced beautiful baskets covered with brilliantly colored feathers (see chapter 5). Central California basketmakers made twined baskets, but relied almost equally on the coiled technique.

Religious cults included the Kuksu cult, which probably originated among the Patwin and was elaborated by the Pomo. The Maidu shared in this cult, as did some other neighboring tribes (northern Costanoans, Coast Miwok, northern Sierra Miwok, and perhaps northern Valley Yokuts). The cult ceremonies, performed by spectacularly costumed dancers, were held in the spacious, earth-covered "roundhouses" which represent the largest and most complex architectural achievement of California Indians. The basic purpose of the Kuksu cult (named after the spirit Kuksu, "South God") appears to have been to renew the world each year and guarantee the continuance of the natural foods (animals and plants) that supported men. Thus its purpose was the same as that of the World Renewal Cult of Northwestern California, but here the resemblance ended. The sacred structures where the dances were held, the dance forms, and the costumes were entirely different. A belief in the need to propitiate the spirits of nature so that they would continue to provide foods for man and prevent natural catastrophes was anciently shared, but the religious observances developed along quite different lines in each area.

The roundhouses, while varying in some details of wooden framing (number of supporting posts, rafters, depth of pit, etc.), were basically similar through Central California (figs. 14, 15, 16). Large ones were 50 to 60 feet (ca. 15 to 18 m.) in diameter, round in ground plan, and partly underground, since they were built in and over an excavated pit. Four or six oak center posts, about 1 foot (ca. 30.5 cm.) in diameter, were set up, cut to form a Y where the trunks branched. Oak stringers, each 6 to 8 inches (15.2 to 20.3 cm.) in diameter, were laid horizontally on the center posts. Radiating out to the edge of the pit were heavy rafters of cottonwood

FIGURE 14 Roundhouse in a Miwok village, with Casus [Jesus] Oliver in the foreground. (Photograph C.H. Merriam, ca. 1905)

FIGURE 15 Maidu earth-covered roundhouse. (After R.B. Dixon, *The Northern Maidu, 1905)*

FIGURE 16 Tall-roofed Miwok roundhouse. (Photograph C. H. Merriam, ca. 1905)

(*Populus fremontii*) and willow (*Salix* spp.) on which were laid a thatch of cottonwood boughs, willow branches, and grass, and then an earth covering. Stringers and rafters were tied to each other with long, green, flexible grapevines (*Vitis californica*), which tightened as they dried. From the outside these ceremonial houses looked like a mound of earth. Some dance houses were made wholly of wood (i.e., lacked the earth cover), but these may have been a form made possible only after the arrival of whites, from whom steel axes and saws were obtained.

The dancers and onlookers entered the roundhouses by way of either a sloping trench or a hole in the roof, descending to the floor by means of a notched log that

FIGURE 17 Earth lodges of the Sacramento Valley, probably Patwin (Southern Wintun). (From S. Powers, *Tribes of California*, 1877)

served as a ladder. The earthen floor was covered with willow branches when a ceremony was held. A drum 6 to 7 feet (ca. 180 to 210 cm.) long, made of a peeled and hollowed-out sycamore (*Platanus racemosa*) log provided accompaniment for the dancers.

Over much of Central California the family dwelling houses (fig. 17) were small editions of the larger ceremonial houses. In mountainous and other areas where redwood or pine grew, large slabs of bark were pried off the trees and used to make dwellings of roughly oval or conical form by bringing the slabs together at the apex (fig. 18).

Society in Central California was based on the tribelet organization, an aggregate of villages in the largest of which lived the tribelet chief. These groups were landowning units and were politically independent. Usually they shared the same language with one or more neighboring tribelets. Money here was in the form of small, flat, round disc beads made of the shells of a marine clam, *Saxidomus nuttalli*,

FIGURE 18 A camp of Northern California Indians. (Illustrated *San Francisco News*, 1869)

which is also an excellent food. Apparently life was sufficiently easy and assured that in the large, permanent villages, perhaps better termed towns (figs. 19, 20), which often numbered 1000 inhabitants, it was possible to develop craft specialists who devoted all their time to particular production activities. Some men concentrated on making arrowpoints, which they traded to their fellow tribelet members for food and other necessities. Other specialists devoted their time to shooting deer, fishing, netmaking, bow manufacture, and so on. In a sense, life in Central California seems to have been rather like modern commercial life, where we "trade" money for specialist productions such as automobiles, meat, vegetables, stationery, telephone service, and so on. In smaller tribelet groups, numbering only 50 or 100 persons, each family took care of its own needs, making its own bows, arrows, baskets, and nets, hunting for its own deermeat, fishing for its salmon, and so on. But with concentrated populations numbering ten to twenty times that number, some kind of organization of activity appears to have been necessary, and specialists appeared.

FIGURE 19 Maidu village on Sacramento River, ca. 1853, by Henry B. Brown.

FIGURE 20 Reconstruction of a Chumash village, Santa Barbara coast, showing houses and plank canoes. (Drawn by A. E. Treganza, ca. 1948)

FIGURE 21 Yokuts tule lodges. (From S. Powers, *Tribes of California*, 1877)

FIGURE 22 A *temescal*, or sweathouse, in Central California. (From Alexander Forbes, *A History of Lower and Upper California*, 1877)

The Yokuts of the southern San Joaquin Valley lined up thatch-covered houses side by side and covered the whole with a sunshade of rushes set on a post framework, to form a kind of "condominium" (fig. 21). Each village also had one or more earth-covered sweathouses (fig. 22) in which men daily underwent a hot air "bath" followed by a plunge

FIGURE 23 Sacramento Valley Indians, probably Patwin, bathing after being in a sweathouse. (After S. Powers, *Tribes of California*, 1877)

in a nearby stream (fig. 23). This sweating was a means of keeping clean as well as healthy, or so the Indians seem to have thought; it was a ritually purifying act which encouraged good health and long life.

GREAT BASIN

In this culture area, which represents a desert adaptation, lived the Northern Paiute and the desert tribes of Southern California. In general the culture was characterized by its comparative simplicity. Oaks and salmon were absent; in some spots there were brackish lakes that contained fish and where waterfowl could be hunted. Some lakes (e.g., Mono Lake) were too alkaline to support fish, but a special food resource occurred in them. This was the "kutsavi," the larval worm of a fly (*Hydropyrus hians*), which was thrown up in great windrows on the lake shore and was gathered, dried, stored, and eaten by the Mono Paiute. The kutsavi was very oily and rich in protein.

In this desert area population density was very low. It probably amounted to not more than 10 percent of that in the better watered, acorn- and salmon-rich areas of California to the west. The desert people were nomadic, visiting valleys where grass seeds were ripe, pine nuts could be gathered, rabbits could be driven into nets, and mountain sheep or deer were seasonally available.

Because each small group was on the move to visit food harvesting spots at particular times, and such groups might make twenty or forty such moves a year, their stock of permanent equipment was limited to what the group could carry. This meant the clothing they wore, rabbitskin blankets for winter wear and bedding, a few baskets for gathering seeds, parching trays, bows and arrows, and not much more.

Some hunting and gathering peoples who lived in cold regions, or at least in regions where the winter temperatures go below freezing, seem to be much more tolerant of cold than people who bundle themselves in clothes. Physical anthropologists and physiologists have studied this matter and have repeatedly observed members of these groups sleeping soundly and apparently comfortably at night with no covering whatsoever on their bodies in temperatures below freezing. Such studies have not been made of Great Basin Indians, who are either long since dead or have adapted themselves to a less strenuous life, but travelers' descriptions of near-naked Indians moving about unconcernedly in freezing weather allow us to suggest that these people, too, had learned to accommodate to weather that would very shortly put a late-twentieth-century person out of commission.

The first Euro-Americans to explore and report on the newly won territory of California after the Mexican War described these desert Indians as "the Arabs of the West" and "the most brutish and despicable Indians of the continent." Such a characterization, inaccurate and cruel as it was, was suggested by the apparent material simplicity of the culture. But it was indeed remarkable that the Indians in the desert areas could wrest a living from an inhospitable environment where food and water were in such short supply.

SOUTHERN CALIFORNIA

A number of Hokan and Uto-Aztekan tribes occupied this culture area, including the Chumash of the Santa Barbara region, the Gabrielino of the Los Angeles basin and farther to the south the Luiseño, the Cahuilla, the Juaneño, and the Diegueño. Of these groups the Chumash and the Gabrielino seem to have been the most skilled in the arts. The Chumash (fig. 20) were the most sea-oriented people of the state, a specialization made possible by their seagoing plank canoes, which were propelled by double-bladed paddles. The Chumash had colonized the offshore islands of Santa Barbara, San Miguel, Santa Cruz, and Santa Rosa, an effort that had occurred far enough in the past for these island groups to have achieved distinctive language dialects. Chumash stonework was of the finest quality, varying from large, beautifully flaked flint blades to capacious flat-rimmed sandstone mortars (fig. 24) to steatite animal effigies (fig. 25)—one of the rare instances of naturalistic

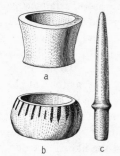

FIGURE 24 Chumash flat-rimmed stone mortar (*a*) and a Chumash mortar containing decorations of beads set in asphalt (*b*). Diameter of *b*, ca. 16 in. [40 cm.]. Flanged stone pestle (*c*). (Courtesy of the Santa Barbara Museum of Natural History)

FIGURE 25 Steatite whale figurine from San Nicholas Island. Length ca. 7 in. [18 cm.]. (Original in State Indian Museum, Sacramento, California)

stone carving among California Indians. Chumash basketry also was of superior quality. No other tribe so impressed the Spanish, and it does seem that in this well-favored region a large native nation did bring its material culture to greater heights of excellence than any other in California.

The Gabrielino of the mainland to the south of the Chumash, who were close rivals, are said to have been the originators of the Chinigchinich cult, which in mission times spread as far south as the Diegueño and northward to the Yokuts. This cult is highly moralistic, and duplicates so many Christian ethical and moral precepts that it has been suggested that it may have been devised after the first Franciscan missions were established—that the inspiration for the cult was Christianity. The southward diffusion of the cult is proved by the fact that all the songs are sung in the Gabrielino tongue. The cult practices include drinking an infusion of the Toloache plant (*Datura meteloides*), also called Jimsonweed, which can cause unconsciousness and induces color visions. The hallucinogen was very dangerous to take, and death at times resulted from too concentrated a dose. Boys being initiated into adulthood and cult member-ship took this drug, became unconscious for many hours, and were carefully watched by elders, who would apply certain measures in the event of too heavy a dose of the drug.* While under the influence of the drug the boy had a vision and through this experience gained "power" of one kind or another—to be a successful hunter, to avoid dan-gers, to be courageous and skillful, and the like. The elders made a sand painting (fig. 26) and lectured to the initiates gathered around it. When the moralistic lecture was com-pleted, the sand painting was destroyed. These paintings, made of different colored earths, were in fact maps that depicted the tribe's concept of the borders of the known

*In recent years in California there have been a number of deaths of young people who have heard of the effects of Jimsonweed and have decided to try it for a thrill. If they had been better informed about how very dangerous the plant is they would have avoided it and saved their own lives. The extreme danger of experimenting with this poisonous plant cannot be too strongly emphasized, since there is no known effective antidote or treatment for a person who has taken an overdose.

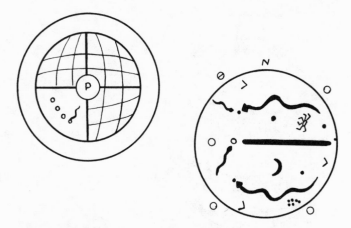

FIGURE 26 Sand paintings used for instructional purposes in boys' initiation rites among Luiseño and Diegueño. Luiseño painting (left): P is a pit in the center of the design; the small circles are ceremonial baskets, and the circle with tail is the rattlesnake. The Diegueño painting (right) has a different emphasis from that of the Luiseño—here the small circles outside the large ground symbolize mountains; the large snakes are rattlesnakes, with the dots in front of them representing Toloache (Jimsonweed) mortars; other elements stand for wolves or jaguars, spider, sun, moon, stars, or constellations (for example, the bar in the center indicates the Milky Way, and the cluster of dots near the edge, the Pleiades). Actual size of Diegueno painting ca. 36 in. [92 cm.]. (After A. L. Kroeber, *Handbook of the Indians of California*, 1925.)

universe as well as prominent geographical features and mythic animal spirits.

Among the Luiseño, when a young man reached about the age of eighteen, he lay in a pit and allowed ants to bite him. If he submitted to this ordeal without flinching or showing pain, it was believed that he would gain the power of not being hurt by arrows. After a time in the pit the young man was taken out and the ants were removed from his body by a brush made of stinging nettles!

The Diegueño, the Cahuilla, and the Kamia made good-quality pottery, in gray, brown, or red (fig. 27). Some pieces

FIGURE 27 Pottery vessels from Cahuilla region. Ht. ca. 22 in. [56 cm.]. (From R. F. Heizer, *Indian Occupation in Southern California*, 1952)

recovered from archaeological sites are decorated with black lines. (See plate 17.)

In Southern California domed, conical or rectangular houses were built with wooden supports for a great variety of brush and thatch roofs of such materials as tule (*Scirpus* spp.), arrowweed (*Pluchea* spp.), or croton (*Croton* spp.).

In the dry and stony Mohave Desert lived a series of Uto-Aztekan tribes, none of them very large in numbers. We know that in 1776 the Colorado River shore was occupied wholly by Yuman tribes (Mohave, Halchidhoma, and Yuma), and the desert tribes kept their distance. But in the 1830s the Yuma and the Mohave banded together, drove out the Halchidhoma, and allowed the Chemehuevi to replace them. The Chemeheuvi (fig. 28) farmed a bit where they could, a practice perhaps learned from their river neighbors, but for the most part they lived on rabbits, mountain sheep, kangaroo rats (*Dipodomys* spp.), woodrats

FIGURE 28 Chemehuevi Indians, Colorado River region, by W. H. Hilton, 1861. (Courtesy of the Huntington Library, San Marino, California)

(*Neotoma* spp.), Raccoon (*Procyon lotor*), Porcupine (*Eri-thyzon dorsatum*), skunks (*Mephitis* spp.), ground squir-rels (*Citellus* spp.), lizards, Mescal (*Agave deserti*), Joshua Tree seeds and flowers (*Yucca brevifolia*), prickly pear cacti (*Opuntia* spp.), Saguaro cactus fruit, seeds, and flowers (*Cereus giganteus*), Mesquite (*Prosopis glandu-losa*), Screwbean Mesquite (*P. pubescens*), and piñon nuts. Much the same can be said for their desert neighbors to the west, the Panamint Shoshoni (sometimes called the Koso), the Kawaiisu, and the Serrano. These groups probably had the least developed material culture in North America, and their territories, which were among the largest in the state, were at the same time the most sparsely populated. We can still see a direct parallel in the human response to this desert region, where today the largest counties and smallest popu-lations of California occur.

Compared with the culture of our own present-day society, the native cultures of California were simple and uncomplex. By the words "simple" and "uncomplex" we are thinking of our highly industrialized culture in which tech-nology is so strongly represented. But these "simple" soci-eties were successful in that they were organized in ways that assured the participants that the even flow of life and events would continue. Threats of annihilation by atomic bombs, warfare, and pestilence were lacking. There was always food-getting to work at, future ceremonial occasions to prepare for and look forward to, and a comfortable level of peace and tranquillity in the day-by-day and year-after-year flow of events in the lives of most persons.

COLORADO RIVER

The Colorado River groups were the only farming tribes of California.* These were large, the Yuma, the Mohave, and the Halchidhoma at the opening of the period of intensive Spanish contact in the 1770s numbering from 2000 to 2500

---

*Some California tribes did cultivate tobacco in special plots which they seeded and weeded. Other tribes collected wild tobacco (*Nicotiana* spp.). The Indians of Owens Valley, also, practiced artificial irrigation of certain wild seed crops. This seems to be one of the few independent inventions of an agricultural technique in North America.

per tribe. War was a national pursuit, carried out by specially trained warriors armed with bows, mallet-headed clubs, and straight clubs of mesquite wood. Scalps of fallen enemies were taken as trophies, as were girls and young women. These female captives were never sexually molested, because such intimate contact with women of enemy origin (and supernatural powers) was thought to cause sickness. The young women seem to have been considered more as living evidence of the military prowess of the tribe. The warriors attacked tribes as far away as 150 miles, such expeditions entailing travel for as much as seven or eight days. The aim of these war expeditions was to settle old grudges, some of which might be harbored for scores of years. Booty and spoils were not the aim; the Colorado River tribes seemed to enjoy fighting for its own sake.

The Colorado River settlements were numerous, generally small, and sited with reference to the bottomland farm plots, which were usually flooded in late spring or early summer. Agriculture provided most of the food. (Colorado farming methods and crops are described in chapter 3.) Large game was scarce, though in aboriginal times there were probably more deer, antelope, and rabbits than there are today.

Face and body painting, using red, yellow, and white clay pigments (fig. 29), was practiced to a greater extent than elsewhere in California.

Houses were substantial. They were rectangular in plan, 20 to 25 feet on a side, and built over a pit dug to a depth of 2 to 3 feet. The door always faced south as partial protection from the cold north wind. Four large interior posts of cottonwood (*Populus macdougalii*) supported rafters running out to side posts. Arrowweed (*Pluchea sericea*) thatch was laid on the rafters and against the side posts, and the whole structure was then covered with earth. In this extremely hot area, where the mean July temperature is 91.0 F. (32.5 C.), such houses were cool inside because of the earth insulation.

The most important ritual was the Keruk, or annual mourning ceremony, whose purpose was to honor the recently deceased. Its origin was attributed to ancient myth

FIGURE 29 Mohave Indians, males and females, with body painting. (From *Hutchings' California Magazine*, 1858)

days when the death of the Creator, Kukumat, was observed. This ritual, in which images of the dead, a male and female, were clothed, danced around, and burned, and which included offerings of goods (clothes, blanket, money) and food, was found generally through Southern California and to the north among the Yokuts, the Sierra Miwok, and the Maidu (figs. 30 and 31). It was the most widespread of the several organized cults of native California. A specialization of the ceremony among the Colorado River tribes was a mock or ritual battle which reenacted part of the myth of the events surrounding the origin of the ceremony. This ceremonial element among these warlike tribes is not surprising.

Special curing doctors received their powers from supernatural spirits. There were snake-bite curers, who treated a patient by puncturing the wound and sucking out the poison. Other specialists cured ordinary sickness, arrow wounds, concussions, fractures, and people plagued by ghosts. When the river failed to overflow and there had been no rain for a long time, farming was impossible and famine

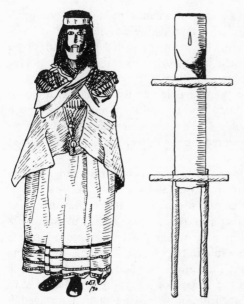

FIGURE 30 Yuma image of the dead and fill-out. (From C. D. Forde, *Ethnography of the Yuma Indians,* 1931)

FIGURE 31 Maidu dead image used in annual "burning" ceremony. (After R.B. Dixon, *The Northern Maidu,* 1905)

threatened. Then a powerful rainmaker would be sent for. A particular ceremony for rainmaking was described to C. D. Forde in 1928 as having been conducted by an old Yuma rainmaker who died in 1893. In the ceremony the doctor quickly smoked four hollow-cane cigarettes filled with tobacco and had the assembled crowd of several hundred people run in a body toward the north and raise as much dust as they could. The doctor then returned home, and soon clouds appeared and a heavy rain fell and lasted four days.

It is difficult for us to believe such stories, and yet there are many of them for tribes all over the state. A mission-period account refers to a drought that caused problems at San Antonio Mission in about 1800. The Franciscan missionary learned of a rainmaker in the congregation. He seized him and put him in the mission jail, with the warning that he would stay there until he relieved the drought. The rainmaker asked for a barrel of water, ordered the priest to lock up the congregation in the mission church, engaged in some occult activity, and, if we can believe the story, shortly made the rain come.

3. ECOLOGICAL TYPES OF CALIFORNIA INDIAN CULTURES

How people live, especially if they derive their subsistence directly from the natural products (both animals and plants) of the land, is determined in part by the conditions under which they live. These conditions are the responses of the plants and animals of the region to such factors as elevation, rainfall, temperature, topography, and soils. In short, the kinds and amounts of food resources that are available are determined in large part by the environment, and human exploitation of such resources will vary from one area to another.

One definition of ecology is "the science of interrelations between living organisms and their environment." The term "human ecology" is widely used, and in simplest terms this means how man uses his environment to the extent he can with the cultural apparatus he happens to possess. Among American Indians this relationship between habitat and man can justifiably be called "creative stewardship," a term intended to convey the idea that the Indians were aware of the fragility of the bonds that hold nature together, and attempted not to injure these bonds lest man himself suffer.

Because California's environment is so varied, with its seacoast, mountains, valleys, and deserts, the Indian cultures of California can be classified in terms of their cultural response to these differing environments. In this natural history guide we have chosen to emphasize the Indian cultures according to the way they were integrated with the natural environment.

Ecological types of Indian cultures are as follows:

I. Coastal
   1. Tideland collectors
   2. Sea hunters and fishers
II. Riverine fishermen
III. Lakeshore fishermen, hunters, and gatherers
IV. Valley and plains gatherers
V. Foothill hunters and gatherers
VI. Desert
   1. Hunters and collectors
   2. Agriculturists

As with any abbreviated classification, some differences are ignored, so that the scheme presented above should be viewed as an abstraction. Sharp distinctions are rare. Most ecological-cultural boundaries should properly be shown as zones where the transition from one to another is a gradual one. The reason for this is that the environment (topography, climate, fauna, and flora) rarely shifts abruptly from one zone to the next, but changes gradually over some distance, and the plant and animal life usually undergoes a gradual shift in numbers rather than species in response to the gradually differing environment. Some Native Californian groups cannot be firmly classified as belonging to either one ecological type or another, for the reason that they found two ecological zones more or less equally accessible to them. Such tribes should properly be classed as mixed, but in the interests of simplicity they are here placed in the category that seems to be predominant.

It should be kept in mind that there was great variety in the methods of fishing, hunting, food preparation, and food storage practiced by the California Indians (fig. 32). Nearly every species of plant and animal has its own habits and peculiarities. By long and patient observation the Indians had learned precisely how to catch each of the kinds of fish, how to hunt down each of the available forms of birds or land animals or sea mammals, and how to gather the nutritious parts of each plant, whether these were leaves, seeds, fruits, or roots, at exactly the moment when they were

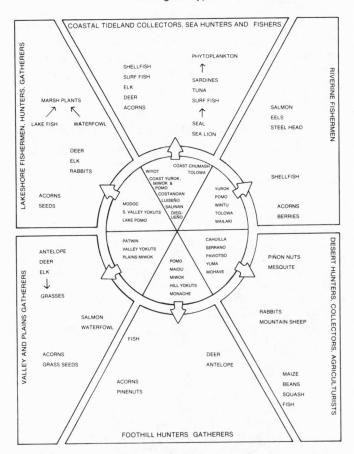

FIGURE 32 Ecological types, principal food resources, and representative California Indian tribes.

best for eating or for preparing for storage. The secret of getting meat to eat lay in learning, through observation, the exact habits, behavior, and reactions of animals and using this knowledge through the means of taking devices, such as bows and arrows, harpoons, traps, and decoys, to carry out a successful hunt.

California Indians were highly accomplished practical botanists and zoologists, perhaps as knowledgeable about subtle differences in form, color, and behavior as some university professors who have spent their adult lives reading and making field observations, but they were also knowledgeable in a different way—a way directed at understanding nature in such a manner as to use it without destroying it. Let us look at their varied means of obtaining a livelihood.

COASTAL TIDELAND COLLECTORS

As will be seen from the map (fig. 33), the coastal tideland collectors occupied the whole California shore from the Oregon to the Mexican border, except for the Santa Bar-

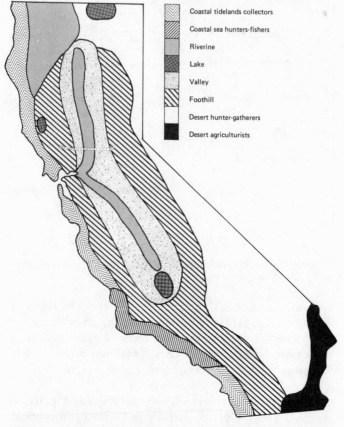

Coastal tidelands collectors

Coastal sea hunters-fishers

Riverine

Lake

Valley

Foothill

Desert hunter-gatherers

Desert agriculturists

FIGURE 33 Ecological culture types of California.

bara Channel and other offshore islands. Some tribes, notably the Pomo, Costanoan, Salinan, Chumash, Gabrielino, Luiseño, and Diegueño, whose land holdings penetrated well into the interior from the coast, have been divided into coastal and interior groups, this distinction being indicated by a dotted line running north-south through their tribal territory areas.

The mainstay of the tideland peoples, whose main bounty came from the ocean shore, consisted of clams dug up in the sandy beaches exposed at low tide, of mussels from colonies attached to the rocks and easily secured at low water, of surf fish that could be hauled in by triangular dip nets wielded by broad-shouldered men standing waist deep in the surge of the waves as they broke on the beach (figs. 34, 35). In

FIGURE 34 Yurok Indians catching surf fish, Northwestern California. (Photograph T. T. Waterman, 1928)

FIGURE 35 Drying smelt on beach near mouth of Smith River, in Tolowa Indian territory, Northwestern California. (Photograph Winton Jones, 1934)

addition there were kelp and dozens of other edibles which the sea produced or nourished and which these wise ancient people had come to learn were nutritious. On or near the shore there were waterfowl, seeds from grasses, acorns, and meat from the various kinds of game—elk, antelope, deer, and rabbits among them. Archaeological sites along the California coast show, through identification of the kinds of mammals hunted and the bony remains of fishes and species of shellfish, that this economy was practiced for at least the last 5000 years.

By right of possession of the Pacific edge, these nearly twenty tribes or subtribes had primary access to the marine shells which, when fashioned, served as ornaments and currency in the form of beads. Bead money served the same purpose that metal and paper currency serve today. It brought what one did not have or could not produce, and it was valued for what it would buy.

COASTAL SEA HUNTERS AND FISHERS

The sea hunters and fishers held the California shore from San Luis Obispo Bay southward to Santa Monica Bay, the Channel Islands, and Santa Catalina and San Clemente islands. Tribally they comprised the coastal and island Chumash and the coastal Fernandeño and Gabrielino. The hunting of sea mammals (Sea Otter, sea lions, and seals), and the taking of quantities of large fish with nets and harpoons as well as small ones with nets, hooks, and basketry traps from the open salt water, were made possible by a unique kind of boat (figs. 20, 36), a canoe about 25 feet (ca. 7.6 m.) long built of numerous small planks sewed together through drilled holes and with the seams caulked with natural petroleum tar, or asphalt, which came from submarine springs in the Santa Barbara Channel. The salt-water fishery was extraordinarily productive because of the extensive kelp beds lying just offshore in water up to a depth of 100 feet (30.5 m.). These kelp beds provided a rich environment and cover for fish, which in turn attracted seals and sea lions. The abundance of fish is partly due to the upwelling of the ocean, which creates ideal conditions for the growth of microscopic phytoplankton, tiny free-floating

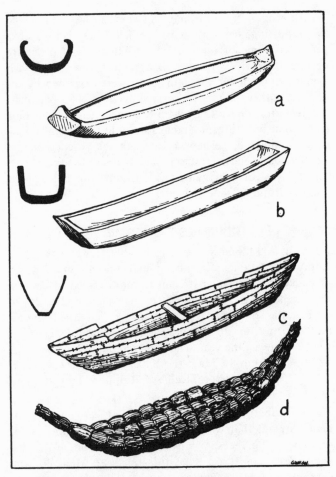

FIGURE 36 Boat types of native California. From top down: Northwestern California river canoe; Klamath Lake region, Northeastern California, canoe; Chumash plank canoe; (bottom) tule balsa, Central California. (After A. L. Kroeber, *Elements of Culture in Native California*, 1922)

aquatic plants, on which the fish spawn feed. Also important in the fishery was the seasonal appearance (concentrated in the summer months) of several species of tuna: California Bonito (*Sarda chiliensis*), California Yellowtail (*Seriola dorsalis*), Albacore (*Thunnus alalunga*), and Bluefin (*Thunnus thynnus*), which were taken in large quantities.

Fish ranging from sardines to swordfish were dried, and this food, together with acorns, which were also storable, permitted some of the coastal sea hunters and fishers to occupy their villages, or perhaps better, towns, the year round. Some of these communities were described by the first Spanish explorers as containing over 1000 persons.

Except for the Santa Barbara Channel area, ocean fishing from boats by California Indians seems to have been lacking or very minimal, perhaps because of the absence of seaworthy boats. The nearest approach to a maritime economy, therefore, was reached among the Chumash peoples of the mainland and offshore islands.

RIVERINE FISHERMEN

North of Monterey the streams that flow westward to empty into the Pacific carried annual runs of salmon, which ascended the freshwater streams to spawn. Such fish, which are hatched in fresh water, live in the ocean, and return to fresh water to spawn and die, are called anadromous. Salmon run from the ocean into the fresh-water streams at various times of the year. The King Salmon (*Oncorhynchus tsawytscha*) runs in May; the Silver Salmon (*O. kisutch*) runs in September; the Steelhead Rainbow Trout (*Salmo gairdneri*) runs in November.

Every tribe north of Monterey held at least one river or major stream that was used by considerable numbers of salmon during the spawning season. The Indians used a wide variety of traps, nets (fig. 37), weirs (fig. 48), and spears to secure as many fish as possible during the run, and they dried and stored surplus fish for winter use (see plate 6). They did not catch salmon in the ocean, probably because hook-and-line methods and adequate boats were not developed, but took them in the rivers all the way from the mouth of the stream to whatever upper natural limit, such as a falls, marked the end of the run. Few of the uppermost reaches of streams tributary to the large rivers contained salmon. Another important dietary item to the people of the Klamath River and its tributaries was the Pacific Lamprey

FIGURE 37 Patwin Indians (Sacramento Valley) fishing for salmon with a boom net. (From J. R. Bartlett, *Personal Narrative of Explorations and Incidents Connected with the United States and Mexican Boundary Commission*, 1854)

(*Entosphenus tridentatus*), which was split open and dried for storage.

As was usual in California, acorns were also an important food resource for the riverine fishermen. They were an especially good one because they were nutritious, could be gathered in great quantity, and were storable.

To different degrees, the coastal tribes from the Costanoans north, whom we have labeled tideland collectors, were also riverine fishermen. By dint of a long walk of, say, 10 to 15 miles to the coast, fish and shellfish could be secured, but beyond this zone people lived largely off the land they occupied, and since settlements were almost always along watercourses, salmon in season were a welcome change in the diet.

The largest and most important salmon streams lay in Northwestern California in the territories of the Tolowa, Yurok, Hupa, Karok, Shasta, and Wiyot tribes, and the Athabascan tribes along the Eel River (fig. 38). The Sacramento and San Joaquin rivers both received very large runs

1. Russian River
2. Klamath River
3. Salmon River
4. Mad River
5. Eel River
6. Trinity River
7. Smith River
8. McCloud River
9. Mill Creek
10. Feather River, North Fork
11. Feather River, Middle Fork
12. Yuba River
13. American River
14. Molelumne River
15. Stanislaus River
16. Merced River
17. Soquel River
18. Pajaro River
19. San Joaquin River
20. Sacramento River

FIGURE 38 Principal salmon streams of Northern and Central California, and upper limits of seasonal salmon runs (shown by circled numbers); streams are not numbered in order of carrying capacity. (Mainly after M. A. Baumhoff, "Environmental Background," in *Handbook of North American Indians*, vol. 8: California, 1978)

of salmon before gold mining in the 1850s silted up their courses. And each of the tributary streams flowing into them from the Sierra Nevadas, from the Kern River in the south to the Pit River in the north, had seasonal salmon runs. Thus, tribes such as the Patwin, Wintun, Wintu, Maidu, and Miwok, whom we class as primarily valley and plains gatherers, were able to harvest considerable quantities of anadromous fish during part of the year. But their other potential food resources were so abundant that fish did not become a staple as it did in Northwestern California.

LAKESHORE FISHERMEN, HUNTERS, AND GATHERERS

Tribes with a lakeshore-adapted economy were the Modoc who lived on Lower Klamath Lake, the Eastern Pomo whose lands bordered Clear Lake some 100 miles (160 km.) north of San Francisco, and the southern Valley Yokuts whose home territories bordered Tulare, Kern, and Buena Vista lakes on the southern San Joaquin Valley floor.

These lakes had an abundant fish life. Oaks and seed-bearing grasses were common on the valley floor, and there was much game, especially antelope, elk, and rabbits. Waterfowl, which were also plentiful, were taken in nets or shot with arrows. Duck decoys, often made with a basketry base with a duck head attached, were commonly used by lakeshore and riverine hunters (see fig. 39) in order to take the birds alive. Mallards (*Anas platyrhyncos*) and Canada Geese (*Branta canadensis*) were probably the most sought after, as they also provided eggs for Indians living around lakeshores or marshes. Other birds important here and in other regions of California were California Quail (*Lophortyx californica*) and Band-tailed Pigeons (*Columba fasciata*). The Pomo employed long, tubular, openwork basketry traps, similar to their fish traps, for catching birds. For quail, such traps were made in sections, the entire "tube" sometimes 30 feet (9.15 m.) long (fig. 40). The Sierra Miwok made a noose of human hair, to be set in a brush fence, for taking quail (fig. 41).

The lake margins supported dense growths of reeds, especially the Common Cattail (*Typha latifolia*), whose starchy roots, growing in the bottom mud, were eaten, and Common Tule (*Scirpus acutus*), which is a heavy producer of nutritious seeds. Lake reeds provided easily available materials for making mats, and in a region where wood may have been somewhat scarce, large mats secured to a willow framework were used for wall and roof coverings (fig. 42).

FIGURE 39 Interior of Northern California Indian house, showing a set of duck decoys, a Pomo Indian type of baby cradle, and other objects used in everyday life. (From J. R. Bartlett, *Personal Narrative of Explorations and Incidents Connected with the United States and Mexican Boundary Commission*, 1854)

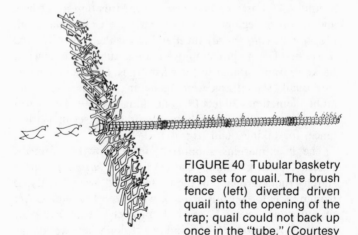

FIGURE 40 Tubular basketry trap set for quail. The brush fence (left) diverted driven quail into the opening of the trap; quail could not back up once in the "tube." (Courtesy of the R. H. Lowie Museum of Anthropology)

FIGURE 41 Hair noose set for quail in openings left in brush fence. (From S. A. Barrett and E. W. Gifford, *Miwok Material Culture*, 1933)

FIGURE 42 Tache Yokuts mat-covered house. (Photograph C. H. Merriam, ca. 1903)

FIGURE 43 Tule balsa in San Francisco Bay. (After Louis Choris, 1822)

The usual watercraft of the Pomo and Yokuts lake people was the cigar-shaped tule raft, or balsa, which would bear two or three persons (fig. 43). Though of simple construction, such rafts served to take fishermen and waterfowl hunters beyond the reeds to open water. They were propelled with long poles, which were pushed into the shallow lake bottom (similar tule balsas, such as those used on San Francisco Bay, were propelled by paddles).

The lakeshore dwellers, though sharing many features of material culture and subsistence procurement, differed in certain ways in the three different areas. Since oaks were very rare in the Modoc area, there Camas (*Camassia quamash*) roots and Wokas (a water lily, *Nuphar polysepalum*) seeds were collected instead. The Pomo around Clear Lake had access to the hilly areas bordering the lake, which gave them a more varied selection of plant and animal foods. The southern Valley Yokuts lake area was surrounded by a relatively barren plain, which was, however, abundantly endowed with seed-bearing grasses and game.

VALLEY AND PLAINS GATHERERS

The area here is the Great Interior Valley of California, which is divided into the northern half, the Sacramento Valley, and the southern half, the San Joaquin Valley. Together they have a length of about 420 miles (675 km.). Each valley is named for its major river, fed by tributary streams flowing west out of the Sierra Nevada. Valley and plains gatherers were the Wintun, Patwin (Southern Wintun), Valley Maidu, Valley or Plains Miwok, and Valley Yokuts tribes.

Their settlements were often very large and were usually on the river bank or the borders of seasonal lakes formed by the spring overflow of the two main rivers. Spaniards exploring the Sacramento River in the early eighteenth century observed villages of over 1000 persons. Many of the settlements were situated on top of very large, high, natural earth mounds so as to keep the houses and villages dry during the spring flood, when the swollen Sacramento went over its banks and dumped its excess waters into a series of natural, shallow, overflow basins along each bank of the lower 70 miles of the river. The white man, by raising high levees, has now largely changed the pattern of flooding, but today's traveler crossing the elevated causeway between Davis and Sacramento may still see in spring a huge expanse of still water which has been diverted through bypasses from the swollen river into the overflow basins to prevent the flooding of more valuable lands.

The diet of the Indian dwellers in the Interior Valley was varied. Small seeds were abundant; oaks grew over most of the valley floor; antelope, elk, and deer were plentiful; and the rivers, together with the slow-moving sloughs and small freshwater lakes, provided mussels and fish.

In the month of February 1833, John Work, leader of a fur brigade of the Hudson's Bay Company, with his group took refuge from the river overflow in the Marysville Buttes of the Sacramento Valley. Valley animals, it seems, were doing the same, and since Work's party was living off the country, they found the hunting good. During this month

Work's hunters killed 395 elk, 148 deer, 17 bears, and 8 antelopes. The figures on this slaughter indicate how abundant game was in this area.

The delta region, where the Sacramento and San Joaquin rivers come together in a maze of tule swamps and sloughs, was the most favorable area of the valley. Waterfowl and fish could be secured in great quantities. The west side of the San Joaquin Valley, in contrast, was dry and barren, and there were no important settlements here.

FOOTHILL HUNTERS AND GATHERERS

The foothill regions were among the most favored in the state for Indian life. Coastal and river tribes were equally well-off, though they differed in the kinds of plants and animals available for food. The foothill regions are the western slopes of the Sierra Nevada, most of the Coast Ranges, and the low mountain areas behind the coast from Point Conception south.

Tribes with a foothill adaptation were the inland Pomo (except for the Lake Pomo), the Interior Esselen, the Salinan people, the Interior Chumash, and the various Uto-Aztekan and other tribes behind the coast south of the Chumash (Gabrielino, Fernandeño, Cahuilla, Luiseño, Diegueño, Juaneño, Cupeño, and Serrano), and the series of tribes living east of the floor of the Sacramento and San Joaquin valleys on the Cascade and Sierran slopes. These people (from north to south) were the Shasta, Wintu, Yana, Foothill Maidu, Sierra Miwok, Foothill Yokuts, Monache (Western Mono), Tübatulabal, Kawaiisu, Kitanemuk, and Alliklik tribes. North and east of the Pomo were the Hill Patwin, the Yuki, and some of the small Athabascan tribes south of the Hupa.

The acorn was probably the most important dietary item in the foothills, with fish and game playing a lesser role. (For more information on acorn gathering, see the section on "Plants as Food" in chapter 4.) In the summer the foothill tribes occupied the Sierra to the crest of the mountains and sometimes traveled east of it, but when the snows began, the people as well as the deer moved down below the snow line, which lay at about 5000 feet (1524 m.) above sea level.

Foothill settlements were, as usual, along streams, but in the more rugged relief of the Sierras, trails and settlements lay on ridges where travel was easier and there was more sun.

In many brushy or chaparral areas the Indians regularly set fires to make a more open countryside, which was easier to travel, hunt, and collect in. The new growth of grass and shoots from shrubs provided food for grazing and browsing animals, and thus led to better hunting. This kind of controlled burning surely on occasion caused great forest fires, although in the valley and foothill areas, where the Indian populations were concentrated, there may have been much smoke but no serious fires.

An experiment has been carried out by foresters on the effect of planned burning. In dense, unburned chaparral areas the deer count was 30 per square mile. After the first burning of the study area the count of deer rose to 98 per square mile. This figure went up to 131 per square mile in the second year, presumably as a result of increased feed. By the fifth and sixth years the count had dropped to 84. Testimony from the Indians is clear on the point that they were well aware of the beneficial effects of burning off chaparral areas at intervals to increase the deer supply. The problem now is how to start the process again after a lapse of more than a century. In many areas today brush growth and accumulated fuel on the ground are so great that any fire soon gets out of control and consumes everything in its path. As land managers, the Indians were in some ways far ahead of us today.

DESERT HUNTERS AND COLLECTORS

Home for the desert tribes was the eastern border of California from the Oregon line south to the Colorado River and the Colorado and Mohave deserts of the southern interior of the state. This region was, and remains, the least populated in the state on account of its low rainfall, its extreme summer heat, and its desert-plant cover. In California the desert hunters and collectors represented the western edge of the larger Great Basin area, which was also populated by Uto-Aztekan speakers. The California representatives were the Northern Paiute (also called the Paviotso), the Panamint, the Chemehuevi (Southern Paiute), the Vanyume (a branch of the Serrano), and the Desert Cahuilla. Some of the Washo, Hokan speakers, were also desert dwellers.

Population density in the desert was low because the region did not afford much food. The piñon pines (*Pinus* spp.) grow in part of the area, and in their years of production there are plenty of nuts to be gathered and stored for the lean winter season. But the crop is irregular, and an area that yields well one year may be barren the next. Perhaps for this reason hard and fast territorial boundaries of bands (the equivalent of the tribelets found west of the Sierras) were not established, and as a result groups could gather piñon nuts wherever they found them. In the south, where piñon does not grow abundantly, Honey Mesquite (*Prosopis juliflora*) and Screwbean Mesquite (*P. pubescens*) seeds were substitutes. Both plants are in the legume family. Hunting and trapping of small game (wood rats, rabbits, and the like) yielded some meat, but the diet was dominated by plant foods.

Occupation sites were located near the occasional springs, some of which were permanent and others seasonal. Nomadism was a way of life, with small bands or family groups moving from one spot to another, the routes being determined by water sources and seasonal plant foods.

As might be expected, the desert peoples, who moved frequently, had a very limited material culture, since everything they needed had to be carried on their backs. Their clothing, baskets for gathering or cooking, a fire drill for making fire, and bows and arrows were the basic stock of equipment.

The information available on population numbers, permanence of villages, and gathering cycles of seasonal movements strongly suggests that these were a reflection of the environment. In a rough way we can say that, for the Indians, the more abundant and varied and assured the food supply was, the larger the social aggregates, the more permanent the villages, and the richer the stock of material culture items.

DESERT AGRICULTURISTS

The Yuma, the Halchidhoma, and the Mohave lived along both banks of the Colorado River. This great stream, before the white man's dams interfered, flooded nearly every year in June. But the exact time of overflowing was uncertain, and it did not flood in some years. The high water which nearly every year covered the wide floodplain and deposited a layer of rich silt was of great significance to the Indians. No other major river in the United States carries as heavy a load of silt as the Colorado River; early white settlers described the stream as "too thick to drink and too thin to plow."

In ancient times, as soon as the floodwaters subsided the Indians planted their crops—maize (five varieties, of which one was a short-season variety from which two crops could be secured with the first planting in June or July), beans (three varieties), pumpkins, and calabashes. These plants remained as staples among the Yuma, and it seems that regular cultivation of muskmelons and watermelons, Old World introductions, did not take place until some time before 1700, possibly 150 years or so after the first probable contact with the Spanish explorer Alarcón, who attempted, unsuccessfully, to introduce such plants as wheat and cowpeas to the Lower Colorado River peoples in 1540.

Colorado River agriculture was simple, compared with modern mechanical methods. A hole was punched with a sharpened stick in the floodplain silt, and the seeds were dropped in. Field tending was minimal, and a luxuriant growth of weeds reduced the crop yield. So many things could go wrong with floodplain farming that these tribes were forced to fall back on Honey Mesquite and Screwbean Mesquite beans and river fish when their crops failed. The Colorado River tribes are best viewed as the westernmost members of the Southwestern farming people, who included the Hopi, Pima, Maricopa, Zuñi, and Havasupai tribes.

An unusual feature of Colorado River agriculture was the sowing of seeds of wild grasses (among then Alkali Sacaton, or Dropseed, *Sporobolus airoides*) in floodplain plots. Since the seeds for planting were collected from wild, uncultivated plants, the effect was to concentrate production and yield of desirable seeds in special plots. Something very like this was also done by the Owens Valley Paiute, who may have learned about it from the Yuma or the Mohave. Among the Colorado River farmers, field corners were marked by raising small mounds of earth. Since these often were washed away when the river flooded, they had to be replaced, and this led to disputes between owners of neighboring plots. To settle their differences each contestant collected a group of friends to aid him in a pushing contest. The chief rivals grasped each other at the waist or the shoulders, and the supporters lined up behind each main contestant. Each line would shove against the other, and the winner placed the boundary marker where he believed it should be. If the loser was still not satisfied, he would then challenge his rival to a stick fight, which was likely to lead to serious bodily injury. The losing contestant, therefore, probably thought carefully before challenging a decision reached in a pushing contest. One possible reason for not placing permanent boundary markers was that without them there was always the potentiality of expanding one's holdings through challenges.

If farm crops ran short in the winter or the harvest was bad, they were supplemented with wild-seed gathering, hunting or fishing. Four main kinds of fish were caught in weirs (fig. 44) built out from the shore: the Humpback Sucker (*Xyrauchen texanus*), Bonytail (*Gila elegans*), Colorado Squawfish (*Ptychochilus lucius*), and Striped Mullet (*Mugil cephalus*). The Colorado Squawfish, often also called whitefish, can run to over 100 pounds (45.4 kg.).

All the Colorado River tribes were interested in warfare, not for the little plunder they might secure but because war was believed to enhance the spiritual power of the tribe as a whole.

FIGURE 44 Mohave Indian fish weir, Colorado River region. (From J. C. Ives. *Report on the Colorado River of the West,* 1861)

In an effort to show, in a simplified manner, the food chain for California tribes living in different environments, four diagrams have been constructed (fig. 45). We do not possess the detailed information on how many deer were killed by the men of a village each year, or how many bushels of acorns per family were gathered in a season before the white man's time, so it is necessary to estimate the relative amounts of dietary items. In general, we believe that we are fairly close to representing the proportional values of major Indian food resources in the days before the European colonists appeared in California.

Without the sun, the ultimate source of all life and energy, there could be no plant or animal life. In the diagrams food plants, such as acorns, bulbs, berries, or seeds, are represented as collected and eaten directly by humans. Land animals, such as deer, elk, antelope, rabbits, squirrels, and the like, are nourished by plants and then hunted by man for food. Here what we have called the terrestrial eco-base is an intermediate step between the sun and man (the secondary consumer) and the animals (the primary consumers). In the ocean or in freshwater lakes, fish and invertebrates (such as mollusks and crustaceans) are supported by microorganisms, but in the end they are subject to predation by larger sea-living forms (bigger fish, sea mammals) searching for

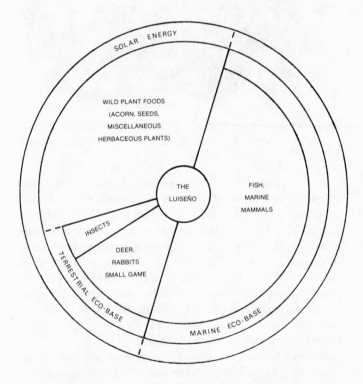

FIGURE 45 Food resource charts of four California Indian tribes. (Sean L. Swezey and George W. Appleton helped us devise these food-chain diagrams.)

food, and ultimately by man. We have not tried to indicate in the diagrams the intermediate predators that are securing meals along the food chain that leads from the sun to man, but they do exist.

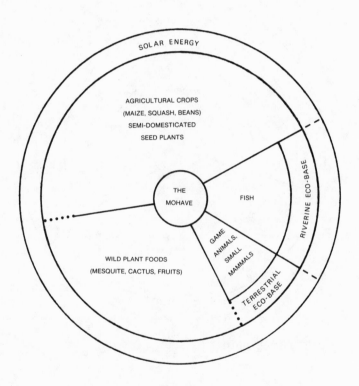

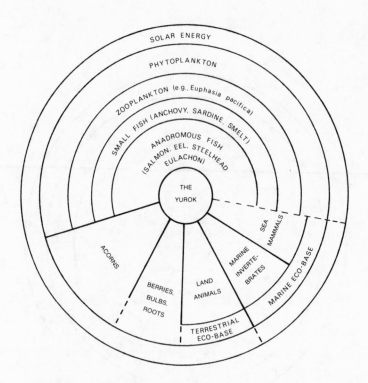

FIGURE 45 continued.

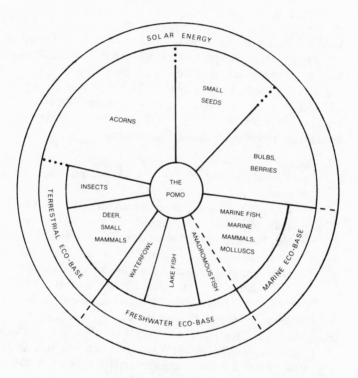

4. THE FOOD QUEST

Wild animals and plants were the source of food for all tribes in the state, except the Colorado River tribes and the Kamia of the Imperial Valley, who also farmed maize, beans, and squash. In brief form we list the preferred foods for each of the ecological types of Indian cultures as described in chapter 3. These foods are given in order of decreasing importance, insofar as possible.

I. Coastal
  1. Tideland collectors: Shellfish (clams, mussels, oysters); surf fish (smelt, sardines, rock fish); acorns (from a half dozen or so oak species); land mammals (deer, elk, bear, rabbit, etc.).
  2. Sea hunters and fishers: Ocean fish (salmon, herring, halibut, tuna, flounder, cod, shark, sturgeon); shellfish; land mammals; sea mammals (seals, sea lions, Sea Otter, stranded whales); acorns.
II. Riverine fishermen: Fish (salmon, steelhead, trout, sturgeon, lamprey eel); acorns; land mammals.
III. Lakeshore fishermen, hunters, and gatherers: Fish (whitefish, sucker, perch); seeds and roots of tule or cattail; water lily seeds; acorns; waterfowl (ducks, mudhens, geese); land mammals (antelope, elk, rabbits).
IV. Valley and plains gatherers: Acorns; grass seeds; land mammals; fish.
V. Foothill hunters and gatherers: Acorns; buckeye; pine nuts (from Digger Pine, Sugar Pine, Yellow Pine); land mammals; fish (trout, salmon, whitefish); insects (grasshoppers, caterpillars).
VI. Desert
  1. Hunters and collectors: Seeds (pine nuts, mesquite, grasses, Joshua Tree); land mammals (rabbit, cot-

tontail, wood rats, deer, mountain sheep, antelope); reptiles; insects.
2. Agriculturists: Cultivated plants (maize, beans,
squashes); wild plant seeds (mesquite, screwbean,
agave); fish; land mammals.

It is probably no exaggeration to say that the California
Indians, taken as a whole, had something like 500 kinds of
plant and animal foods to use. Some resources, such as
acorns, salmon, elk, and deer, were staples in the areas
where they occurred; other animals and plants that were
more restricted in their distribution were only regionally
exploited.

GENERAL DIET INFORMATION

Stephen Powers estimated in 1877 that the California
Indian diet consisted of 56 percent acorns, 28 percent fish,
and 14 percent small seeds, the amount of seeds varying
according to locale (fig. 46). E. F. Castetter and W. H. Bell
say that the Colorado River Yuma divided their food-
getting as follows: agricultural crops (maize, beans, squash),
40 percent; wild plant products (Honey Mesquite, Screwbean, grass seeds), 35 percent; fish, 15 percent; animal foods
(rabbits, wood rats, ducks), 10 percent. R. C. White estimates that the Coastal Luiseño, who were mainly fishers
and collectors, secured about 30 percent of their livelihood
from wild plants (acorns, seeds, greens); 20 percent from
game and marine mammals; and 50 percent from fish.

David Prescott Barrows in 1900 studied the ethnobotany
of the Cahuilla Indians and recorded 60 plants they used for
food and 28 for narcotics, stimulants, and medicines. A
partial list of food plants included Honey Mesquite or
Algaroba (*Prosopis juliflora*) and Screwbean Mesquite (*P.
pubescens*) beans; Indian Ricegrass (*Oryzopsis hymenoides*)
and Fremont's Goosefoot (*Chenopodium fremontii*) seeds;
Desert Agave (*Agave deserti*) blossoms, cabbages, and
stalks; Mojave Yucca (*Yucca schidigera*) green or ripe
fruit pods; Wild Plum (*Prunus ilicifolia*) fruit and pits;
dates (*Washingtonia filifera*); berries of juniper (*Juniperus*

FIGURE 46 San Joaquin Valley Indians gathering grass seed. (From H. R. Schoolcraft, *Indian Tribes of the United States*, 1865)

spp.); acorns (*Quercus lobata, Q. dumosa*); pine nuts (*Pinus lambertiana, P. edulis, P. quadrifolia, P. monophylla*); Chia seeds (*Salvia columbariae*); and cactus buds (*Opuntia basilaris*). They could gather plant foods from April through December and needed to store food only for the four winter months. Barrows wrote:

A review of the food supply of these Indians forces in upon us some general reflections and conclusions. First, it seems certain that the diet was a much more diversified one than fell to the lot of most North American Indians. Roaming from the desert, through the mountains to the coast plains, they drew upon three quite dissimilar botanical zones. . . . And yet this habitat, dreary and forbidding as it seems to most, is after all a generous one. Nature did not pour out her gifts lavishly here, but the patient toiler and wise seeker she rewarded well. The main staples of diet were, indeed, furnished in most lavish abundance.

What is doubtless the most complete and detailed ethnobotany for any California tribe is titled *Temalpakh* (1972) and was written by an ethnographer, Lowell Bean, and a Cahuilla woman, Katherine Saubel. They describe native uses for 174 different plants known to and used by the Cahuilla, but they admit that their listing is incomplete.

One of the most thorough ecological studies of California Indians is that made by M. A. Baumhoff (1963). By calculating the density of acorn-producing oaks, the anadromous fish resources in streams, and the amount of large game in tribal areas, he secured a set of figures which show the differing degrees of reliance each tribe placed on these three primary food resources. Table 3 is taken from his report.

FISH AND SHELLFISH AS FOOD

As we said in chapter 3, every tribe north of Monterey used its stream to advantage during the seasonal salmon runs. Salmon fishing with spears, nets, or weirs (figs. 47, 48, 49) was very productive. Ethnologists have taken the rough figures for the salmon catch by California Indians and have estimated that 15 million pounds (6,804,000 kg.) were caught each year. There are statements dating from the last century that it was not uncommon for a Klamath River Yurok family to have a ton of dried salmon hanging from the rafters of the house (fig. 50).

The Klamath River Yurok stored dried salmon in baskets, each layer of fish being separated by a layer of leafy twigs of the aromatic California Bay or Laurel tree (*Umbellularia californica*). The Yurok say that the leaves "kept out the moths," which presumably would otherwise have laid eggs on the salmon and whose larvae would have eaten the fish.

TABLE 3. The Reliance of California Tribes on Three Primary Food Resources

Tribe	Popu-lation	Tribal area (in square miles)	Resource*		
			Acorns	Fish	Game
Tolowa	2,400	955	686	510	845
Yurok	3,100	741	582	1,265	650
Karok	2,700	1,053	775	880	798
Wiyot	3,200	297	149	865	269
Hupa	1,475	428	496	390	496
Mattole	1,200	219	171	335	315
Wailaki	2,760	416	611	160	634
Coast Yuki	750	179	122	170	141
Yuki	6,880	1,169	1,269	830	1,504
Northern Pomo	7,010	1,194	1,234	485	1,656
Eastern Pomo	1,410	285	299	270	514
Central Pomo	3,440	693	762	505	913
Southeastern Pomo	1,070	207	328	270	408
Southwestern Pomo	1,480	275	310	275	338
Wappo	4,600	519	760	250	964
Plains Miwok	14,350	1,290	872	3,340	2,580
Central Miwok	2,130	2,870	2,626	880	2,883
Southern Miwok	2,725	1,905	2,025	600	2,789
Southern Valley Yokuts	15,380	6,572	4,583	?	12,781
Monache	3,640	3,417	1,971	350	2,481

* The acorn figure is an index of the potential yield per square mile of tribal territory. The fish figure is an index of the potential yield of anadromous fish in tens of linear stream miles. The game figure is an index of the potential yield of large game (deer, elk, antelope) in square miles of tribal territory. What is significant is the differential weight of the three main food resource categories in the native diet in different tribes.

The indexes are abstract figures for comparative purposes only. For example, the table shows that the Yurok had fewer acorn and game resources than the Tolowa had, but more than twice the Tolowa potential in fish.

FIGURE 47 Karok Indians fishing from scaffold with A-frame net in the lower Klamath River, ca. 1900. (Courtesy of the Lowie Museum of Anthropology)

One may suppose that the pungent herb leaves also imparted a flavor to the dried fish, a fact known to many American cooks today.

Judging from the presence of shells in California Indian archaeological occupation middens and from reports from recently living Indians, there were few molluscan species that were not gathered for food or other purposes. All along

FIGURE 48 Hupa Indian fish weir, ca. 1906. (Courtesy of the Lowie Museum of Anthropology)

FIGURE 49 California Indian spearing salmon. (From *Hutchings' California Magazine*, 1860)

FIGURE 50 Salmon drying in Indian house, lower Klamath River, ca. 1901. (Courtesy of the Lowie Museum of Anthropology)

the Pacific coast the rocks and beaches were exploited for shellfish, and the sites of former villages are composed largely of the shells of species collected. Many interior people came to the coast to gather and dry shellfish, which they took back with them, and many of the resident people on the Pacific shore gathered and dried large amounts of shellfish as well as salt and kelp to trade for other food or goods with tribes living in the interior.

Some village groups along the Central California coast would spend the summer months living on the ocean shore at the mouth of a stream, but in the fall and winter they would move several miles back into the steep mountains where acorns could be collected and deer hunted. Here the group would spend the winter, often above the coastal fog, where it was warmer. To supplement their acorn soup, some members of the group (probably the women) would make the long, steep hike down to the shore to dig clams and gather mussels and abalones, which they carried back in baskets. Big shellmounds are found at some of the hill sites, for example in the Big Sur region of Monterey County, even though they lie five or more miles by trail from the ocean coast.

The shellfish in the following list are all edible, unless otherwise noted. The non-food uses for various species are included.

Abalone (*Haliotis cracherodii, H. rufescens*): Beads, ornaments, C-shaped fishhooks, bowls (siphon holes closed with asphaltum or other substance).

Barnacles (*Mitella polymerus*) (Goose Barnacle): Stem eaten after being cooked in hot ashes (not coals).

Chitons (*Cryptochiton stelleri*) (Gum Boot): Heated near fire to loosen epidermis on back, then cooked in coals or earth oven.

(*Katharina tunicata*) (Leather Chiton): Cooked in coals or earth oven.

Clams (*Saxidomus nuttalli*) (Washington Clam): One of the chief sources of shell beads in northern California.

(*Macoma nasuta*) (Bent-Nosed Clam): Abundant and widely used around San Francisco Bay and Tomales Bay.

(*Tivela stultorum*) (Pismo Clam): Large clam abundant on the southern coast and Monterey Bay.

(*Chione californiensis*) (California Venus).

(*Protothaca staminea*) (Rock Cockle).

Cockle shells (*Clinocardium nuttallii*) (Nuttall's Cockle, Button Shell).

Cowries (*Cypraea spadicea*) (Chestnut Cowrie): Found on the southern coast; probably used for ornaments or amulets only.

Limpets (*Lottia gigantea*) (Owl Limpet).

(*Megathura crenulata*) (Giant Keyhole Limpet): Not a true "limpet" and probably not important as a food species, since it occurs below low-tide level. It was evidently found on the beach and then painted as ornament.

Mussels (*Mytilus californianus*) (California Mussel):

Shells used in the manufacture of C-shaped fishhooks and eating spoons (whole); Yurok used shells for adze-blades. (Note that California Indians were aware of the poisonous effect of the "red tide" on these and some other molluscan species—see chapter 6, under "Medicinal Plants.")

(*Mytilus edulis*) (Blue or Bay Mussel): Found especially in San Francisco Bay.

Olive shells (*Olivella biplicata*) (Purple Olive): One of the favorite shells for beads; not a food species.

Oysters (*Ostrea lurida*) (California Oyster): Small oysters, but abundant along the coast, especially in the San Francisco Bay region and Tomales Bay.

Scallops (*Pecten* spp.): Common on the coast south of Monterey.

Sea urchins (*Strongylocentrotus purpuratus*) (Purple Sea Urchin): Yellow egg mass eaten raw.

Tusk Shells (*Dentalium pretiosum*) (Tusk Shells; "Indian Money"): Tusk shells occur in California waters, but this species, not used as food, came from the north (Washington). It was prized as currency and decorative beads in Northern California (see fig. 78).

ACORNS AND OTHER PLANT PRODUCTS AS FOOD

In Central California no fewer than seven species of oaks (*Quercus* spp.) were used for their acorns (fig. 51). These were extremely productive wild tree crops, and foresters have measured the yields for many species. These range from about 500 to 1000 pounds (225 to 450 kg.) of acorns for a large tree. The total annual acorn crop for Central California would have run into the millions of tons, but only a small fraction of the yield was gathered each year by the Indians. The bearing season for oaks is only a few weeks, and Indians were not the only collectors of acorns. Squirrels, insects, woodpeckers, and bears competed with the Indians for the acorn crop.

All acorns produced by the several species of California oaks contain tannin (some observers refer to this as tannic acid), which is bitter in an untreated state and makes the

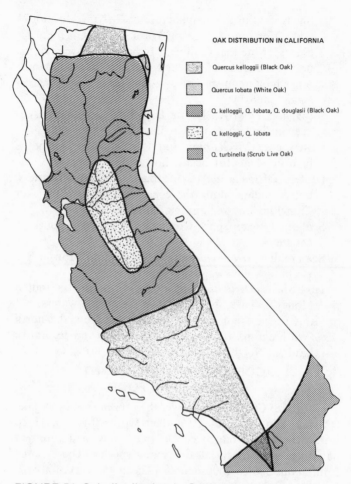

OAK DISTRIBUTION IN CALIFORNIA

Quercus kelloggii (Black Oak)

Quercus lobata (White Oak)

Q. kelloggii, Q. lobata, Q. douglasii (Black Oak)

Q. kelloggii, Q. lobata

Q. turbinella (Scrub Live Oak)

FIGURE 51 Oak distribution in California.

acorns unpalatable. Two methods of removing the tannin were employed. One was to bury the whole (i.e., unshelled) acorns in mud, usually on the edge of a stream or a swamp, for a period of several months, up to a year. This mud immersion method neutralized the bitter element, so the acorns became "sweet." The most common method was to remove the acorn hull, grind the interior "meat" into a flour in a stone mortar or on a flat grinding slab (metate) and then pour warm water repeatedly over the flour, to leach out the tannin. A shallow concave pit was dug in the earth, lined with grass or conifer needles, and the acorn meal was put in the pit. The water was heated in a basket by dropping in hot stones that had been placed in a fire, and it was gently poured over the meal. Several such applications of warm water percolating through the meal sufficed to rid it of the bitter taste.

The leached meal was next mixed with water in a watertight basket and boiled by dropping hot stones, usually about fist size, into the gruel. The cooked mush was then edible, and was either drunk or eaten with a spoon made of half of a bivalve shell, or carved of wood or antler. Figure 85 shows Indians engaged in leaching and other processes of acorn preparation. At times the leached acorn meal was made into a cake and baked on a flat stone heated in the fire, but most tribes preferred to consume acorns as mush. It was not customary to enhance the taste of the mush by adding spices or other flavoring.

Indians collected large quantities of acorns during the fall bearing season of the oaks and stored them for winter use in granaries (figs. 52, 53). In September 1849, Lieutenant George Derby, while camped on the bank of the lower Feather River, wrote:

About 200 yards above the farm house is situated a rancheria of Indians, about 300 in number. They had just commenced the collection for their winter stock of acorns, and had many high baskets, containing probably 40 or 50 bushels of this species of provender lying about.

Captain John C. Frémont in 1844 on the American River noted that he saw an Indian village with "two or three huts,"

FIGURE 52 Miwok Indians and acorn granary, Yosemite Valley. (Photograph C. H. Merriam, ca. 1898)

FIGURE 53 Miwok acorn granaries. (After S. Powers, *Tribes of California*, 1877)

and near each house was "a crate [granary] formed of interlaced branches and grass, in size and shape like a very large hogshead. Each of these contained from six to nine bushels [of acorns]." This was in April and presumably was the chief winter food of this small village.

Table 4 gives the chemical analyses of acorns, yucca, California Buckeye, Tanbark Oak, Honey Mesquite, piñon, and several cultivated plants (peanuts, beans, barley, maize, wheat). It will be readily seen that acorns are an excellent food, although fattening unless supplemented with high protein foods such as fish or deer meat.

Foresters have collected and weighed all the acorns produced in one year by certain species of oaks. The average per tree production of acorns of the Valley Oak is 350-500 pounds (160-227 kg.); Interior Live Oak, 200 pounds (90.7 kg.); Blue Oak, 160 pounds (72.6 kg.); and California Black Oak, between 200 and 300 pounds (90 and 136 kg.). A single stand or grove of oaks within the tribal territory could adequately satisfy a village's demand for this food item.

Carl B. Wolf of the Santa Ana Botanic Garden made field studies in the 1940s of a number of wild tree crops in California. Table 5 gives production figures for some of these wild crops (all of which were heavily exploited by the Indians) and the time required for one person to collect measured amounts of seeds. It may be seen from this that a family, by diligent work over a short period, could have collected a considerable amount of storable food. Let us take a family of five (mother, father, children aged 15, 10, and 8) and estimate how many pounds of Valley Oak acorns they could have collected in two weeks in a good bearing year. Let us assume that the two youngest children worked at 50 percent of the efficiency of the parents and the older child, so that in effect there were four collectors. And, since the yield of individual trees is different, and there would have been some time loss in moving from tree to tree and in shaking acorns from the branches, let us say that an adult could have collected 75 pounds of acorns in an hour. Working for 8 hours a day (though Indians certainly worked from early morning to dusk in the bearing season of oaks)

TABLE 4. Chemical Analyses of Indian and Non-Indian Plant Foods (all figures are percentages)

Seed	Water	Protein	Fats	Fiber	Carbohydrate
Quercus agrifolia (Coast Live Oak)	29.10	4.88	13.05	9.04	42.52
Q. chrysolepis (Golden Cup or Canyon Oak)	42.10	2.63	5.50	8.10	40.42
Q. douglasii (Blue Oak)	33.60	4.00	5.90	7.15	47.80
Q. garryana (Oregon Oak)	30.70	3.00	3.40	9.10	52.45
Q. kelloggii (California Black or Kellogg Oak)	31.40	3.44	13.55	8.60	41.81
Q. lobata (Valley Oak)	40.80	3.19	3.60	6.15	44.91
Yucca brevifolia (Joshua Tree)	5.90	10.56	34.40	10.45	37.04
Aesculus californica (California Buckeye)	64.70	2.88	0.45	1.75	28.87
Lithocarpus densiflora (Tanbark Oak)	36.00	2.06	8.50	14.15	38.29
Prosopis juliflora (Honey Mesquite)	?	8.34	2.40	?	52.02
Pinus monophylla (Piñon)	2.2	3.8	35.4	?	15.3
Indian corn (maize)	12.50	9.2	1.9	1.0	74.4
Wheat	11.5	11.4	1.0	0.2	75.4
Barley	10.10	8.70	1.90	5.70	71.00
Peanuts	9.4	19.4	27.5	?	15.3
Kidney beans	?	24.2	1.2	?	?

TABLE 5. Wild Tree Crops Collected by California Indians

Tree	Time expended (hours)	Amount collected		Amount edible	
		lbs.	kg.	lbs.	kg.
Yucca brevifolia (Joshua Tree)	3.75	450	204.2	211	95.7
Quercus lobata (Valley Oak)	1	150	68.1	112	50.8
Q. agrifolia (Coast Live Oak)	1	50	22.7	35	15.9
Lithocarpus densiflora (Tanbark Oak)	?	100	45.3	49	22.2
Q. chrysolepis (Golden Cup or Canyon Oak)	1	300	136.1	147	66.7
Q. kelloggii (California Black or Kellogg Oak)	?	100	45.4	78	35.4
Aesculus californica (California Buckeye)	1	200	90.7	64	29.0

for two weeks (14 days), our family could have collected 33,600 pounds (17 tons or 15.4 metric tons) of acorns.

Each species of oak does not bear with equal abundance every year. The Oregon Oak (*Quercus garryana*) bears abundantly only one year in every three or four; the Valley Oak (*Q. lobata*), the Blue Oak (*Q. douglasii*), and the Golden Cup Oak (*Q. chrysolepis*) each have good crops one year out of three; the Interior Live Oak (*Q. wislizenii*) and the California Black Oak (*Q. kelloggii*) bear well every other year. If the acorn crop was light, the gatherers would have had to work harder to collect enough to see them through the winter. If it failed, they were in trouble and would have had to turn to other storable food resources, such as Buckeyes. Famines are not reported, apparently because there were always some other foods to fall back on, even though these were not the preferred ones. An anthropologist has reported a typical Sierra Miwok chief's exhortation to his fellow villagers:

> Get up! Get up! All the people get up! Wash yourself; wash your face. After you wash yourself, eat breakfast. Go hunt for something [to eat]. You will get hungry. After you get something, you will eat it. Get up!

A federal Indian agent assigned to care for the Indians of Placer, Nevada, Sierra, and Yuba counties in 1855 reported that the acorn crop had "failed completely in the last three years" but also noted that on the Yuba River one week's fishing would yield enough salmon to last the people through the winter. The Southwestern Pomo said that when food ran short in the winter they would search through the woods for bark-covered trees that had been used by woodpeckers to store acorns. By prying off the bark, they could release the acorns and pick them up. Indian testimony had it that considerable amounts of acorns could be gathered in this way. A tree without thick bark in which woodpeckers had cached acorns was not exploited because the natives had no means of cutting down such trees. (The Pomo also observed that ground squirrels stored "anise" [probably

Fennel, *Foeniculum vulgare*] roots in their burrows, and discovered that an easy way to collect these roots was to dig out the squirrels' hoard and remove it. As much as one and a half quarts of roots could be recovered from a burrow.)

A common practice was to collect enough acorns in one season to last a family for two years. Since all species of oak (*Quercus*) do not bear each year, there was always the possibility of a short crop during the alternate years. And perhaps, since the nuts were so easy to gather, excess quantities would be collected so that guests could be fed on ceremonial occasions without reducing the acorn supply needed to support the family through the winter months.

Granaries for acorns were of variable size, and some of these were measured by ethnologists. S. A. Barrett and E. W. Gifford saw a Sierra Miwok granary that was 5 feet (1.52 m.) in diameter and 12 feet (3.66 m.) high. Kroeber saw a Patwin granary 3 feet (0.914 m.) in diameter and over 8 feet (2.44 m.) tall. The volumes of Sierra Miwok granaries have been calculated, ranging from 94 to 196 cubic feet (2.64-5.5 cu. m.).

A. S. Taylor, observing the Indians of the northern California coast in the 1860s, noted that "to keep the rats, squirrels, and ants away from his stores, the Indian smears the trunk [of the oak tree holding the granary] round with pitch, which is furnished in abundance by the pine trees." Seeds and nuts (such as acorns) that were stored in baskets or granaries could also be protected from insect damage by putting with them leaves of the California Laurel or Bay tree, which are very pungent.

The reader may be interested in some calculations of the food energy (calories and proteins) contained in acorns. Assuming that the Sierra Miwok granary mentioned above, measuring 5 feet in diameter and 12 feet in height, was the yearly storage of a single family (averaging 6 persons), it can be calculated that it held, with a conical bottom, about 170 cubic feet (4.7 cu. m.) of nuts, which would weigh 5366 pounds (2439 kg.) and yield 5636 kilocalories per day per person, which is in excess of actual bodily needs. This same cache would produce 50.1 grams of protein per day per person. An adult male weighing 143 pounds (65 kg.) needs only 37 grams of protein per day.

The Indians themselves preferred the acorn of the so-called Tanbark Oak, saying that it tasted better than those from trees of the *Quercus* genus. Chemically it tends to be lower in protein and higher in fiber than the acorns from *Quercus* species. The Tanbark acorns have thicker shells or hulls than other acorns, which makes them less susceptible to rot, and they are not so readily attacked by insect pests. These advantages may have contributed to the Indian preference for this acorn. The low protein content of the Tanbark Oak was not a serious drawback, because the tree grew most abundantly where salmon, a high-protein food, was readily available.

Greens such as Spanish Clover (*Lotus purshianus*) and pond lily roots, mushrooms, tree fungi, and small grass seeds might occasionally be mixed with acorn mush to add flavor (and, incidentally, vitamins). Clay earth was at times added to the mush by the Pomo and the Sierra Miwok so that it would absorb any bitter tannic acid remaining after leaching. The clay additive might have had some nutritional value in supplying useful minerals to the diet.

The California Buckeye tree (*Aesculus californica*) produces generous quantities of large, round, meaty seeds, about two inches in diameter. Foresters calculate that a dense stand of Buckeye trees will produce 4.4 tons (4 metric tons) of seeds per acre per year. These contain a bitter and poisonous alkaloid (aesculin) and have little fat or protein. For several reasons the Indians did not consider them a staple food, but rather one which they could fall back on if the acorn crop failed. The volatile poison in the Buckeye seeds had to be removed by leaching or baking in an earth oven. The leaching process took a long time, and if it was carried out by hand (i.e., by heating water in a basket and pouring it through the ground meal), it would have been onerous. The Buckeye seeds are very watery, and 100 pounds will yield only 32 pounds of meal, whereas all acorns will yield a much higher proportion of edible meal. Finally, the taste of Buckeye mush was not liked as much as that made of acorns.

A plant utilized by both the desert gatherers and agriculturists was the mesquite (*Prosopis* spp.). Its growth is determined by ground water and is not wholly dependent on local rainfall, which may be either overabundant or very deficient in any one year. Thundershowers at the time the pods are ripe may strip the trees and cause the fallen pods to be lost by rotting on the damp ground. But on the whole the crop is fairly reliable.

LAND ANIMALS AS FOOD

Food derived from land animals was varied. It included numerous birds, both permanent residents and seasonally migratory species; rodents such as wood rats, squirrels, and rabbits, which were found nearly everywhere; and large game.

But snakes, small lizards, carrion eaters, and scavengers (vultures and coyotes, for example) generally were not eaten, and we do not understand precisely why. Perhaps if the desert collectors were faced with real hunger, they would eat lizards or snakes, but since these were so widely tabooed, it is more likely that eating them was considered deleterious to health. Religious taboos, we think, would have been outweighed by practical ones in this region where food was very scant and people were often hungry. Coyote meat, like that of the other scavenger, the buzzard or vulture, is usually considered to be so rank as to be downright unpalatable, and this fact could account for the Indians' failure to utilize the animal as a meat source.

Large game (deer, elk, antelope, Mountain Sheep, and bear) were each present over half or more of the state, and wherever they occurred they were hunted (fig. 54). Deer were driven along trails where slip-noose snares were placed, or were hunted by men wearing a set of deer antlers tied to their heads as decoys. By creeping slowly on all fours, a hunter was able to approach a deer from downwind at close range and shoot it with an arrow.

The Pronghorn Antelope (*Antilocapra americana*), which usually lived in the open valley plains, was a difficult animal to hunt because it was wary and fleet of foot. The antelope's one weakness was its curiosity, which was recognized and

FIGURE 54 Indian stalking an antelope, probably in Sacramento Valley. (By C. A. Walker, 1870)

exploited by Indian hunters. They would erect a long pole bearing a banner several miles from where the antelope herd was grazing. After a few days, any apprehension the animals felt was dissipated, and apparently out of curiosity, they would approach the banner, which was inside a corral made of brush piles, around whose outer borders bowmen were hidden. Once in the enclosure, the confused animals were shot.

Mountain Sheep (*Ovis canadensis*) are also difficult to kill, and various tricks were employed to take these wary animals. A hunter might pound a moccasin on a rock to bring a ram within arrow range, the animal mistaking the noise for the sound of two rams fighting with their horns. Sometimes sheep were driven past hunters lying in ambush.

The most dangerous animal the California Indians encountered was the Grizzly Bear (*Ursus arctos*). Grizzlies had about the same diet as Indians: acorns, roots, berries, elk, deer, and fish. As a result these powerful and aggressive bears often encountered Indians when the latter were on hunting or gathering trips. Indians were, quite sensibly, afraid of the huge animals and did their best to avoid them. A group of women collecting acorns would station pickets to watch for bears and sound the alarm if one came in sight. Black Bears (*Euarctos americanus*), which are smaller and less pugnacious than Grizzlies, would be attacked by a group of hunters. (From several prehistoric village sites in Central California there have been recovered complete skeletons of young Black Bears, which were apparently kept as pets until they became so large and dangerous that they had to be killed.)

Deer, one of the important food resources of Indian California, were rare in the Mohave Desert and on the floor of the Great Interior Valley. In those deer-scarce areas there were other large game animals, such as the mountain sheep of the desert ranges, and the antelope and the Tule Elk (*Cervus nannodes*) in the valleys.

Zoologists calculate that today more than 50 percent of the state (57,000,000 acres) is occupied by deer, that the present deer population is now at least 1,250,000 animals, and that the deer density is about 13 per square mile. If the Indians "harvested" 125,000 deer per year, this would amount (at 100 pounds [45.4 kg.] of usable meat per animal) to slightly over one pound (½ kg.) of venison per day per person. Wildlife biologists think that the present deer population is about the same as it was before the white man came. Between 1850 and 1900, white hunters reduced the deer herds, as did natural predators, such as the wolf and the Grizzly Bear, but the predators are now extinct or nearly so in the state. Domestic sheep, which caused severe over-grazing, were for long a threat to the deer population. But with the recent emphasis on land management, conservation of natural species, hunting laws, and scientific game management, the deer are doing very well.

INSECTS AS FOOD

To the Indians, insects were a highly useful though not essential source of food. Table 6 lists the most important insect foods of California Indians.

Stephen Powers in 1872 referred to earthworms (*Lumbricus* sp.) as "aboriginal vermicelli" and said that the Yuki cooked them in a soup "which is much esteemed." Many

TABLE 6. Insects as a Source of Food*

Insects	Taxonomic identification	Stage of life cycle utilized	Area/Tribe
Grasshoppers	*Melanoplus* spp.	Nymphs, adults	Widespread
	Camnula pelucida	" "	"
	Schistocerca spp.	" "	"
Crickets	*Anabrus simplex* (Mormon Cricket)	Nymphs, adults	Northeastern California
	Gryllus achaeta (Field Cricket)	" "	Central Valley
	Stenopelmatus fuscus (Jerusalem Cricket)	" "	Central Valley
Stone Flies	*Pteronarcys californica* (Salmon Fly)	Nymphs, adults	Northeastern California
Aphids, scales, white flies, and other sucking insects	*Hyalopterus arundinis* (Mealy Plum Aphis)	Honeydew "sugar"	Southern and Eastern California dry regions
Army worm	*Homoncocnemis fortis*	Caterpillars	North Coast Ranges
Silk moths	*Platysamia (Hyalophora) euryalus* (Ceanothus Silk Moth)	Caterpillars	Central California
	Eumorpha achemon (Achemon Sphinx Moth)	Caterpillars	Central California
Pandora Moth	*Coloradia pandora*	Larvae and pupae	Mono Paiute
Wood-boring and soil-inhabiting beetles	*Prionus californicus*	Larvae	Mountain areas
	Ergates spiculatus (Pine Sawyer)	"	Mountain areas
	Polyphylla spp. (June Bugs)	"	Mountain areas
	Monochamus spp.	"	Mountain areas
Bees	*Bombus* spp. (Bumblebee)	Honey, larvae	Widespread
	Andrena spp.	Honey, larvae	Chumash
Ants	*Camponotus* spp.	Larvae, adults	Central Sierra Nevada
	Pogonomyrmex californicus	" "	Southern California
Yellowjackets and hornets	*Vespula* spp.	Larvae	Widespread
	Polistes spp.		"
Flies	*Hydropyrus hians*	Pupae	Eastern California

*This table was drawn up by Sean L. Swezey.

California tribes ate earthworms, recognizing them as a valuable source of meat (protein). The Eastern Pomo collected earthworms in large numbers from damp patches of ground. They brought the worms to the surface either by tapping the ground with a stick and singing a special "worm-enticing" song or by thrusting a pointed digging stick into the ground at an angle and working it up and down to disturb the earth.

The Owens Valley Paiute collected large quantities of "peaggie," the larvae of the Pandora moth (*Coloradia pandora*), in July. J. M. Aldrich in the 1920s observed one Indian group which had collected and stored a ton and a half of these caterpillars. The larvae were picked up from the ground, put in baskets, and killed by holding the basket in the smoke over a fire. They were then cooked by being buried in a heap of earth that had been previously heated by a fire built on the pile. The peaggie were separated from the dirt by being sifted in a coarse basket or were winnowed on a flat basketry tray and set out in the sun to dry thoroughly. The dried peaggie were then taken into the mountains in sacks and put in shady rock overhangs where they would be out of the sun and remain cool. In the fall, when the weather grew colder, the sacks could be brought down to the village in the valley. They were eaten after being boiled in baskets or pottery bowls.

Grasshoppers were obtained by firing a circular area or by beating the young insects toward a fairly deep hole with bushes; when they were thus captured, they could be put in containers, saturated with salt water, and then roasted in a kind of earth oven with hot rocks.

Native California bees do not produce and store much honey, but the Indians eagerly collected and ate what they could find. Bees were more valued for their tender larvae, and the larvae of yellowjackets and hornets were much esteemed as delicacies.

Aside from honey, there were few natural sweet things. (Manzanita berries, after being lightly crushed and having cold water poured on them in a sieve basket, produced a sweet drink like cider.) In the drier parts of California a honeydew sugar was collected. This "sugar" is the sweet excreta of aphids, which crystallizes and collects on the leaves of certain plants, especially Common Reed (*Phragmites communis*) and Common Tule (*Scirpus acutus*). The plants were cut off at the base of the stem, placed on a flat tule mat, and beaten with sticks to dislodge the crystalline sugar. Winnowing by tossing the sugar and leaf bits on a flat basketry tray yielded the pure sugar, which was then dampened slightly and molded into balls. Such sugar, eaten as a treat or a dessert, was a welcome change from the rather pallid staple, acorn mush.

The Pomo welcomed the rare appearance of army worms, red-striped caterpillars, which they called "lip," that appeared at irregular intervals of six or ten or even fifteen years. The caterpillars ate the leaves of ash (*Fraxinus* spp.) trees, and appeared only in summers when there had been an unusual amount of fog. Partly because it was considered such a great delicacy and partly because of its rare appearance, it was thought to be a special gift of the Thunder God. The people would surround an ash tree covered with caterpillars, preserving the utmost gravity of mien and remaining silent. They dug narrow trenches around the base of the trees and began to sing a refrain used only on this occasion, the words of which were "Li, li, li, li." The caterpillars are said to have listened to the song, shaking their heads from side to side, dropping, and slowly descending the tree into the lower branches from which they were gathered in baskets. The caterpillars were drowned in cold water, then toasted (fig. 55) or boiled, and stored. They were handled gently, and while gathering them no person could speak crossly to another under sanction of later being bitten by a rattlesnake. In 1904 S. A. Barrett observed that "several hundred pounds" of army worms were gathered in a few days by the inhabitants of one small Pomo Village.

We here provide two insect recipes:

YELLOWJACKET-MANZANITA BERRY DESSERT (YOKUTS)

Locate a yellowjacket nest hole in the ground. Early in the morning before the yellowjackets are aroused by the light, build a

FIGURE 55 Pomo woman with basketry tray containing army worms. (Photograph S. A. Barrett, 1904)

fire close to the hole and force the smoke down the hole with a fan. After the yellowjackets are stupefied by the smoke, dig out the nest and carry it carefully to a prepared bed of coals. Roast the nest, shake the dead larvae out on a basketry tray, mash them, and put them in a basket to be boiled with hot stones. After the larvae are boiled, drain and eat with manzanita berries or acorn meal.

MORMON CRICKET SOUP (HONEY LAKE PAIUTE)

Gather Mormon Crickets early in the morning before they become too active. Dig a pit and build a fire in it, allowing it to burn down to coals. Put crickets in the pit on the coals and immediately cover with earth. From time to time extract a cricket and sample it to see if it is done. When roasted to taste, remove crickets from the pit and place in the sun to dry. The crickets can then be boiled to make soup.

CONDIMENTS AND SALT

Judging from the comparatively small number of plants that have been reported by Indians as condiments, we can conclude that the staple diet was probably bland according to our taste. This is not to say that the total diet was dull, for many of the plants of minor importance which they used as food have distinctive and sometimes spicy flavors.

It has been established that, with but few exceptions, all California Indians used salt in one form or another. It seems to have been used separately, not out of sheer necessity (many of the natural foods they ate contained a sufficiency of salt) but as a social custom, regardless of physiological need. There were four sources for salt in native California: (1) grass; (2) seaweed; (3) saline waters (marshes, lakes, springs, the ocean); and (4) dry mineral deposits.

In the interior, north of Tehachapi, Salt grass (*Distichlis spicata*) was roasted or burned in a pit over wood coals. The melted salt dropped to the bottom of the pit and was collected there as a cake. Along the coast a purple seaweed (*Porphyra perforata*) was gathered, pressed tightly into cakes, dried, and nibbled at during meals. (*Porphyra* is the genus so widely cultivated by modern Japanese and used as *nori*.)

A few tribes boiled salt water to extract the salt. At least one group put sticks of rotten punky wood into a salt spring; when these were well soaked they were removed and burned to "melt" out the salt into a cake. The Tolowa of coastal Northwestern California used seawater to salt their food. Salt was also gathered from deposits near salt springs or seepages. Sometimes the Indians then dissolved it in water and decanted and evaporated it in order to purify the salt product. Rock salt deposits occur in the Owens Valley, along the Colorado River near Overton, and in some places in the territory of the Western Mono near Sequoia National Park. From these and several other well-known places where it appeared either as rock salt or as heavy crustal depositions from springs, salt was used as an item of trade with surrounding interior peoples.

Finally, salt was also reputed to have curative properties for ailments such as stomach aches and colds.

CULTIVATION

Partly because of the "back-up guarantee" in the mesquite crop, we believe that the River Yuman tribes did not devote themselves wholeheartedly to supplying their food by raising corn and beans and pumpkins. In regard to vegetal foods, the Colorado River tribes seem to have been about half dependent on cultivated plants and about half on wild crop seeds. To have relied wholly upon one or the other might have been more risky than dividing the diet equally between agricultural and wild plant foods.

The Kamia, a Yuman-speaking tribe who lived in the Imperial Valley, were mainly farmers, growing maize, Tepary Beans (*Phaseolus acutifolius*), pumpkins, gourds, watermelons, and Cowpeas (*Vigna sinensis*). These last two crops were probably introduced so soon after the European settlement of Mexico that some Indians stated in the 1770s that they had grown them for as long as they had maize and beans. The Kamia lived west of the Colorado River Yuma farmers and east of the coastal Diegueño hunters and collectors; they traded their watermelons to the Diegueño for acorns. The Diegueño were apparently partial to the watery, sweet melon as an alternative to their usual acorn mush, and the Kamia presumably found the oil-rich acorns a welcome change from their corn and beans. Both tribes could have gotten along perfectly well without the other's foods, but by having them both tribes may have found their diets a little more interesting.

THE SEASONS IN RELATION TO FOOD

The Cahuilla divided the year into eight seasons, each recognized partly on the basis of the growth cycle of the mesquite, whose beans were an important food resource (fig. 56). The seasons were named budding of trees; blossoming of trees; trees beginning to form seed pods; time of

FIGURE 56 Mohave dwellings, Colorado River region, showing mesquite bean granary (left foreground); children are playing hoop and pole game. (Drawn by H. B. Möllhausen, ca. 1860.)

ripening of seed pods; falling of the pods; midsummer; cool days; cold days.

The Eastern Pomo divided the year in several ways, but the most common way was into thirteen moons, beginning with the winter moon. The terminology used to refer to them centered on the main work of food getting.

POMO LUNAR CALENDAR

First moon (or month):	It will be difficult to go out and hunt game.
Second moon:	The fish won't come to shore.
Third moon:	Fish will begin to come out.
Fourth moon:	There will be better weather; we can fish and hunt.
Fifth moon:	You can get clover.
Sixth moon:	Fish begin to run; we will move nearer the lake.
Seventh moon:	We will be moving back, carrying the fish.

Eighth moon:	If the moon is good [?] we will go to Bodega Bay and get clamshells [for beads].
Ninth moon:	We will go home and even will be sent out to find good acorn crops.
Tenth moon:	We will be camping and gathering acorns.
Eleventh moon:	We will still be gathering acorns.
Twelfth moon:	We will finish the acorn gathering, move home, and get settled again.
Thirteenth moon:	We will be settled and resting, for there will be nothing to do.

SUMMARY

Let us tabulate a sample of California tribes with reference to their life-zone habitat territories (see table 7). The preferred lands were obviously the foothill and forest areas, with the desert and high mountain zones less attractive.

TABLE 7. Percentages of Tribal Territories in Different Life Zones

Tribe	Lower Sonoran (valley)	Upper Sonoran (valley)	Transition (mid-altitude mountains)	Boreal (high mountains)
Yurok	—	—	82	18
Hupa	—	6	85	9
Yuki	—	17	69	14
Shasta	—	18	57	25
Yahi	—	44	49	7
Northern Pomo	—	25	72	3
Washo	—	11	44	45
Monache	—	18	33	49
Nomlaki	39	45	13	3
Southern Maidu	22	28	32	18
Central Sierra Miwok	6	33	33	28
Owens Valley Paiute	20	32	25	23
Serrano	69	18	11	2
Cahuilla	59	32	7	1
Southern Pomo	—	45	53	—
Northern Diegueño	22	65	13	—
Coast Miwok	—	58	42	—
Costanoan	6	66	19	—
Luiseño	47	45	7	—
Chumash	13	87	—	—
Yuma	100	—	—	—
Southern Yokuts	88	12	—	—

Although tribal territories were carved out by occasional aggression, adjudication, and agreement with neighboring tribes in a process that may have taken centuries, there must have been an underlying awareness that there were great advantages in owning and being able to exploit two or more life zones and their varied products. Referring to this as "ecological adaptation" is only one way of saying that Indians used common sense for their continued existence and comfort.

There is in the anthropological literature a native account of a war between the Southern Pomo and the Wappo, in which the latter prevailed and which resulted in the withdrawal of the Pomo from Alexander Valley along the Russian River above Healdsburg. This event occurred about 1830 and before the first Spanish-Mexican settlements were established in the region. Kroeber, in commenting on this bit of native history, pointed out that the Pomo would have withdrawn from this tract only if there was assurance that there would be enough food to support them among their Pomo kinsmen to the north, among whom they found refuge; otherwise, they would have remained and continued to contest their land with the Wappo. Kroeber further observed:

It does not follow that the population of aboriginal California was increasing at the time of discovery. A high mortality may have held numbers steady. Nor is it maintained that only a fraction of the resources were utilized; it was rather the bulk; and a material increment to the population would undoubtedly have resulted in hardship, until new methods of utilization of the food supply had been developed. But there was a margin; it was fairly liberal; and the variety of resources probably led to its exhaustion only at intervals, and to acute want still more rarely. The Californian could not go for any considerable period without busying himself with procuring food, in which respect he was handicapped against the Indians that had specialized their food production; but the very diversity and multifariousness of the supply, and of his quest of it, while robbing him of leisure and of concentration, gave him also comparative security against want.

But choices, based on long experience of living in a restricted area, must have been made in the past by most native Californian societies. Some tribes chose a dietary base that relied heavily on salmon or shellfish or acorns or another food, but there were always supplementary foods to fall back on when the main diet sources failed or were in short supply. It was this flexibility that enabled California Indians to survive, and even to prosper, during the thousands of years they occupied the land.

UNESCO and the National Academy of Sciences have in recent years made intensive investigations into the productivity of wild tree crops as well as a wide variety of abundantly producing seed plants that are not generally used as food. Many of these trees and plants could be placed under direct or semicultivation (i.e., tending) and are food resources of great potential as the world fills with hungry people. Humans who become accustomed to a particular diet are reluctant to change their tastes—this perhaps was one of the primary factors in preventing the California Indians from changing their food preferences from acorns to maize—but they would do so rather than starve to death. The day may come when Californians will have cause to regret the destruction of so much oak parkland for firewood or for use as pasture land.

The California Indians, then, understood the principle of artificial planting (for more on this, see below, chapter 6, under "Tobacco"); they seemingly also understood the relationship between soil quality and plant growth. There is little question that in many open parts of California during optimal Indian residence the country was less overgrown with brush than at present. Photographs of the floor of Yosemite Valley taken almost a hundred years ago, compared with modern photographs of the same area, amply bear this out. The increase of forest is ascribable to the cessation of Indian burning, which was apparently done for the purpose of improving the forage for such animals as deer. Foresters today observe that deer, and cows as well, prefer to graze or browse on recently burned-over land, probably because shoots from burned-back brush and from new grass growing in ash compost contain more minerals attractive to the animals.

5. MATERIAL CULTURE

The things made and used by California Indians for their living were endlessly varied. Wood was the most common craft material, and next probably came stone, then leather, bone, and cordage (for more information, see chapter 6). The Indians used no metals, although the tribes of the Sierra knew what native gold looked like and took the earliest gold miners to places where big nuggets occurred. Gold simply did not interest Indians until they became aware that the whites were eager to secure it and that it would buy white men's things. So far as we know, no gold, either in unworked nuggets or fashioned into some object, has ever been recovered from a prehistoric California Indian occupation or burial site.

BASKETRY AND POTTERY

Baskets were made everywhere, though the forms and techniques of manufacture differed from area to area. Baskets were used to collect and store and cook food in (fig. 57). Pottery was not widely produced, being made only among the southernmost tribes (Yuma, Mohave, Kamia, Diegueño, and Cahuilla) and the southernmost Yokuts and Monache. Pottery was doubtless known to all the tribes of Southern California and most of those of Central California, but they did not seem to accept it as a substitute for basketry, probably because pottery cannot be used for as many purposes as baskets can. Although food can be boiled in a fired clay pot set on the fire, a tightly woven basket can serve the same purpose if stones heated in the fire are dropped into the liquid in the basket. And a clay vessel is not nearly as handy for lugging a load of firewood or a half-bushel of acorns or buckeye nuts from the gathering place to

FIGURE 57 San Joaquin Valley Indians transporting water and grass seed. (From H. R. Schoolcraft, *Indian Tribes of the United States*, 1865)

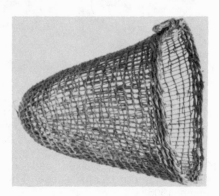

FIGURE 58 Wappo open-work carrying basket. Ht. ca. 24 in. [60 cm..]. (Courtesy of the Lowie Museum of Anthropology)

the granary near the village (fig. 58). California Indians did more carrying about of things than, say, the town-living Southwestern Pueblo people, and they would have found pottery much more breakable than flexible baskets.

MORTARS

Mortars for grinding small seeds or acorns were ordinarily made of stone hollowed out to form a bowl (fig. 59). A cylindrical stone pestle was used to pound the seeds. A substitute for the globular stone mortar was a flat stone slab with a grinding depression over which a twined basketry hopper was set, held in place with pitch or asphalt. Fixed mortars are found throughout most of the state in the exposed bedrock, except in the valley areas, where there are few or no stone outcrops. These are sometimes called "community mills," where the women of a village congregated to grind acorns and to socialize while doing so. (For more on this, see chapter 6, under "Mineral Commodities.")

FIGURE 59 Mortars, pestles, and bedrock mortars in a Nisenan (Southern Maidu) village. (Photograph C. H. Merriam, ca. 1905)

WEAPONS AND TOOLS

Everywhere the bow and arrow was the standard weapon for hunting and occasionally for war, though their constructions differed. North of Santa Barbara the back of the bow was covered with sinew strips to increase its pull, applied with glue made, for example, from boiled sturgeon bladders or a substance produced by roasting a fish head. Elsewhere a simple bow with no reinforcement was used. Southern California Indians preferred an arrow made of Common Reed (*Phragmites communis*), whereas those in the rest of the state used wooden arrowshafts. Tips either were of sharp wood or were chipped out of flint or obsidian. Sir Francis Drake's men, some of them armed with the famous English longbow, referred contemptuously to the poor bows of the Coast Miwok among whom they summered in 1579, but at medium range the California Indian was a deadly marksman. Ishi, "the last wild Indian" of California, made a bow with which he could send an arrow 185 yards. Charles Wilkes, in command of the United States Exploring Expedition, visited Mt. Shasta in 1841 and observed men who could hit a button three times out of five at a distance of 60 feet. Loeffelholz, a German gold miner at Trinidad Bay in 1851, wrote that he witnessed the Yurok "strike a ten-cent piece, at a distance of twenty paces, six times out of ten."

The arrow shot from a California Indian bow (fig. 60) was probably not very effective against game at a distance of over 200 feet. But there were many stratagems that permitted a bow hunter to release an arrow at a much closer range. Ishi (fig. 61), for example, was accustomed to crouch behind a low wall of piled-up boulders erected along a deer trail and to shoot the deer when it passed. If a man does not make sudden movements, especially with his legs, deer are likely to ignore him and the arrow he discharges. Saxton Pope, a medical doctor who learned archery from Ishi, reported that he had many times shot four missed arrows at a big buck deer, which stood calmly watching the arrows fly past.

In pre-Cabrillo California, man was really not very much feared by wild animals, but was fairly effective as a predator.

FIGURE 60 Costanoan Indian at Monterey, with bow and animal-skin arrow quiver. (By T. Suria, 1791)

FIGURE 61 The Yahi Indian Ishi poised with bow and arrow. (From S. T. Pope, *Yahi Archery*, 1914)

Although deer were not alarmed by a bow hunter, they have in recent times evidently learned to associate men with guns.

In Southern California a flat curved throwing club was used by the Indians for hunting rabbits. It is also said to have been capable of breaking the leg of a deer. This is a true boomerang, though not of the special returning type known from Australia.

In the Santa Barbara area, and in fact all along the Pacific coast of California, dead whales were occasionally cast up on the shore, and this bounty of the sea was gladly received. Not only were the meat and blubber removed and eaten, but also the large bones of the whale were useful for making implements. No California tribe hunted live whales in the ocean.

Specialized implements for food-getting would fill a volume of description. Harpoons, either fixed to the end of a shaft or with a retrieving line attached so that an impaled fish could be drawn to shore, were used wherever fish were speared. Nets in a bewildering variety were used to gather fish, and basketry fish traps were common (fig. 62).

The grooved stone ax was not known, except for occasional examples recovered from prehistoric sites, which appear to have been secured by intertribal trade from the Southwest (i.e., Arizona).

Boats have been mentioned elsewhere (in chapter 3). Wooden dugouts (fig. 36) were known in the northernmost part of the state. In Central and Southern California the cigar-shaped tule bundle raft (balsa) was used (figs. 36 and 43). And the Chumash had their unusual plank canoe, which has been likened to canoes built in Polynesia.

E

FIGURE 62 Pomo basketry fish trap, with funnel or "fly-trap" entrance. Length about 5 feet [1.5 m.]. (Courtesy of the R. H. Lowie Museum of Anthropology)

HOUSEHOLD FURNISHINGS
AND CLOTHING

Indian dwellings and ceremonial structures are discussed and illustrated in chapter 2. Household furniture was sparse. People usually simply sat on the floor on woven tule mats, but Northwestern tribes made low round wooden stools on which the men sat, and the Chumash made raised beds on which to sleep. In mild climates, clothing was minimal. Men usually went naked; women covered the lower parts of their bodies. In cold weather, men, women, and children wore fur robes of deer or rabbit skin. Leather or rush sandals were standard in the southern part of the state, possibly because of the intensity of the sun on the bare ground. Leather moccasins, used chiefly when traveling, were made in Central and Northwestern California, but for the most part people went barefooted. The tribes of the central and northern Sierra knew how to make a simple round snowshoe (see fig. 80).

Animals were killed for other uses than food, and some were taken for their fur alone. (The Southwestern Pomo killed skunks by a sharp blow on the head with a stick rather than by shooting them with an arrow when the animal threatened to release its scent. The skin and the meat were not used, but the fat was removed and heated, and the oil extracted was used to rub into the hair to prevent baldness and graying.)

MUSICAL INSTRUMENTS

California Indians liked to sing, and a considerable body of their music was preserved on early recording devices. The songs are often repetitive and run in a narrow range of scale.

Musical instruments were simple. Rattles were made by inserting small pebbles in dried insect cocoons tied to a stick (fig. 63). Another type of rattle was fashioned by tying several dry deer hoofs to a stick. The most common rattle was made by half-splitting a stick and wrapping it so that the two halves clapped together (fig. 63). Whistles made of hollow bird bones, with one or two holes drilled in them, were used nearly everywhere. A flute (fig. 64) made of

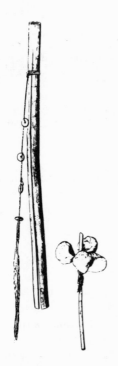

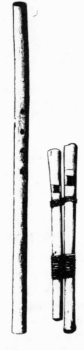

FIGURE 63 Maidu clapper rattle and cocoon rattle. (From R. B. Dixon, *The Northern Maidu*, 1905)

FIGURE 64 Maidu flute and whistle of bird bones. (From R. B. Dixon, *The Northern Maidu*, 1905)

elderberry wood, usually with four holes and blown at the end, was known widely and played for recreation or by a young man a-courting. The usual drum in Central California was the footdrum, a flat wooden plank set over a resonating hole in the floor of the dance house. It was sounded by a man pounding on it with his heels while dancing. The drum made of a cylinder with a skin head was unknown.

TOBACCO PIPES

Pipes for smoking tobacco were, nearly everywhere, tubular (fig. 65) and made of stone or wood. An obtuse-angled tube of pottery was used by the southernmost tribes.

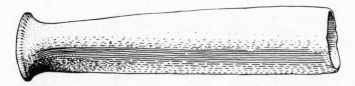

FIGURE 65 Archaeological stone pipe, probably for tobacco, 4 in. [10 cm.] long. (Courtesy of the Lowie Museum of Anthropology)

Men usually were the smokers. A pipeful was smoked at night before bedtime, probably because the tobacco was very heady and is said to have induced drowsiness.

FIREMAKING AND LUMBERING

To cut down a tree, Indians built a fire at the base and prevented it from climbing by applying a plaster of wet mud. The fire was designed to burn through the trunk so that the tree could be pulled or pushed down. Sections of trees could also be burned in this way. Planks were made from sections of straight-grained trees (pine, cedar, redwood) by splitting them lengthwise with a wedge made of elk antler or whale-bone, which was pounded with a cobble. In Northwestern California, where planks were much used, a bell-shaped stone maul was made for driving wedges.

Fire was made with an upright drill twirled between the palms of the hands, rotating in a hole in a flat hearth stick (figs. 66, 67). Another kind of drill—which, however, was usually employed for perforating shell beads—was introduced to the Pomo by the Mexicans in the 1800s. This was a pump drill (fig. 68), which had a shaft equipped with a flywheel and a cross-stick with a loose thong that passed through a hole in the upper end of the shaft. The shaft was rotated with a strong downward stroke of the hands on the cross-stick. The momentum from the flywheel allowed the thong to rewind itself as the cross-stick went back up the shaft.

 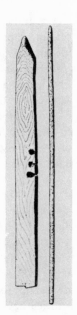

FIGURE 66 (left) Karok Indian using fire drill. (From J. P. Harrington, *Tobacco Among the Karok Indians of California*, 1932)

FIGURE 67 (right) Maidu fire drill shaft and hearth. (From R. B. Dixon, *The Northern Maidu*, 1905)

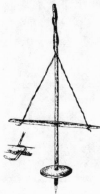

FIGURE 68 Pump drill of wood, with hide thongs. (From *Handbook of North American Indians*, vol. 8: California, 1978)

USES OF BIRDS

The Indians found many uses for parts of birds' bodies. The most practical application of feathers was as fletching for arrows, for which the quills of the Red-tailed Hawk (*Buteo jamaicensis*) seem to have been most frequently used. The leg bones of pelicans (*Pelecanus* spp.) were used as whistles or flutes.

Some tribes fashioned whole skins of large birds into clothing or used them in feather blankets. Large feathers, such as those of the Turkey Vulture (*Cathartes aura*), the Bald Eagle (*Haliaeetus leucocephalus*), the Raven (*Corvus corax*), the Yellow-billed Magpie (*Pica nuttalli*), the Great Horned Owl (*Bubo virginianus*), or the California Condor (*Gymnogyps californianus*), could be used in blankets, cloaks, or robes.

Probably the most spectacular uses to which bird feathers were put were in a whole range of ceremonial dress (see plates 1-3) and in basketry decoration. Headbands, elaborate headdresses (figs. 69, 70), plumes, and sticks covered with feathers were employed frequently in the northern and central parts of California. The most common of the

FIGURE 69 Klamath River Indians with feather headdresses. (Photograph A. W. Ericson, ca. 1900)

FIGURE 70 San Francisco Mission Indians with ceremonial headdresses. (By L. Choris, 1816)

headbands seen at dances were probably those made from the yellow quills of the Common Flicker (*Colaptes auratus*); flicker-feather headbands were also sometimes worn by shamans, or curing doctors. In northern California red headbands of Pileated Woodpecker (*Dryocopus pileatus*) or Acorn Woodpecker (*Melanerpes formicivorus*) feathers, or blue headbands of Steller's Jay (*Cyanocitta stelleri*) feathers, were also worn. In the south, flicker bands were not seen so commonly, but headbands found in a cave just north of Los Angeles included the Common Flicker feathers as well as those from the Bald Eagle, the Common Crow (*Corvus brachyrhyncos*), the Red-tailed Hawk, the Red-winged Blackbird (*Agelaius phoeniceus*), and the California Condor. Black or white eagle and condor feathers were used as ritual plumes (fig. 71) or bound on sticks and appeared on headdresses, which also contained feathers from the Great Horned Owl, the Yellow-billed Magpie, and the Common Crow. The spectacular "Bighead" pieces of the Pomo Indians were of a "pincushion" design, with slender dogwood rods emanating from a tule-bundle foundation worn on the head; the wooden shoots were tipped with white quill sections, probably from the tail feathers of the Bald Eagle.

FIGURE 71 Maidu "feather-plume sticks." (From R. B. Dixon, *The Northern Maidu*, 1905)

Ear tubes placed through holes pierced in the lobes were often made of pelican leg bones decorated with brilliant feathers, such as those of the Mountain Quail (*Oreortyx pictus*).

Down from the Bald Eagle or the Golden Eagle (*Aquila crysaetos*) was inserted in the string of net hats. Such down was incorporated into strips for dance skirts, which also may have included eagle or condor feathers.

The Pomo Indians, who excelled in covering some of their most precious baskets with feathers (see plate 18), used the black feathers from the California Quail (*Lophortyx californicus*); black or red feathers of the Red-winged Blackbird; red scalp feathers of the Pileated Woodpecker or the Acorn Woodpecker; yellow feathers of the Western Meadowlark (*Sturnella neglecta*) and oriole (*Icterus* spp.); and green feathers of the Mallard (*Anas platyrhyncos*).

Bird feathers, as we have seen, were used in several kinds of ceremonial as well as ordinary regalia, and certainly birds, such as hawks, eagles, condors, ravens, owls, and even hummingbirds, figured strongly and in different personifications in Indian mythology. Nevertheless, we have only a few hints in many regions of California about the formalized beliefs in the sacredness of these birds or about their place in religious or other special cults. In Northern California there was a belief in a mythic bird of supernatural shape, while in the south a bad-luck symbol in the form of a bird or at least of a man in feathers was feared. In North Central California, among the Pomo, for example, parts of the ceremonial dance cycles were named "duck" or "goose" dances, but neither dance seems to have been considered a central expression of cult activities. By contrast, in Southern California, especially in the regions of the Chinigchinich religion described by Father Gerónimo Boscana, there appeared to be an annual rite, essentially funerary, which involved the ceremonial killing of eagles or condors. The comparatively wide distribution of this cult ritual suggests that it was of considerable antiquity.

Indian names for birds were given in imitation of their call, or song, or for a bird's eating preference, or from some belief about its particular powers. Nearly everywhere in California the Western Meadowlark (*Sturnella neglecta*) was said to be a "bad bird" with powers to harm people. The raptorial birds (condors, hawks, eagles) were spiritually powerful but were not feared in the way the meadowlark was.

6. NON-FOOD RESOURCES: PROCUREMENT AND USE

The California Indians seem to have found a use for almost any natural product they encountered on the land. They learned, probably over thousands of years of experimentation, how to extract poisonous or bitter elements from food plants (see chapter 4). They also learned to use other plants, minerals, and animals for a great number of purposes in medicine, basketry, ropemaking, woodworking, and other arts needed to prolong life or make it more comfortable in a generally lush but sometimes capricious environment.

PLANTS

Medicinal Plants

In our survey of plants used in medicine, only a selection of the more important species will be mentioned; a full descriptive listing would literally require an entire book. Possibly as many as one-fourth of all medicines in the modern United States Pharmacopoeia were derived originally from plants known for their curative powers to North American Indians in general. The California Indians, though perhaps not notably more inventive in this respect than Indians in other regions, nevertheless had an extremely varied range of plants from which to choose, and they did not neglect their opportunities. Modern drug researchers have extracted and purified chemicals from some of these plants, testing them with laboratory animals for their effects on known diseases, and many new drugs beneficial to man have been discovered in this way. By trial-and-error and patient observation, native societies around the world hit upon a great number of drug plants that are effective as remedies for bodily complaints and diseases.

While every California Indian probably knew a few standard plant remedies for common complaints such as headache, sore muscles, rheumatism, and cramps, more serious matters were ones for the herb doctor (a professional distinct from the shaman), who was called in to diagnose and then to prescribe, gather, prepare, and administer plant remedies.

Not all herbal cures were effective. Some had magical connections, which may have had psychotherapeutic value only. The sick person doubtless believed that taking a potion from the herb doctor was better than doing nothing at all. Many doctors the world over and in all times have probably depended to some extent on such medicines.

A few years ago research was done at the University of California on *Gonyaulax*, a saltwater microorganism that causes the so-called red tide. This organism is taken in as food by some filter feeders, such as mussels, clams, and oysters, and by small surface fish. These animals retain the microorganisms in their gut, and if humans eat them the result can be severe illness and even death. Today the state posts quarantine signs prohibiting the collecting of shell-fish from May 1 to October 31, which is the "red tide" period. Indians had learned that in the summer months eating the big Ocean Mussel (*Mytilus californianus*), which grows on rocks in the tidal zone, would cause sickness or even death. Whether they associated the "red tide" season with the dangerous time for eating mussels, we do not know. Many coastal tribes had "remedies" for mussel poisoning caused by *Gonyaulax*, but recent tests done on a number of these alleged cures indicated that none was in the slightest degree effective against the poison.

There are, however, two native medicines that are known to be effective. In the early 1960s, when interest was generated in oral contraceptives, much testing of native plants reputed to prevent conception was done. Many were found to be worthless, but two proved effective in preventing pregnancy. Some Northern Paiute women of western Nevada and eastern California who did not want children are said to have drunk an infusion of the roots of *Litho-spermum ruderale*, a low shrub, and after six months' time sterility resulted, though we are not informed whether it was permanent. The Modoc are reported to have given a decoction of Squaw Carpet (*Ceanothus prostratus*) to girls who menstruated too heavily, and it too, when taken for "a long time" in small doses, allegedly prevented conception.

These extreme examples do not apply to most of the plants in the list below (see also Appendix 1), which were used to treat ordinary ailments afflicting humankind and were probably as efficacious as any modern remedies. Infusions, or steepings of leaves in hot water, seem to have been the commonest medicines, but it will be seen even in this short list that no parts of the plants were overlooked, and some parts were evidently thought to be better than others for effecting cures.

Alders (*Alnus* spp.): Bark infusion used for stomach aches, as a blood purifier, and to facilitate childbirth; dry rot from tree mixed with powdered willow bark as poultice for burns.

Buckhorn Cholla (*Opuntia acanthocarpa*): Ashes applied to cuts and burns.

Buckwheat (*Eriogonum fasciculatum*): Dry heads or leaves taken in decoctions for headaches and stomach disorders.

Calabazilla (*Cucurbita foetidissima*): Roots chewed and applied to skin ulcers, open sores; also used as soap, shampoo.

California Everlasting (*Gnaphalium decurrens*): Leaves used as poultice on swellings; decoction of leaves taken for colds and stomach troubles.

California Laurel (*Umbellularia californica*): A medicine in the sense of an insecticide. Several tribes affirm that boughs of Laurel hung in the house, or leaves strewn on the floor, kept the house free from fleas.

California Mugwort (*Artemesia douglasiana*): Decoction of leaves taken for headaches, colic, bronchitis, rheumatism; taken after childbirth to promote blood circulation.

Cascara Sagrada (*Rhamnus purshiana*): Infusion of bark used as a laxative; berries eaten as an emetic.

Coyote Mint (*Monardella villosa*): Leaves as tea used to cure colic and purify the blood.

Creosote Bush (*Larrea tridentata*): Tea from stems and leaves drunk for colds, stomach cramps; solutions and poultices used to heal wounds, draw out poison, prevent infections.

Croton (*Croton californicus*): Mashed and cooked stems and leaves used as poultices for earaches; also tea from stems and leaves said by some to induce abortion.

Dogwoods (*Cornus* spp.): Tea from roots and bark taken as remedy for colds.

Elderberries (*Sambucus* spp.): Tea from flowers taken as a diuretic and a purgative.

Elk Clover (*Aralia californica*): Root decoctions taken for colds, fevers, open sores, and for diseases of lungs and stomach.

Great Basin Sagebrush (*Artemesia tridentata*): Tea from leaves taken for colds and sore eyes; used to produce sweating during fever.

Gum Plants (*Grindelia* spp.): Decoction from leaves, stems, buds, taken internally for lung troubles and applied externally for skin diseases.

Incised Cranesbill (*Geranium oreganum*): Decoction from roots rubbed on aching joints.

Jimsonweed, or Toloache (*Datura meteloides*): Ointment from powdered leaves applied to severe wounds, aching teeth, and swellings.

Lupines (*Lupinus* spp.): Tea from leaves or seeds used for bladder trouble and failure to urinate.

Milfoil, Common Yarrow (*Achillea millefolium*); Tea from leaves and flowers taken for stomach ache, headache, colds; lotion put on sore eyes.

Mistletoes (*Phoradendron* spp.): Berries pounded to a flour and applied to wounds; powder mixed with water to bathe sore or infected eyes.

Mormon Teas (*Ephedra* spp.): Tea from leaves or stems used as a tonic; also used to cure diarrhea and to bathe sore eyes.

Mountain Misery (*Chamaebatia foliolosa*): Hot tea from leaves drunk for rheumatism and for diseases manifested by skin eruptions.

Oregon Grape (*Berberis aquifolium*): Roots steeped in water for general debility or to create appetite.

Rattlesnake Weed (*Euphorbia albomarginata*): Leaves and stems in solution used for bathing snakebites and drunk to cure sores in the mouth.

Spice Bush (*Calycanthus occidentalis*): Bark infusion used for severe colds.

White Sage (*Salvia apiana*): Tea from leaves drunk as a cure for colds and also applied as a shampoo; crushed leaves applied to eliminate body odors (i.e., to cleanse sweat glands).

Wild Ginger (*Asarum caudatum*): Fresh leaves used in poultices for boils.

Willows (*Salix* spp.): Bark tea for lumbago.

Yerba Santa (*Eriodictyon californicus*): Tea from leaves and flowers used to cure colds, coughs, sore throats.

Basketry Materials

A wide variety of plant materials, including stems, leaves, stalks, and roots, was used all over California for the foundations (warps) and for the wrapping, or weft, elements of baskets (figs. 72-76; plates 7, 15). Plants for basketry were not chosen at random from among those available, but apparently were rigidly selected. Seventy-eight different species have been counted from several nearly comprehensive basketry collections, and even these 78 species represent a limitation when all the plants that *could* have been used are considered. Throughout the entire region, local traditions of techniques of weaving, design motifs, and materials were built up over the centuries. Some tribes, for example, might use a certain material for warps exclusively, while another would use it only for wefts.

Willows (*Salix* spp.) were probably the most widely used materials because of their strength and resiliency. Peeled willow stems were used for both warps and wefts, and often also for hoops or rim bindings.

FIGURE 72 San Joaquin or Sacramento Valley Indian making a basket. (From H. R. Schoolcraft, *Indian Tribes of the United States*, 1865)

Among the other common materials used for baskets were the following, not necessarily in the order of greatest frequency:

California Hazel (*Corylus cornuta*): For warps; used heavily in Northwestern California.

Redbud (*Cercis occidentalis*): For both warp and weft, especially for ornamentation.

Common Tule (*Scirpus acutus*): For both warp and weft, especially in the Modoc region.

Sedges (*Carex* spp.): Mostly for wefts.

FIGURE 73 Pomo twined basket. (Photograph S. A. Barrett, 1904)

FIGURE 74 Pomo coiled basket. (Photograph S. A. Barrett, 1904)

FIGURE 75 Chumash Mission Indian coiled basket. (From A. L. Kroeber, *Basket Designs of the Mission Indians*, 1922)

FIGURE 76 Various Mission Indian coiled baskets. (From A. L. Kroeber, *Basket Designs of the Mission Indians, 1922)*

Bear Grass (*Xerophyllum tenax*): For decorative overlay, dyed yellow, used in Northwestern California; dyed porcupine quills were also used in this region for the same purpose.

Squaw Bush (*Rhus trilobata*): For warp and weft, and only by several tribes in Southern California, even though the species occurs widely in the state.

Spiny Rush (*Juncus acutus*): For warp and weft, especially in Southern California.

Deer Grass (*Muhlenbergia rigens*): For foundation bundles (warps), mostly south of San Francisco.

Pines (*Pinus* spp.): For wefts, in many northern tribes; *P. monophylla* pitch used for sealing water bottles in the south.

Common Cattail (*Typha latifolia*): Rushes for replaceable padding in baby craddles.

Dyes

The Indians used dyes for several different purposes, such as painting the body for ceremonials and the permanent facial tattoos of the women of some tribes (fig. 77). Proably the most important uses of plant dyes were for decorating baskets. Several plant stems, like Redbud (*Cercis occidentalis*) (red) and Willow (*Salix* spp.) (near-white), were selected for their naturally contrasting colors in basketry and could be left untouched.

The following list includes most of the plant dyes and colors known to have been used by the Indians and the parts of the plant from which they were derived:

Alder (*Alnus rhombifolia*): Red (bark).

Barberries, Oregon grapes (*Berberis* spp.): Yellow (root).

Buttercups (*Ranunculus* spp.): Yellow (flowers).

California Blackberry (*Rubus vitifolius*): Black (berry juice).

Coast Blue Larkspur (*Delphinium decorum*): Blue paint (applied with glue and berries of Oregon Grape on bows) (flowers).

Common Sunflower (*Helianthus annuus*): Purple, black (seeds); yellow (flowers).

Cow Parsnip (*Heracleum lanatum*): Yellow (leaves).

Creek Nettle (*Urtica gracilis*): Yellow (roots).

Elderberries (*Sambucus* spp.): Black (stems).

Honey Mesquite (*Prosopis juliflora*): Black (gum from roots).

Indigo Bush (*Dalea emoryi*): Yellow-brown (stems).

Leather Root (*Psoralea macrostachya*): Yellow (roots).

Manzanitas (*Arctostaphylos* spp.): Black (green wood and charcoal).

Mistletoe (*Phoradendron* spp.): Black (leaves).

Mountain Mahogany (*Cercocarpus* spp.): Red (bark and roots).

Poison Oak (*Rhus diversiloba*): Black (juice).

Sea Blite (*Suaeda diffusa*): Yellow (whole plant).

Spanish Needles (*Palafoxia linearis*): Yellow (probably leaves were most used).

FIGURE 77 A Wailaki woman with facial tattoos. (From S. Powers, *Tribes of California*, 1877)

Valley Oak (*Quercus lobata*): Black (bark plus iron oxide from the soil).

Wolf Moss (*Evernia vulpina*): Yellow (whole plant).

Cordage, Mats, Nets, and Clothing

Fibers for cordage, strings, and ropes needed by the Indians were obtained from a lesser number of plants than were used in basketry. When stripped or split off from the leaves or stems of plants, the fibers were usually twisted or rolled on the thigh of the maker to bind them together; two-ply cordage was most common, but after the intrusion of the whites, the Indians sometimes made three-ply string from native materials. There is some archaeological evidence that the Indians were once familiar with the use of stone spindle whorls, perforated disks set on sticks, which could be rotated easily while fibers were twisted at the free end so as to produce cordage. The closest approach to loom weaving in California was done with a two-bar frame, this sometimes being made of two saplings or vertical stakes; strips of rabbit skin were made into blankets on this "loom."

The most frequently used cordage fibers were from the following plants:

Desert Agave (*Agave deserti*): Used mostly in Southern California.

Dogbane, or Indian Hemp (*Apocynum cannabinum*): Apparently the most frequently used fiber throughout California, except in desert areas.

Ground Iris (*Iris macrosiphon*): Most commonly used along the coast of Northern California.

Milkweeds (*Asclepias* spp.): Probably most frequently used in the south, except in desert lands.

Mojave Yucca (*Yucca schidigera*): Like Desert Agave, used mostly in Southern California.

Nettles (*Urtica* spp.): used in Central and Northern California.

Mats for sitting and sleeping on were universal in California; they were usually made in a twining technique, like the basketry. Common Tule (*Scirpus acutus*) and Common Cattail (*Typha latifolia*) were the materials most frequently used.

Nets, mostly made of knotted string or cordage, were used in fishing. In Northwestern California iris shoots were the preferred material for fishing nets. In Southern California especially, nets were also in the form of carrying bags, small hammock-like contrivances worn on the back and supported by integral cords at both ends. For these, yucca or agave fibers were probably the most frequently used materials. Among the Cahuilla, the hammock-like carrying net is said to have been used in the house to hold a sleeping baby.

Plant materials for clothing were secondary to animal products, although underskirts for women were in some places contrived from the soft inner bark of cottonwood (*Populus* spp.) or willow (*Salix* spp.) twisted on a cord, or the skirt was made from the usual string material. Women of the lower Klamath River region had skirts made from braided Bear Grass (*Xerophyllum tenax*) alternated with a course of husk beads made from pine nuts (*Pinus sabiniana*) (fig. 78). Sandals in the arid south were commonly made from Mescal (*Agave* spp.) fibers, worked back and forth across a looped cord. Moccasins (fig. 79) were the footwear

FIGURE 78 Hupa woman with twined basketry hat, *Dentalium* shell necklace, buckskin back skirt, and front skirt of braided Bear Grass (*Xerophyllum tenax*) and Digger Pine (*Pinus sabiniana*) seed beads. (From S. Powers, *Tribes of California*, 1877)

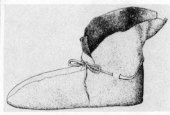

FIGURE 79 Maidu moccasin. (From R. B. Dixon, *The Northern Maidu*, 1905)

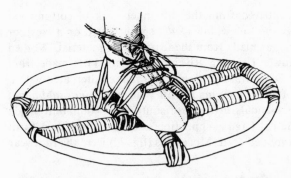

FIGURE 80 Maidu snowshoe. (From R. B. Dixon,
The Northern Maidu, 1905)

of the north, and there, as well as in the mountainous
regions generally, snowshoes (fig. 80) were known. These
were made from a small wooden hoop strung with grapevines (*Vitis* spp.).

Wood Products

The uses to which wood was put were almost endless. We
shall mention only the most common, besides its use as a
fuel; these were for bows and arrows (see plate 13); as
haftings for knives, spears, or other weapons; as boxes and
stools (fig. 81) in the north; as acorn mush stirrers; for
dugout and plank canoes (see fig. 36); and for houses (see
chapter 2).

FIGURE 81 Yurok stools of redwood. (From A. L.
Kroeber, *Handbook of the Indians of California*,
1925)

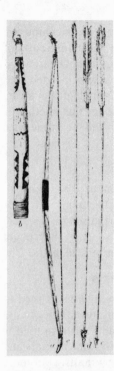

FIGURE 82 Maidu bows and arrows. (From R. B. Dixon, *The Northern Maidu*, 1905)

The favored material for bows in Northern California (north of Santa Cruz and Tulare counties) was Western Yew (*Taxus brevifolia*) (fig. 82). Elsewhere, particularly in Southern California, willows (*Salix* spp.), junipers (*Juniperus* spp.), and mesquites (*Prosopis* spp.) were used to advantage, although they could not compare with yew in allowing the recurving that imparted more power to the weapon. Coincidentally, yew was also the preferred wood in Europe for bows.

For arrows, in the south, the Common Reed (*Phragmites communis*) and Arrowweed (*Pluchea sericea*) were favored materials. Reed arrows were straightened with the use of heated steatite (see p. 149 and fig. 89). Syringa (*Philadelphus lewisii*) or Cluster Rose (*Rosa pisocarpa*) were used for arrowshafts in the north. Here a piece of wood containing holes for insertion of several sizes of shaft was used to straighten the shafts to the desired degree.

Arrows (fig. 82) were either of one piece or composite. Composite arrows were equipped with short foreshafts of hardwood, particularly in the arid lands, where Greasewood (*Sarcobatus vermiculatus*), for instance, was inserted into jointed cane shafts and secured with pine-pitch glue or string or both. Arrows, of course, could have stone tips whether or not they had foreshafts; some arrows had no stone tips, only sharpened wood points.

Abrasives

Horsetail "fern" (*Equisetum* spp.) was used as a kind of sandpaper for polishing arrows and other items. Also for smoothing arrows many tribes in the north used stones, such as sandstone, grooved longitudinally so that they could easily be drawn along the shaft, sometimes in pairs.

Adhesives and Sealants

Pine pitch (especially of *Pinus monophylla*) was used to seal basketry water bottles in arid regions, just as the coastal people used asphaltum (see p. 150). Pitch was also used in some places to attach basketry hoppers to stone mortars and to secure wooden foreshafts to cane arrowshafts. (For more about Indian glues, see above, chapter 5, under "Weapons and Tools.")

Fish Poisons

To poison fish, the stems and leaves of certain plants were crushed and thrown into shallow quiet pools in streams. The fish were stunned or stupified, coming to the surface where they could easily be caught by hand. Evidently the poisonous elements were present in such low quantity that they were harmless to humans or were dissipated in the cooking process. The most commonly used plants for this purpose were:

Soap plant (*Chlorogalum pomeridianum*).

Turkey Mullein, or Dove Weed (*Eremocarpus setigerus*): The second common name for this plant may derive from the fact that doves are very fond of it; the

Indians were aware of this, and evidently caught many doves while they were feeding on it.

California Buckeye (*Aesculus californica*) nuts.

Hallucinogenic and Stimulant Uses of Plants

California Indians apparently did not produce any alcoholic beverages. On the other hand, they were well aware of the hallucinogenic or mind-altering qualities of certain plant infusions, like that of *Datura meteloides*, Toloache, or Jimsonweed. The drug was prepared mostly for puberty initiation rites in certain Southern California tribes (see chapter 2), and it therefore fell into the category of esoteric or formal periodic usage.

Tobacco

Much more regularly used, even outside shamanistic rites, was tobacco (*Nicotiana* spp.), which was used for smoking, mostly for soporific effects. Pipes of stone or clay, of the same general type as those used by Indians at the time of contact with the whites (fig. 65), have been found in archaeological sites in many parts of California, and it must be presumed that some of these were used for smoking, probably of tobacco. Hence the practice seems to be ancient, perhaps more than 2000 years old. Among some ethnographic groups, such as the Gabrielino, the Yokuts, and the Costanoans, tobacco was mixed with lime from seashells and eaten. A kind of "intoxication" resulted, though the main effect seems to have been vomiting.

Tobacco is remarkable because it was raised in a semi-horticulture: special plots were chosen, the brush was burned, seeds were planted in the ashes, and the plot was tended by thinning and weeding. Tobacco was grown even in far Northern California, removed a great distance from the influences of agricultural peoples. The Achomawi of Northeastern California originally secured tobacco seed to plant from the neighboring Shasta because wild tobacco did not grow in their territory. This instance points up what was suggested in chapter 4, that the "wild acorn industry" was in fact so well developed that formal agriculture was not adopted by the tribes north of the Colorado River region. It appears that the Indians understood that agriculture was less reliable than the well-established acorn gathering and processing methods that had been perfected over many millennia. But from the larger complex of agriculture that diffused out of Mexico as far as the Colorado River, tobacco culture was selected to diffuse even farther.

MINERAL COMMODITIES
Grinding Stones

Compared with the variety of plants, an equal range of choice of minerals was not available to the California Indians. To be sure, they did not recognize metals such as gold as having any great value, nor did they possess the technology to extract metals such as silver or copper from ores. Nevertheless, whatever was immediately at hand they utilized, and judging from recorded trade patterns, they had evidently learned where the best sources of a given mineral were.

Throughout the granite formations of the Sierra Nevadan foothills, especially along streams near oak groves, literally thousands of holes have been found ground in the bedrock, holes used for grinding acorns, along with pestles also made from granite. Elsewhere, other types of grinding surfaces were used: flat portable milling stones, or metates (fig. 83), used with manos, or handstones; globular seed-grinding mortars; or flat slabs used in conjunction with attached basket hoppers (fig. 84). These could be of nearly any kind of granular stone, such as hard sandstone. Where vesicular basalt (the variety of volcanic rock ridden with air holes or pockets) occurred, it was used advantageously as bowl mortars or metates in the process of preparing seeds and acorns, for the grinding surface was "self-sharpening"; it did not have to be deliberately pitted or otherwise roughened to permit good flour-producing action. In certain places where large stones were not available, such as in the delta region of the lower Sacramento Valley, stones were carried in from elsewhere, or lighter wooden slabs with suitable depressions in them could be substituted for the stone mortars.

FIGURE 83 Milling stone, or metate, for grinding plant seeds, from prehistoric Southern California. Length ca. 16 in. [40.6 cm.] (From A. E. Treganza and A. Bierman, *The Topanga Culture*, 1958)

FIGURE 84 Maidu basketry hopper and mortar for grinding acorns. Diameter at top, ca. 16 in. [40.6 cm.]. (From R. B. Dixon, *The Northern Maidu*, 1905)

FIGURE 85 Indians making "chemuck" (acorn mush) probably near Yosemite. (From W. C. Bryant [ed.], *Picturesque America*, 1872)

Ground acorns were usually cooked in baskets by means of dropping hot stones in the mass of watery meal and stirring vigorously, so that baskets would not be burned (fig. 85). Where natural stones were not abundant, sub-spherical or loaf-shaped pieces of baked clay were manufactured to serve as substitutes for the stones. Although baskets were the chief storage or cooking vessels in California, the Colorado River peoples and a few others in Southern California and in the southern Sierra Nevada region used pottery vessels for these purposes, a feature apparently derived from the Southwest. Certain clay deposits recorded in Southern California were evidently known for their superior qualities in pottery production.

Soapstone Cooking Vessels

The peoples of the Santa Barbara coast used yet another kind of cooking vessel besides basketry. They procured large chunks of soapstone (steatite) and fashioned them into globular pots (figs. 86 and 87; see plate 8) by carving and grinding with harder stone tools. Sometimes it was possible to rough out the shape of the bowl, inside and out, before it was detached from the parent outcrop. The particular property of steatite is that it can be heated to a very high

FIGURE 86 Stone quarrying and steatite bowl-making on Santa Catalina Island. (From R. F. Heizer, *Indian Occupation in Southern California*, 1954)

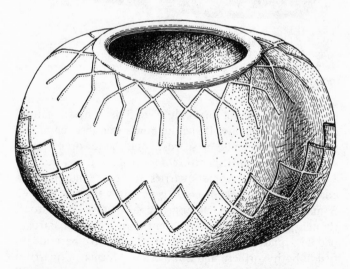

FIGURE 87 Steatite bowl with incised decoration, Santa Barbara coastal region. Diameter ca. 15. in. [38 cm.]. (Courtesy of the Santa Barbara Museum of Natural History)

FIGURE 88 Steatite *comal*, or frying pan, Santa Barbara
coastal region. Width ca. 6 in. [15 cm.]. (From R. F.
Heizer and A. E. Treganza, *Mines and Quarries of the
Indians of California*, 1944)

temperature without breaking. No other known natural
stone has this quality. If steatite bowls were broken in use,
the carved fragments, or sherds, could be reworked into a
sort of frying pan (Spanish *comal*) (fig.. 88).

Evidently the favored quarries for the Santa Barbara
coast and the southern coast generally were outcrops on
Santa Catalina Island. Other groups also utilized soapstone,
though probably to a lesser extent than the Santa Barbara
peoples; quarries and finished specimens have been identified in both Northern and Southern California. A quarry in
the vicinity of Lindsay (Tulare County) was especially well
known and exploited by the Indians of the southern Sierra
Nevada region.

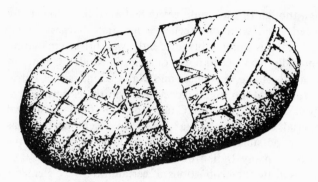

FIGURE 89 Steatite arrowshaft straightener from San Bernardino County. Length about 3½ in. [9 cm.]. (From R. F. Heizer and A. E. Treganza, *Mines and Quarries of the Indians of California*, 1944)

Soapstone was used for a variety of implements besides cooking vessels: "charmstones" (see chapter 8) have been found almost exclusively in archaeological sites, which indicates that they were not being carved in historic times. Stone straighteners for cane arrows, from both prehistoric and historic times (fig. 89), were carefully shaped and grooved; when heated, such stones would not burst apart, and the joints of the arrow cane could be placed in the grooves, allowing enough "relaxation" in the joint to facilitate the straightening of the shaft. Soapstone was also used for making tubular smoking pipes (see chapter 5), and among the Yurok Indians of Northwestern California, soapstone dishes, often in the form of boats, would be placed under salmon being smoked, to catch grease drippings.

Obsidian and Other Stones for Chipped Implements

Every California Indian was familiar with obsidian (black volcanic glass), and in more recent centuries it was probably the most frequently used material for arrow and spear points, knives, scrapers, choppers, and the like. This natural glass, though brittle, could easily be flaked into almost any desired form with the keenest edge and sharpest point. Trade in this commodity evidently was brisk, emanating principally from well-known quarries in Modoc County in the north, Lake, Sonoma, and Napa counties in Central California, Mono and Inyo counties in the eastern Sierra Nevada region, Ventura County on the south coast, and Imperial County in the far south. In recent years it has become possible for researchers to identify precisely the source of many Indian obsidian implements because they can associate the proportions of certain rare trace elements in the obsidian with specific quarries. By this method, it has been found that some San Francisco Bay region archaeological sites, although they contain much obsidian from sources such as those in nearby Napa County, also have a significant amount of obsidian tools made of material originating in the mountains of Mono County, indicating long-range prehistoric trade. The trade in obsidian is documented in sites as old as 4000 years, and obsidian has thus proved to be one of the earliest items of exchange known in prehistoric California.

Other minerals containing silica, such as jasper, chert, flint, chalcedony, and petrified wood, have been identified as coming from specific sources; all were used in about the same manner as obsidian, that is, for projectile points, scrapers, and the like.

In the northern Sierra Nevada and the southern Cascade mountains, a region where there are abundant formations or outcrops of basalt, this material, though less easily chipped than obsidian, for example, was used for thousands of years for projectile points and other implements. Seemingly it was not replaced by siliceous materials for these purposes until about 1500 years ago, and then not entirely.

Asphaltum as a Sealant

Asphaltum, or bitumen, was known principally along or near the southern (Channel Island) coast and in the interior

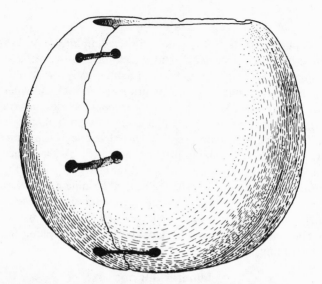

FIGURE 90 Repaired steatite bowl. Drilled holes containing thongs were later filled in with asphaltum to make a tight seal. Santa Barbara coastal region. Diameter at center ca. 17 in. [43 cm.] (From R. F. Heizer, *Indian Occupation in Southern California*, 1954)

to the east (Kern County); the California Indians were the first people to utilize the main petroleum resources of the state. The tar was used for almost countless purposes among the Chumash and their neighbors as a sealant and an adhesive; in areas where it was not easily available, pine pitch (see p. 142) was used as a substitute. The Chumash or their immediate prehistoric predecessors took asphalt blobs floating up from undersea springs and used them to seal (caulk) the joints of their seagoing plank canoes, to plug the holes of abalone shells to make dishes or containers for liquids, and to attach basketry hoppers to acorn grinding stones. To seal basketry water bottles, they melted asphaltum with heated small pebbles in the interior of the vessels. They also used the tar as an adhesive to mend broken implements (fig. 90) and to set knife blades into wooden handles.

Pigments

Paint pigments in the colors most commonly found in minerals (red, especially, and black, green, white, and yellow) were commonly used by Indians, mostly for ritualistic purposes, such as in body painting and in rock drawings (see chapter 8), or in producing decorative designs on everyday implements. A red pigment, probably hematite, is said to have been employed as a prophylactic against skin eruptions in small children. Cinnabar, used as a red face paint, was mined; that is, holes and tunnels were dug in the ground to obtain it. The principal cinnabar mine was at New Almaden near San Jose. The main economic significance of this particular source was that it was well known by distant peoples, and there seems to have been much traveling for and trading in the commodity.

Mineral Springs

Indian archaeological sites have been identified near or at mineral springs, and it is known that living tribes used many of the hot springs that are now modern resorts in Sonoma, Monterey, and San Diego counties. Tribal members afflicted with ailments that all humankind is heir to, such as stiff joints or the general fatigue of aging, drank and bathed in the waters.

Minerals in Foods

It was a common culinary practice north of San Francisco and west of the Sierra Nevada to mix small amounts of iron-bearing red clay with acorn meal to produce native bread. Acorns contain bitter tannic acid, which was usually removed from the meal by a special leaching process. The red clay was added to the meal to remove any remaining tannic acid by converting the latter to an insoluble compound at cooking temperature, by action with the iron oxide in the clay; the tannic acid passed out of the eater's system instead of being absorbed.

It has been observed that the teeth in the jaws of skeletons of adult persons recovered from prehistoric archaeological sites are very worn, often literally ground down to the level

PLATE 1. Indian dancer from San Francisco Mission, artist and date unknown; probably after Louis Choris, ca. 1816.

PLATE 2. A and B. Patwin Indians (Sacramento Valley) in ceremonial costumes, with "Big Head" headdresses (C.H. Merriam, photographer, ca. 1920-hand tinted)

PLATE 3. "Big Head" dance costume, Pomo Indians.
(Photograph S. A. Barrett, ca. 1960)

PLATE 4. Mohave glass-bead collar, collected
ca. 1908. Shows reworking of traditional designs in introduced materials. (Courtesy of
the R.H. Lowie Museum of Anthropology)

PLATE 5. Alabaster charmstones from Sacramento Valley, Early Horizon (ca. 2000 B.C.). Size of largest specimen 10½ in. [27 cm.]. (Courtesy of the R. H. Lowie Museum of Anthropology)

PLATE 6. Bone fish harpoons from prehistoric sites in Sacramento Valley. Largest specimen ca. 5 in. [13 cm.] long. (Courtesy of the R.H. Lowie Museum of Anthropology)

PLATE 7. Various baskets from Central California; cordage fishnet in background. (Courtesy of the R. H. Lowie Museum of Anthropology)

PLATE 8. Decorated steatite bowl from archaeological site on San Clemente Island. (Courtesy of the R. H. Lowie Museum of Anthropology)

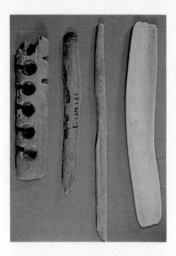

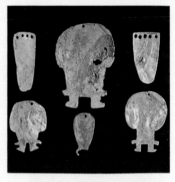

PLATE 10. Abalone ornaments from a Late Horizon archaeological site in Central California. (Courtesy of the R. H. Lowie Museum of Anthropology)

PLATE 9. Artifacts from a dry cave in the Death Valley region: Wooden hearth and drilling stick for making fire; wooden arrow foreshaft with blunt end—inserted in cane shaft, would serve as hard wooden arrowpoint; polished bone tool, probably used for scraping flesh from hides. Length of hearth, ca. 3 3/8 in. [8.4 cm.]. (Courtesy of the R.H. Lowie Museum of Anthropology)

PLATE 11. Prehistoric tubular stone pipes from San Francisco Bay region. Largest specimen 7 in. [18 cm.] long. (Courtesy of the R. H. Lowie Museum of Anthropology)

PLATE 12. Red obsidian blade, stone projectile points, and bone harpoon parts from sites in Northwestern California. (Courtesy of the R. H. Lowie Museum of Anthropology)

PLATE 14. A. Top: Painted limpet shell (*Megathura crenulata*); abalone disc ornament (*Haliotis* sp.). Center: Abalone disc; cowry shell bead (*Cypraea spadicea*). Bottom: Limpet ring ornament; two abalone fish hooks. From Santa Cruz Island.

B. Prehistoric painted shells. Top: keyhole limpet (*Megathura* sp.) from Southern California coast. Bottom: Clam (*Macoma* sp.) from Marin County. Length of clam shell, 2 3/8 in. [6 cm.]. (Courtesy of the University of California Archaeological Research Facility)

PLATE 15. Wiyot twined basket. Ht. ca. 14 in. [35 cm.]. (Courtesy of Katherine Branstetter)

PLATE 13. Hupa bow, painted in traditional manner. Length 38 in. [97 cm.]. (Courtesy of the R. H. Lowie Museum of Anthropology)

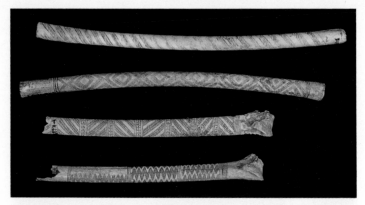

PLATE 16. Incised bird bones tubes, probably for insertion in earlobes, from a Late Horizon archaeological site in Central California. Length ca. 7 in. [17.8 cm.]. (Courtesy of the R. H. Lowie Museum of Anthropology)

PLATE 17. Prehistoric decorated pottery olla (or storage jar, probably for seeds) from Colorado Desert region, east of San Diego. Width ca. 18 in. [46 cm.]. (Courtesy of the Southwest Museum)

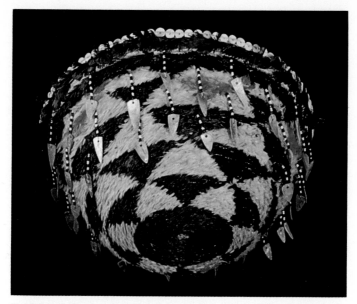

PLATE 18. Pomo feathered basket. Ca. 10 in. [25 cm.] diameter.
(Courtesy of the R. H. Lowie Museum of Anthropology)

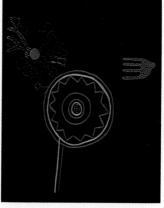

PLATE 19. Pictographs from Santa Barbara coast region. (Reproduced
by courtesy of Campbell Grant, Carpinteria, California)

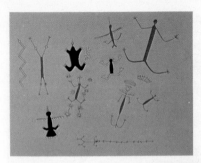

PLATE 20. Pictographs from Santa Barbara coast region. (Reproduced by courtesy of Campbell Grant, Carpinteria, California)

of the bone of the jaw. This extreme tooth wear is attribut-
able to a lifetime of eating cooked or raw roots and bulbs
that were not completely cleaned of adhering soil; to ashes
and grit transferred from stones heated in a fire and dropped
into a basket of acorn gruel to boil it; and to stone powder
contained in meal ground from various seeds, derived from
wear between the mortar and the pestle or the mano and the
metate. Also, there must have been dust everywhere, which
would have contributed to tooth wear. Tooth decay and
abscesses are evident in some of these prehistoric skulls, but
some at the same time show no such dental anomalies.

Indian Explanations of Some Geological Features

There is no question but that when Indians looked at
outstanding and impressive geological features such as
Yosemite Valley, great snow-covered peaks such as Shasta
and Lassen, or the immense land-locked bay of San Francisco, they wondered how these had come into existence.
And always, some person invented a myth that accounted
for these places; the myth was accepted and repeated; and in
the end it answered for the Indians the questions of when
and how and why. We give here three examples:

San Francisco Bay has, as we know, a single narrow
opening to the sea—the Golden Gate, a name given to it by
Captain J.C. Frémont in 1846. Indian legend tells that the
Bay was once a great freshwater inland lake and that in the
ancient past an earthquake opened the Coast Range to form
the Golden Gate and allow the sea to enter. (Despite the
logic of the myth, it is geologically incorrect.)

According to the Southern Sierra Miwok, Yosemite
Valley was formed as follows: Half Dome (then a person)
lived with her husband, Washington Tower, near the edge of
the San Joaquin Valley along the Merced River. After a
quarrel with her husband, Half Dome ran away to the east
and in the process made the Merced River and gouged out
the Valley of the Yosemite. She was carrying her baby in her
arms and the baby's cradle on her head. Washington Tower,
on finding that his wife had left him, cut a white-oak club
and pursued her. Reaching her, he beat her with the club.

Half Dome threw the baby's cradle, with its arched basketry sunshade, against the north wall of the valley, where it became the Royal Arches. Half Dome herself was transformed into the great rock bearing that name. What became of her baby we are not told; perhaps the baby only served as the reason for her carrying the cradle that became the Royal Arches.

Lake Tahoe is ascribed by the Washo to a great natural convulsion at which time an immense wave was sent across the continent by the Great Spirit. A half-month later a great volcanic eruption, accompanied by earthquakes, occurred with such intensity that the Sierra Nevada was formed. The few human survivors were thrown by the Great Spirit into a cavern on the east side of the lake (perhaps Cave Rock), where they are fated to remain until another earth upheaval releases them.

ANIMAL MATERIALS

Although animal products not consumed as food seem to have provided a much smaller inventory of economically usuable items than either plants or minerals, it must not be assumed that the Indians wasted any animal parts. Bones of mammals were used for awls (for coiled basketry), as needles, pins, daggers, and spear points, particularly as harpoon heads for hunting sea mammals or fish, as well as for a great many kinds of beads or amulets. Elk antlers, hollowed and slotted for the purpose, were used in the north for coin purses for *Dentalium* bead money. Handsome carved spoons were made from elk antler and bone as well (fig. 91). Large wedges of elk antler were employed by the Yurok, together with heavy, shaped, stone mauls (fig. 92), to split redwood and cedar planks for housing. Such planks were often finished with adzes having carefully carved stone handles (fig. 93) and blades of slate or shell. Elk or deer antlers were frequently used in the pressure flaking of stone tools and for shuttles and concave-sided tabs of a standard size, used to keep the meshes of uniform size throughout, in the manufacture of fish nets among the Northwestern peoples. The Modoc employed a thick fighting armor made of double elk skins.

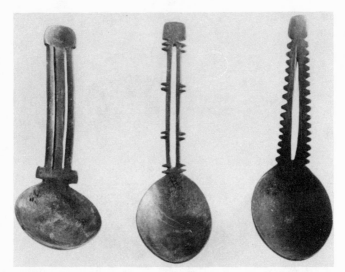

FIGURE 91 Elk antler spoons from Northwestern California. Length about 8 in. [20 cm.]. (From A. L. Kroeber, *Handbook of the Indians of California*, 1925)

FIGURE 92 Stone mauls for pounding antler wedges, used in spolitting redwood for planks, Northwestern California. Length ca. 7 in. [18 cm.]. (From A. L. Kroeber, *Handbook of the Indians of California*, 1925)

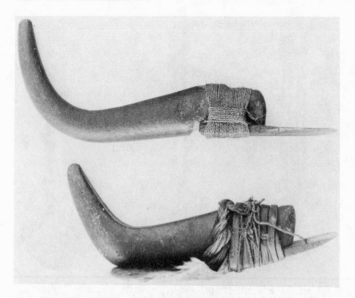

FIGURE 93 Carved stone adze handles with two kinds of blade lashing, Northwestern California. Steel blades have replaced those of hard shell originally used. Length ca. 10 in. [25.4 cm]. (Courtesy of the Lowie Museum of Anthropology)

Deer sinews were important for bowstrings, and strips of sinew were also used to strengthen the backs of bows; these were applied, mostly in the north, with a glue made of fish skins.

Abalone shells were used as dishes, as was already noted, and other seashells were worked on their edges so that they could be used as scoops or spoons. In one recorded case, shells were specially worked on the edges so that they could be used to strip suitable cordage fibers from certain plant parts.

The Indians were well aware of the processes of curing skins, especially deerskins, so that they could be comfortably worn as clothing or used as blankets or robes. In addition, they sewed Sea Otter skins together to make a quite luxurious garment (fig. 94) and made arrow quivers from single Sea Otter skins. Rabbit skins were cut in strips,

FIGURE 94 Monterey woman wearing otter skin cloak. (By José Cardero, 1791)

wound around lengths of cordage, and twined with a double weft of such strips into warm and serviceable blankets or capes. Even feathers, especially of large birds, were used for making capes, skirts, blankets, or elaborate headdresses; perhaps most important, they were used as fletching materials.

7. ARCHAEOLOGY

Although this book is devoted primarily to California Indians living just before or in the historic period, that is, after the Spanish conquest of Mexico in A.D. 1519, some knowledge of the lives of Indians during the many millennia before that is of utmost importance. Much concerning the earliest occupation period will always remain speculative, since remains of people dating back to the end of the Pleistocene epoch (about 12,000 years ago) are extremely rare. Assumptions about the early Indian presence may be based on the dating of questionable material, such as charcoal in its various forms, or on the interpretation of the functions of sites or of certain classes of stone objects alleged to be the work of man's hand and occurring in ancient geological deposits. Thus, for several localities, such as Mission Valley in San Diego, Santa Rosa Island in the Santa Barbara Channel group, or the Manix (dry) Lake shore in the western Mohave Desert, claims have been made of human occupancy more than 15,000 years ago. We take the position here that none of these claims has yet been adequately documented or vindicated, and therefore such sites will not be discussed further.

SOUTHERN CALIFORNIA

A small number of human skeletal finds from Del Mar near San Diego, from Laguna Beach and Los Angeles ("Los Angeles Man"), and in the Yuha Desert near El Centro have been dated by one means or another at far older than 15,000 years. It has not been possible to connect any of these human remains with a definite culture, although at least one find, "Los Angeles Man," was apparently associated with bones of now-extinct Pleistocene animals. Some of the methods of interpreting the meaning of the finds, or even the dating methods themselves, might be questioned. Quibbling over such matters, however, may be fruitless when so relatively few specimens are available for scrutiny.

San Dieguito Culture

Even though Indians may have been present in California more than 15,000 years ago, the story here will begin with a culture called San Dieguito, named after a stratified, dated (around 7000 B.C.) site found in the broad bed of the San Dieguito River near San Diego. This is the Harris site (fig. 95). Although it is located near the coast, its culture has been identified not as maritime, but as one more likely following mainly a land hunting mode of life. The culture represented at this site has been associated with other finds from a large portion of what is today called the Southeastern California desert region. It has been suggested that some so-called San Dieguito I sites in this vast area date back to 9000 B.C. These are possibly associated with the beginning of a wet period called Anathermal or Pluvial, which followed the end of the Pleistocene epoch, or "Ice Age." Certainly the locations of these finds in present dry desert terrain do not suggest initial occupation in markedly arid circumstances. Many of the sites are found on hilltops, though not far from "fossil" stream channels or the edges of playas, present-day dry lake basins.

The distribution of San Dieguito sites is scattered. The late Malcolm Rogers of the San Diego Museum of Man, who first formulated the concept of this ancient culture, suggested that it included several "centers" or aspects in Southern California and surrounding regions. The largest of these centers extended well beyond the borders of present-day California; one relatively small, detached locality in Northern California at Borax Lake, adjacent to Clear Lake, was suggested as a sort of outlier of the San Dieguito culture. The Borax Lake and Harris sites both have layered cultural deposits, but the information about San Dieguito sites in the Mohave or Colorado deserts is derived only from surface collections. Thus the possibilities of properly desig-

FIGURE 95 Map showing some important archaeological site locations in California.

nating various stages or separate periods of the culture (with Roman numerals) are reduced. Nevertheless, it has been suggested that the Harris site dates from the late end of the sequence, often being termed San Dieguito III in the literature. (In archaeological usage, the earliest known stage of a culture is designated stage I; the later stages, found on layers above it, are numbered II, III, and so on.)

No definite skeletal remains are known for the San Dieguito sites. "Sleeping circles" (fig. 96), areas about 10-12 feet (3-4 m.) in diameter cleared in the stony desert or

FIGURE 96 "Sleeping circles" attributed to the ancient San Dieguito culture, ca. 12 ft [3.6 m.] in diameter, near Indian Pass, Colorado Desert. (Photograph Rudolf Miller, courtesy of Imperial Valley College Museum, El Centro, California)

FIGURE 97 Chipped stone "crescents" from Southern California, attributed to time of ancient San Dieguito culture. Size of specimen on left: ca. 2 in. [5 cm.] across.

outlined in stone, and chipped stone implements, like small crescents (fig. 97), generally serve as distinguishing features of the culture, especially in its desert aspects. Milling stones (metates) for grinding seeds are not included in the San Dieguito inventory, but stone tools have been found with retouched or reworked edges, and with pressure flaking, by which small flakes are detached from the original relatively crude edge by means of a tool, perhaps of bone, applied to the old edge by hand pressure. These tools include large projectile points, probably used with thrusting spears or as

FIGURE 98 Idealized drawing of method of grasping throwing stick (atlatl), with end of spear resting against hooked end.

darts in conjunction with a throwing stick, or atlatl (fig. 98), and a variety of scrapers or knives. The small crescent-shaped chipped objects, because of their sometimes approximately animal shapes, have been suggested as amulets, but most likely they represent some specialized kind of projectile point. These and the relatively well-made "domed scrapers" (fig. 99) are probably the most distinctive tools for sites generally termed San Dieguito. However, particular shapes of certain classes of projectile points that may be associated with San Dieguito are more intriguing from the standpoint of estimating age.

In many parts of North America besides the San Dieguito area, researchers have found a form of concave-based point

FIGURE 99 Domed scrapers from Southern California. Size of both, ca. 2½ in. [6.25 cm.] diameter at bottom.

with "flutings" extending toward the point from the concavity. This style is called the Clovis point, named after an ancient site in New Mexico, where it was first found. In some places it has been found in lower levels of sites dating around 10,000 B.C. Clovis-like points have been recovered from California sites at Borax Lake (fig. 100), Tulare Lake and Lake Mohave, for example, and in all three of these

FIGURE 100 Fluted stone projectile point (obverse and reverse) from ancient Borax Lake culture, Lake County. Length 2½ in. [6.25 cm.].

places they have been found associated with stone crescents. At Borax Lake the fluted points and crescents are made of local obsidian, which has been subjected to tests based on the observation that native volcanic glass acquires on its surface over time a measurable amount of water, or a "hydration layer." In theory, the thicker the layer, the older the specimen. While this method of dating is not entirely dependable, it seems to have some usable approximate results for some localities, and the Borax Lake material may provide a good example for application of this dating method. At least, the Borax Lake findings appear otherwise to be consistent with those from what have been called San Dieguito sites elsewhere in California.

Two other types of allegedly ancient projectile points are from the Mohave Desert and are known as Lake Mohave or Silver Lake points (fig. 101). It is possible that these points also are of the same approximate time range as that suggested for the San Dieguito culture and may represent a specific local variation of that culture.

To an archaeologist it would appear that the San Dieguito peoples were primarily hunters of big and small game who had not yet begun to develop specialized implements like milling stones for exploitation of plants, although they almost certainly included plant foods in their diet.

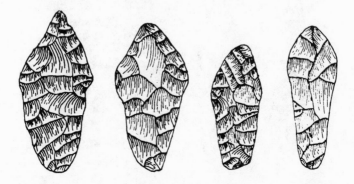

FIGURE 101 Projectile points from Mohave Desert region, Southern California. Length averages about 2¼ in. [5.7 cm.]

Milling Stone Horizon

Following the San Dieguito in time were cultures that can conveniently be grouped in the category "Milling Stone Horizon." (The term "horizon" as used by archaeologists denotes the similarity of numbers of cultural elements covering a large geographical area during a particular span of time.) This period may have had its beginnings about 5000 B.C. in Southern California. The term itself was evidently devised to refer at first to essentially coastal peoples, who perhaps more evenly divided their time between hunting and seed-gathering. However, desert groups like the so-called Pinto peoples, living during this time in or around the Mohave Desert, which was then in the grip of an extremely warm climatic period, the Altithermal, could also be included in this horizon. They are usually identified as people using a particular type of projectile point, the "Pinto point" (fig. 102), but they had also adopted the use of the milling stone (fig. 83) for grinding seeds. Excavations at Little Lake, south of Owens Lake, have revealed evidence of a group using Pinto points and milling stones, as well as the Lake Mohave or Silver Lake points characteristic of an earlier period.

According to some investigators, these desert Pinto people were followed in time by people called Amargosa, perhaps after 1000 B.C., at the beginning of the Medithermal climatic period, which in general was cooler and wetter than the Altithermal; the Medithermal climate seemingly extends to present times in California. The Amargosa people differed from their predecessors in their stoneworking tech-

FIGURE 102 "Pinto" culture projectile points from Southern California. Length ca. 1⅜ in. [3.5 cm.].

nology; they may have adopted from elsewhere the idea of using the bow and arrow rather than continuing to use the spear thrower as their hunting weapon. Such a change can be inferred from the size and shape of projectile points; that is, small notched or finely stemmed points can easily be associated with the use of lightweight arrows rather than with spears. In later Amargosa times pottery, undoubtedly from the Southwest (i.e., Arizona), was introduced into the Mohave Desert. It has not been possible to estimate precisely when pottery-using Shoshonean-speaking groups like the Chemehuevi, Cahuilla, Luiseño, and Gabrielino tribes came to their present locations, but it was probably some time after A.D. 800 or 1000.

On or near the Pacific Coast, a number of post-San Dieguito sites extending from Santa Barbara south to La Jolla have been designated centers of the Milling Stone Horizon. Some of these—for example, the Topanga site—have in their lower levels indications of the San Dieguito culture, such as chipped stone crescents and domed scrapers (see figs. 97, 99). Various culture designations have been given to these coastal or near-coastal Milling Stone Horizon sites, such as Oak Grove (Santa Barbara region), Topanga (Los Angeles), or La Jolla (San Diego), but all seem to share the kind of stone implements that indicate a strong seed-gathering economy. Hunting was undoubtedly still important, although Milling Stone Horizon projectile points were generally large and crude. There were present also other fairly crude stone flake-and-core tools (made by striking a stone chunk, or core, to knock off a flake, which might then be further worked to produce the particular tool needed, such as a scraper or a plane). There were few bone objects, and shell implements were rare at any time in earlier California prehistory. In Milling Stone Horizon sites, at least on the mainland, shell tools were either nonexistent or have disappeared through chemical action, having been embedded in the soil for thousands of years.

During the Milling Stone Horizon the Channel Islands (such as Catalina and Santa Rosa islands—though without milling stones) probably began to be occupied by peoples who for some unknown reason were only beginning to realize the great potential food resources to be had from fishing and mollusk-collecting. (There are, however, some radiocarbon dates as early as about 10,000 years ago from sites on Santa Rosa Island. If these dates are in any way connected with peoples engaged in gathering food, then, considering the locations, that food must have included many marine products.) Some archaeologists believe that before 5000 B.C., sea level was lower than at present, and that sites containing evidence of marine adaptation by human occupants may long since have been obliterated by the rising sea level.

After about 1000 B.C., to use an arbitrary date, Milling Stone Horizon groups began to differentiate. They obviously did not give way to successors in any abrupt way, nor even at the same time in different places. The La Jolla peoples around San Diego, for instance, may have continued to follow the traditional ways without any great changes for hundreds of years after 1000 B.C. For the rest, however, it is reasonable to assume that from about that date the homeland stage was being set by the ancestors of some of the peoples whom the sixteenth-century Hispanic explorers found established in the region. Among these would be, in order north from the ethnographic Diegueño, the Luiseño, the Gabrielino, and the Chumash.

It may be noted that in the center of this land, that is, between the Hokan speakers (Chumash and Diegueño), the ancestors of the Shoshonean-speaking Luiseño and Gabrielino possibly at some undetermined time drove a wedge and, in the process, occupied the southern Channel Islands. But the archaeological evidence does not seem to register the cultural magnitude of any such intrusion. If the first pottery users in the Mohave Desert around A.D. 800, an estimated date at best, were also Shoshonean speakers, as are the Indians there today, it is difficult to see why pottery did not come to the coast not long afterwards. The introduction of pottery into the territory of the coastal Diegueño has been suggested as no earlier than about A.D. 1400. At this time their northern neighbors (the ancestral Luiseño?), still perhaps getting along with vessels of steatite from Catalina Island, were clearly not in possession of much pottery.

At best, the period immediately after 1000 B.C. is not very well known. Approximately representative of this time may be the so-called Hunting, or Intermediate, cultures of the Santa Barbara region, which probably had begun to take shape earlier, perhaps about 2000 B.C. During this time (say, after 2000 B.C.), the important curved abalone-shell fish-hook had made its first known appearance; stone mortars and pestles, suggesting an increased use of acorns with more efficient grinding implements, were now used, although the flatter milling stones were not abandoned. In addition, the hopper mortar, a bottomless conical basket attached around the edge of a depression in a grinding stone by means of asphaltum, was introduced; the hopper mortar also was probably best employed with acorns. Late in the period, the bow and arrow were evidently introduced, although the atlatl may have continued in use.

Canaliño-Chumash Culture

Finally, in the centuries just before the first century A.D., the culture called the Canaliño began to develop. These people appear to be the direct ancestors of the Chumash. Evidence now suggests that at this time there was a thriving mainland-island community, including what are called to-day Santa Cruz, Santa Rosa, and San Miguel islands. The Canaliño-Chumash probably reached the highest point of achievement in bone, shell, and stone technology in California. With their seagoing boats of planks fastened to-gether with cordage and sealed with asphaltum, they could exploit their rich environment to the full. Juan Rodriguez Cabrillo was the first European to see these people, in 1542, and he described them favorably. Referring to the Santa Barbara coastal region, he reported it as "very well settled. . . . Fine canoes each holding twelve or thirteen Indians came to the ships. . . . They have round houses, well-covered down to the ground. They wear skins of many different animals, eat acorns and a white seed the size of maize which is used to make tamales [probably the kernels of pits of the

Holly-leaved Cherry, or Islay (*Prunus ilicifolia*)]. They live well."*

CENTRAL CALIFORNIA

Central California consists of the vast region comprising the Great Central Valley, the drainages of the San Joaquin and Sacramento rivers, and the San Francisco Bay area. Dating of sites thought to be earliest in this region is not altogether satisfactory. The Tulare Lake finds, already mentioned, for example, are of stone implements thought to be ancient, but they are from surface collections. From Buena Vista Lake, south of Tulare Lake, a radiocarbon date of about 5500 B.C. from a buried cultural stratum has been associated with the find of a chipped stone crescent. Sites at Buena Vista and Tulare lakes, together with that at Borax Lake, in the north Coast Ranges not far from the western margin of the Central Valley, all contain material pointing to affinities in time with the San Dieguito culture. (See fig. 95.)

Near Fresno, at the Tranquillity Site, human bones have been found and are allegedly associated with fossilized bones of extinct Pleistocene mammals (camel, horse, and bison) probably from at least 10,000 B.C.; but the artifacts with the human remains resemble those from more definitely dated sites of about 1000 B.C. in the San Joaquin River delta area. Farther north at the Farmington site east of Stockton, a large assemblage of crudely flaked stone tools (e.g., choppers and scrapers) has been found in buried gravel deposits. No radiocarbon dates or bones of extinct animals are available at this site to help date these implements.

Early Horizon

It is not until we come to the region of the Sacramento-San Joaquin River delta and San Francisco Bay that we find an already flourishing hunting-gathering culture, whose

*Quotations are from an abstract of a surviving account of Cabrillo's voyage, translated by H. R. Wagner in the *California Historical Society Quarterly*, 7 (1928): 41-54.

earliest radiocarbon dates are about 2500 B.C. This has been named the culture of the Early Horizon in Central California, and it represents the beginning of a well-documented sequence that extends right up to the time of contact between Indians and whites. From the relative sophistication of artifacts of shell, bone, and stone, especially the latter (fig. 103), among these Early Horizon people, we may assume that the antecedents of the culture are much older than the 2500 B.C. date, but we cannot be certain just where the point of origin was—that is, whether it was local (California) or some more distant part of North America. From the distribution of language stocks (see fig. 1) in California, it may be postulated that members of the Hokan stock were Early Horizon people, that they were the early occupants of Central California, and that they were later displaced by the Penutians, who remained in the Central Valley until the time of contact with the whites.

The archaeological record does show some kind of cultural change in about 1000 B.C., mainly a change of emphasis in certain practices. The new archaeological culture is referred to as Middle Horizon. The people of this culture continued many of the usages of their predecessors in shell, stone, and bone, although they seemingly elaborated bone artifacts like awls, needles, and harpoons far beyond the Early Horizon people. The finding of a fair number of Middle Horizon skeletons with stone projectile points embedded in their bones may indicate that this period was a time of violence or upheaval, or it may merely signify some esoteric ritual burial practice having nothing to do with war or intrusion by foreigners. Evidently these people spread beyond the confines of the Sacramento-San Joaquin delta and the region of San Francisco Bay, for evidences of their presence have been found in abundance on the Central California coast and far up both main rivers.

Late Horizon

From these beginnings, practically the whole of Central California apparently was settled, probably by peoples speaking Penutian languages. As they spread farther from

EARLY	MIDDLE	LATE

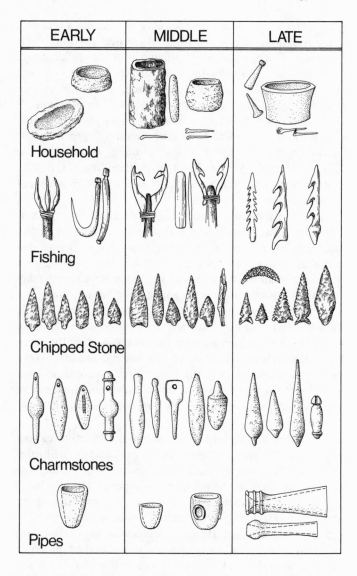

FIGURE 103 Significant artifacts of stone, bone, and shell from Early, Middle, and Late archaeological horizons, Central California. (After R. K. Beardsley, *Cultural Sequences in Central California Arcaheology*, 1948)

the center—from San Francisco Bay and the delta region—
they seemingly adapted to different physical conditions and
began to differentiate in culture and probably in language.
Nevertheless, probably through the agencies of common
language stock and continuing trade, a distinct culture
evolved which has come to be called Late Horizon. It
appears to have taken its essential form by about A.D. 300,
when the bow seems to have almost entirely supplanted the
spear thrower as the principal hunting weapon for the
Middle Horizon people. The Late culture, like its Canaliño
contemporary around Santa Barbara, excelled in bone and
even more in shell work.

That the Late people were highly developed acorn gatherers is indicated archaeologically by the numbers of implements used in processing this nutritious nut. Besides the
familiar mortars and pestles, there is other evidence of a
strong commitment to the acorn industry: charred fragments of baskets, bone awls for making baskets, and even
objects of baked clay, which were almost certainly used as
substitutes for heated natural stones for cooking acorns in
baskets. There is even a legitimate suggestion that the acorn
complex, and especially its strong integral use of baskets,
was reason enough why the Late Horizon peoples did not
adapt pottery vessels to their inventory of cooking devices;
pots would not have appreciably improved the total processing technology.

Late Horizon sites show certain minor distinctive features
in each of several different parts of Central California.
Figure 103, however, illustrates salient parts of the material
culture of peoples living in the supposed "hearth land"
around the Sacramento-San Joaquin delta only during the
past 800 years or so, until the time of contact with whites.
(See plate 16.) Late Horizon peoples in any part of the
Central Valley and its immediate environs had probably
already settled about 1000 years ago in the localities where
they were later observed by ethnographers, who identified
the areas as the territories of the Costanoans (San Francisco
Bay region and the Pacific Coast south to Monterey); the
Southern Wintun, or Patwin (western Sacramento Valley),

the Maidu (eastern Sacramento Valley and the adjoining Sierra Nevada), the Miwok (Coast Ranges north of San Francisco, the northern San Joaquin Valley, and a long section of the southern Sierra Nevada), and the Yokuts (almost all of the southern San Joaquin Valley and parts of both the Sierra Nevada and the south Coast Ranges).

OTHER AREAS OF CALIFORNIA

The main crest of the Sierra Nevada has probably represented a significant cultural barrier for a long time. The most recent important breach appears to have been made by the Numic-speaking Monache (Western Mono) in the southern part of the range, whose ancestors probably came over the crest from Owens Valley during the last 600 years or so. The Monache probably brought with them the knowledge of a crude kind of pottery called Owens Valley Brown ware, used by them and by some neighboring Yokuts groups until very recent times.

Ancestors of the Hokan-speaking Washo of the Lake Tahoe region, essentially to the east of the Sierran crest, possibly came to that territory at some ancient time, or they could have been removed from frequent contact with the west side of the mountains after the so-called Penutian invasion.

For a vast stretch of the western side of the Sierra Nevada, including Yosemite Valley, researchers have discovered a series of culture sequences, perhaps beginning about 1000 B.C., which are related in stoneworking technology and other features to Middle and Late Horizon Central California cultures and to those of the Great Basin as well. Again, these relationships may have been strengthened by trade, since great numbers of Pacific Coast shell artifacts have been found at habitation sites in the Great Basin east of the Sierra, and Sierran obsidian has been found in considerable quantities in the Central Valley and on the Pacific Coast. Limestone mortuary caverns of the western foothills in the southern Sierra Nevada also contain Middle Horizon types of coastal shell beads and ornaments.

For the southern Cascade-Modoc Plateau in Northeastern California, the archaeological picture is roughly
similar to that of the Sierra, with perhaps even earlier sites,
going back to about 3000 B.C., in the region of the upper Pit
River. One site with a date of about 1350 B.C. has been
found on a tributary of the Pit River; this may be associated,
with some archaeological evidence, with the Hokan-Penutian transition in California. In any case, affiliations with
both Central California Middle Horizon and coexisting
cultures in the Great Basin have been noted in the region. It
is possible that the ancestral Hokan-speaking Yana, Atsugewi, and Achomawi peoples were all displaced by the
Penutians and arrived at approximately their recent locations in about 1000 B.C. Whether this is so or not, it seems
apparent that by Late Horizon times all of these southern
Cascade peoples were receiving influences from Central
California.

In the south Coast Ranges, between the territories of the
ethnographic northern Chumash around San Luis Obispo
and the Costanoans of Monterey, lay a sort of cultural
backwater, the land of the ethnographic Salinans, also Hokan speakers. No markedly ancient implements have been
found here so far, although it may be noted that at Diablo
Canyon, near San Luis Obispo, a site with an early culture
deposit dated about 7000 B.C. has been recorded. The
earliest carbon 14 date of any known site in the Salinan
region is about A.D. 50, from a coastal site, corresponding
with the late Middle Horizon in Central California. Evidently this region was influenced strongly from the Santa
Barbara coastal area as well as the San Francisco Bay
region. The main villages known were marine oriented.
Seeds, and especially acorns, were ground in hopper mortars, a style probably derived from the Santa Barbara region
as were, apparently, the curved-shell fishhooks.

The post-Pleistocene climatic patterns (with the sequen-
tial periods Anathermal, Altithermal, and Medithermal denoting marked fluctuations during the past 10,000 years)
appear to have had powerful cultural effects in what are
today the arid or desert parts of California. Along the coast,

in the mountains, and in the northern part of the Central Valley and its margins, such effects surely must also have been felt, although not so critically or over such a wide area as in the desert region.

We have already noted, in the north Coast Ranges, at Borax Lake, some stone artifacts, "fluted" projectile points and crescents, which resemble those found in the San Dieguito sites in Southeastern (i.e., "arid") California. Whatever the exact age of the Borax Lake specimens may be, they almost certainly represent the beginning or early stage of a cultural sequence that has been detected in various parts of the range. In the Napa Valley, for example, numerous crude stone implements have been found, which are undated as yet but which probably represent a slightly later stage of the basic Borax Lake period.

A site near Willits, radiocarbon-dated at about 1800 B.C., had in its lower levels a number of concave-based (unfluted) projectile points, also seemingly related to the early Borax Lake complex, though of a much later time. These points have been assigned to a culture called the Mendocino complex, which in turn appears to have some relationships to Middle Horizon Central California and to various Great Basin sites as well. The Mendocino complex included milling stones as well as bowl mortars. Shell beads, which have been used extensively in Central California for cross-dating many sites from which materials for radiocarbon dating have not otherwise been obtained, were not present at early time levels at many sites in the north Coast Ranges. Later sites, corresponding to Late Horizon Central California, have been found at numerous localities in the north Coast Ranges. In upper levels, often designated as of the Clear Lake complex, hopper (slab) mortars, beads of magnesite, and small, triangular, side-notched projectile points were found. These are points with small notches near the base on both sides, used for securing the point to the wooden arrow with cordage. At least once, a carefully made stone-lined earth oven was also excavated. All these could be attributed to either the ethnographic Pomo or the Yuki of the region.

The question of regional ancestry of both the Pomo and the Yuki is a difficult one. The earliest Borax Lake people could conceivably have been Hokan speakers from whom the Pomo were derived; alternatively, the Pomo could have come into the area after the "Penutian invasion," perhaps in about 1000 B.C., or even much later. The Yuki (and the related Wappo in Napa County) pose an even greater dilemma, for they represent the one linguistic group in California for whom at this writing no outside linguistic relatives have been determined. They may therefore be the oldest occupants of the region, perhaps with ancestors dating from San Dieguito times; or their forebears may have come in at some later time, possibly separating themselves from antecedents who have not been identified or whose languages have not yet been sufficiently analyzed to allow an estimate of the date of separation. (See also chapter 2.)

The last region to be considered in this survey is the northwestern corner of California and a small part of southwestern Oregon, comprising parts of the north Coast Ranges as well as the Klamath Mountains, which form a good proportion of the drainage of the Klamath River. Along the lower course of that river, groups representing three great linguistic stocks lived: Athabascans (e.g., Hupa), Algonkians (Yurok), and Hokans (Karok). Little is known of the prehistory of the Klamath River itself, since so few sites have been excavated, none of an antiquity beyond about 800 years ago. The ethnographic Klamath River peoples, Hupa, Yurok, and Karok, had virtually identical ways of living. The Yurok also occupied a stretch of coastal land on both sides of the mouth of the Klamath River. From there and from coastal land to both the south and the north (about 50 miles into Oregon), we have sufficient information to allow discussion of Northwestern California prehistory in some depth.

Although the mouth of the Klamath appears to have been the center of a rich and unique cultural development, we can assume for convenience that a similar adaptation to the coastal environment prevailed throughout the entire strip, from just south of Humboldt Bay to the territory of the

Athabascan-speaking Chetco in southern Oregon. The earliest dates in this region come from a site in the land of the ethnographic Chetco, at the mouth of the Pistol River. A carbon 14 date of about 3000 B.C. is recorded here from a cultural level with large heavy points having a suggestion of edge serration. At a site at Point St. George, in ethnographic Tolowa territory (the Tolowa were also Athabascan speakers), near Crescent City, California, a date of 300 B.C. has been obtained from a sandy level apparently containing some crudely chipped stone tools. Neither of these early dates is late enough to be associated with the earliest Athabascan presence in the region, nor can the dates be associated with the characteristically rich later prehistoric culture of this coastal area, especially that aspect of it just south of the Klamath River (figs. 104, 105). Here there are carbon 14 dates of only about A.D. 900, which seem to date the rich culture, apparently a fully developed maritime culture that was discontinuous with the complex marine culture north of the Columbia River. Some archaeologists suggest that the beginnings of this coastal culture in the lower Klamath River region must largely have occurred at a time of lower sea level, and hence that its early sites must today be buried offshore.

With but few exceptions, the known archaeological culture of the region is approximately the same as that of the ethnographic coastal Yurok and their neighbors, Tolowa to the north and Wiyot to the south. Emphasis was on sea-lion hunting, fishing, and shellfish gathering, although hopper mortars suggest forays into the interior for acorns. Bone spearheads, barbed bone or antler harpoons—some slit at the tip to receive chipped stone points with concave bases—bone shuttles used in the manufacture of fishnets, grooved stone sinkers, and bone fishhooks similar to those from the Santa Barbara region were important in the local technology. Besides the stone harpoon points there were finely chipped large barbed arrowheads and arrowshaft smoothers consisting of two pieces of abrading stones with grooves. Finely shaped steatite bowls were used for catching the grease from cooking salmon. Stone mauls and elaborate

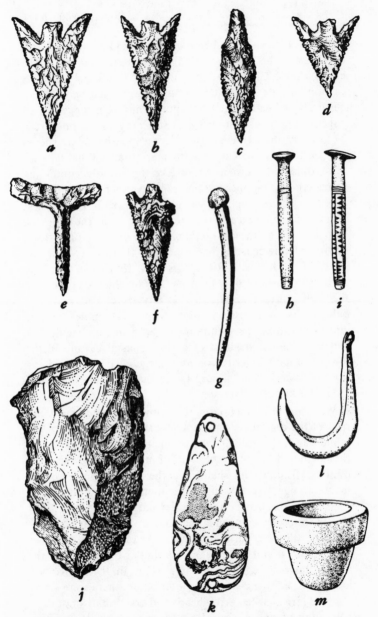

FIGURE 104 Northwestern California late prehistoric artifacts of chipped stone (*a-f, j*); polished stone (*m*); bone (*g-i, l*)
and shell (*k*). Size of *k*, ca 2 in. [5 cm.]. (From R. F. Heizer and
J. E. Mills, *The Four Ages of Tsurai*, 1952)

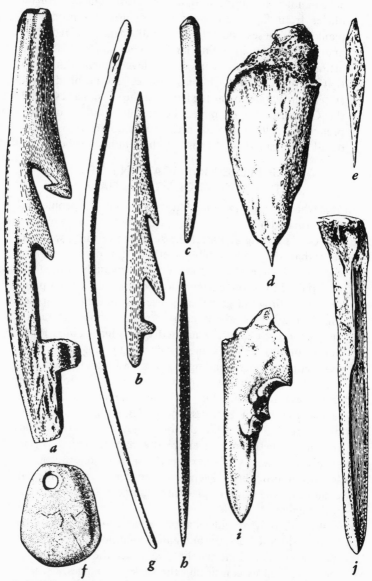

FIGURE 105 Northwestern California late prehistoric artifacts of bone (*a-e*, *g-h*) and stone (*f*). Size of *a*, ca. 4¾ in. [12
cm.]. (From R. F. Heizer and J. E. Mills, *The Four Ages of
Tsurai*, 1952)

adze handles (to receive, at first, shell blades, and later, metal blades from European sources) were used for producing planks for houses and for shaping all manner of redwood and cedar items, including large dugout canoes. All these artifacts point to another climax development similar to that of the Canaliño-Chumash. Since the Yurok did not suffer near-extinction at the hands of the missionaries as did the Chumash, for example, the gradual grading of their prehistoric culture into the present was observed in greater detail than can that of most of the southern tribes.

FURTHER IMPLICATIONS OF THE ARCHAEOLOGICAL DATA

In the attempt to trace the origins of the peoples of California who were encountered by the Spanish explorers and others during and after the sixteenth century, we have seen that the only feasible methods for detecting basic customs of the earlier periods depend on analysis of stone materials. Stone implements surely express important parts of the hunting and gathering processes, but there is something unsatisfying about characterizing whole groups of people simply as those who used Clovis-like points, Pinto points, or even milling stones. Such categorizing only means that people were responding in certain ways to different and changing environments, and that we are able to discern these responses with but a limited number of kinds of artifacts. When it is necessary to define cultures in such broad terms, it is easy to lose sight of the facts that transitions between conventionally named periods often required hundreds of years to occur, and that any given transition, probably in keeping with different environmental conditions, did not take place at the same time throughout a wide region.

We can only speculate about what brought about the major transitions. Environmental conditions, that is, climatic events, must ultimately have played the chief role, but local preferences concerning the sites for villages, perhaps even in aesthetic terms, must also have been important. Another major factor was the effect of accelerating human inventions, such as those involved in the whole complex of acorn preparation.

From San Dieguito times onward there appears to have been an exchange of ideas or goods, through either peaceful trade or migration, and perhaps through physical invasion. Although certain valid inferences about migrations can be drawn from the present geographical distribution of linguistic stocks, especially those relating to Hokan-Penutian, we can presently use these data only in the crudest way to make statements about the time of such migrations.

In all, no matter what forces were in play, it is possible for us to see, from a time beginning about 11,000 years ago, a sporadic but consistent series of efforts to better the human condition, or at least to ensure survival, in the ever-changing environment of California.

California is rich in archaeological sites. Many of these, perhaps four or five thousand, were occupied when the whites first appeared, but were soon abandoned when village populations were drawn into missions in the Spanish period. The depopulation that began during the mission period was hastened by epidemic diseases introduced by the Europeans. The malaria epidemic of 1830-1834 in the Great Interior Valley continued the trend; and the outright killing of Indians was a common occurrence in California during the Gold Rush.

No full count of prehistoric village sites in California has ever been attempted, because large sections of the state have never been surveyed by archaeologists. About 30,000 sites of all categories (temporary campsites used perhaps only once or twice; stone quarries; petroglyph sites; permanently occupied village sites; seasonal hunting, fishing, or collecting camps; cemeteries) have been recorded to date, and it is probable that the full total would run to about 100,000. Many known archaeological sites were abandoned long before the whites appeared and began to disrupt the native settlement system. Many prehistoric sites that were once occupied were later abandoned. Among the reasons given by Indians for leaving one village site and for establishing a new one were floods; attacks by hostile villages situated nearby; internal quarrels between families, which might cause a village population to split in two; dread of ghosts of former occupants, who were believed to return and "haunt" the village; uncontrollable infestation of fleas; and others. Father Pedro Font in 1776 observed that a number of Chumash villages along the Santa Barbara Channel were not occupied, because "the year had been without rain and their watering places gave out." Anthropologist T. T. Waterman reported in 1920 on several reasons why the Yurok in the northwestern part of the state founded new towns:

Like most primitive people, the Yurok change their places of abode very abruptly. No doubt the relative size and importance of towns has shifted from time to time. I think the Yurok may have been more prone to change their places of abode than the average tribe. In addition to all the usual causes of change of abode (disease, floods, attacks of enemies, bad dreams, and plain fidgetiness), the Yurok are extremely quarrelsome. Prominent among their traits is a certain sinful pride, a love of squabbling, and readiness to take offense. These result indirectly in the shifting of habitations. . . . If an individual commits a homicide, . . . that individual is an uncomfortable person to have around. Unless his cause is so just, his character so upright, or his personality so winning that his towns-people are ready to join in his defense and make common cause with him, the village usually makes it so unpleasant for him that he leaves. . . . In most cases in which a man moves off in this way he begins sooner or later to "pay for" the man he has killed. The price for a homicide is pretty high, however, and a number of years are often occupied in making up the full sum, which is paid in installments. When he has completed his payments, he often does not feel like moving back. If he makes his new home a permanent one, and raises a large family there, the addition of new houses gradually lends the place the character of a settlement. . . . Some very important towns are said to have started in this way.

Waterman also describes natural calamities as a cause for changing village locations:

[Klamath] River towns are usually more than a hundred feet above the stream, which has in places an annual rise of more than seventy vertical feet. A tremendous flood in the winter of 1862 . . . somewhat changed the location of settlements; a good many towns were permanently moved to higher sites, and others where the houses were washed down the river were abandoned.

The occupants of a village spent much of their time foraging the countryside, bringing home all kinds of useful items: killed game animals, firewood, seeds, houseposts, stone for making implements, rocks to be heated for stone-boiling in baskets, and so on. Graves for the dead were usually dug somewhere on the village site. The residues of all these activities became part of the deposit which we see today as an archaeological site.

To what extent Indians, during their occupancy or use of the land of California for many thousands of years, caused an appreciable effect on topography or plant and animal distribution is not known. There are hints that repeated burning off of valley areas may have considerably reduced the growth of oaks and that these areas became parklands or even grasslands. In places where Indians lived for many generations and accumulated substantial piles of refuse ("Indian mounds," "shell mounds," etc.), there was created a distinctive soil chemistry especially rich in phosphorus and calcium. It appears that the growth of certain plants useful to the Indians (such as tobacco, doveweed, and thistles) was especially favorable in these soils, so that even today old Indian village sites can often be easily identified at a distance because of the exuberant growth of one or another of these particular plants, more than a century after the sites were abandoned.

The California black walnuts (*Juglans* spp.) and Buck-eye (*Aesculus californica*) often cluster in isolated grooves on prehistoric living sites, and these too must be vol-unteers that found a favorable microhabitat in ancient campsites where the seeds or nuts were brought for food. Present-day Washoe Indians are aware that old summer campsites tend to support a rich growth of Western Choke-cherry bushes (*Prunus virginiana* var. *dimissa*), clumps that presumably were generated long ago from berries brought back to camp from food-gathering trips.

A careful study of the botany of prehistoric Indian campsites might show that Indians did act as important agents for the dispersal of certain grasses, berry-producing shrubs, and trees. So far as is known from the archaeological record, California Indians never overhunted any animal to the point of extinction. Some animals may have been so heavily exploited that their numbers were locally reduced, but as predators Indians do not seem to have affected the overall distribution of any game animals or birds.

With no reason or means to create large earth disturbances, the Indians did not make topographical changes. There is, however, a report of two Pomo tribelets who got into an altercation over ownership of fish in a small stream flowing into Clear Lake. One of the groups managed to divert the stream so that it flowed, undeniably, through its own tribal grounds. It has also been said that some Sacramento Valley villagers deliberately piled up earth to raise the level of the surface above spring flood waters, but archaeologists who have carefully examined the layering of such mounds have never found any evidence of the deliberate piling up of soil. Rather, the mounds are simply accumulations of refuse that resulted from intensive living in a restricted area over centuries.

Taken altogether the Indians of California do not seem to have appreciably changed the topography or the biota of California. No animal extinctions can be attributed to them, but some local distributions of plants or animals could have been slightly changed through their activities. Evidence of such change has not been carefully looked for by biologists, and so we should not at this time take too positive a position on the matter.

During the Spanish period in California many new plants were introduced. Some of them, such as Wild Oats (*Avena fatua*), managed to spread very widely in the new environment. The Anglo-Americans after 1850, with their gardens and field crops, made many more such introductions. It is surprising to some persons to learn how many familiar shrubs and weeds have been introduced in the historic period and have thus affected the flora and the appearance of California.

8. ANCIENT CALIFORNIA INDIAN ART OBJECTS

With the possible exception of shell beads, the greatest number of man-made objects recovered from archaeological sites are of a directly functional nature, although sometimes even the homeliest implements bear decorations, such as incised lines or inset shell designs on stone mortars for acorn grinding. Whether or not tools or other devices are refined or finished, we are dealing here with components of highly developed crafts, usually devoted to economic pursuits, with decoration only incidental. The numerous shell beads manufactured largely by the coastal tribes and found in quantity among interior tribes were evidently trade goods, which in some cases functioned as money itself. However, many kinds of beads and a variety of painted or carved abalone and other shells (fig. 106; see plate 14), together with a lesser amount of shaped or incised bone and stone objects, possibly were used only as personal decoration, although a ceremonial use for some of these cannot be discounted.

Another class of evidence in California archaeology of human activity can be ascribed with more certainty to a ceremonial or an essentially spiritual function. This consists primarily of paintings or carvings on rocks, rocks themselves arranged in specific designs, and several kinds of small, shaped or specially decorated stone or clay pieces. We can conveniently classify all of these aesthetically pleasing productions as art, at least in the sense that they have no ascertainable direct utilitarian function. However, they probably had, in the context of California Indian life, an important underlying economic function, as symbolic expression of desires for continuing the fertility of human life,

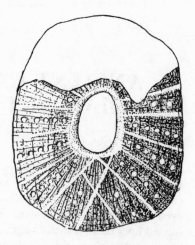

FIGURE 106 (left) Clam shell (*Macoma nasuta*) painted with hematite, from Marin County. Length 2½ in. [6.2 cm.]. (right) Painted Limpet shell (*Megathura crenulata*) from Southern California coast. Length ca. 2⅜ in. [6 cm.]. (From A. E. Treganza and L. L. Valdivia, *Painted Shell Artifacts from California*, 1957)

for the increase of animal species, for control of the weather, or for success in hunting or gathering food. In this light, inclusion of these works in this book needs no further justification.

SMALL ART OBJECTS
Charmstones

Charmstones are carefully shaped stones (fig. 107; plate 5), sometimes referred to as "plummets," and are found in great numbers, usually accompanying a burial, in Central California archaeological sites, beginning, in a highly developed state, in the Early Horizon, or about 2500 B.C. The phallic shapes, probably denoting the life force, are unmistakable, but the spindle-shaped pieces, which are more common, suggest fish. Both types of stones almost always have holes or contracted necks and were obviously intended

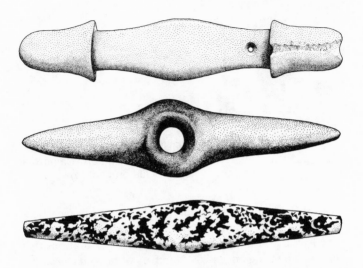

FIGURE 107 Charmstones from the Early Horizon of Central California. Length of mottled granite specimen, ca. 6½ in. [16.5 cm.]. (From R. F. Heizer, *The Archaeology of Central California: The Early Horizon*, 1949)

for suspension; some ethnographic information indicates that they were suspended over preferred fishing spots along streams, marking either an individual's claim or hoped-for luck by the owner. Some charmstones are made from hard stone such as grano-diorite, evidently chosen especially for its attractive appearance, and are carefully shaped and polished, while others are homely, apparently battered from heavy use; these could conceivably have been employed for some less amuletic function, such as fishnet or fishline sinkers.

Plummet-shaped charmstones have so far not been found in Southern California south of recently known Chumash territory. Other kinds of shaped stones, usually called "cog stones" (fig. 108), have been recovered from several sites along the southwestern coast. These appear to be associated in time with the Milling Stone Horizon, possibly around 2000 B.C. Cog stones may be the southern counterpart of the

FIGURE 108 "Cog stone" from an ancient Southern California site. (Scale on picture)

0   5 cm

Central California charmstones, for, of the many specimens found, none appears to have been worn through heavy practical use, although some have central perforations that suggest mounting on a stick. Numbers of broken cog stones were evidently mended with asphaltum, and this repair also suggests their value as some kind of amulet.

Stone Animal Effigies

Confined to archaeological sites dating from around A.D. 1000 in the northwestern part of the state, animal effigies in stone, usually called "clubs" but sometimes "slave killers," were not used by such Indian peoples of historic times as the Yurok or Wiyot. Almost all the pieces (fig. 109) are of a dark polished slate about 14 in. (35 cm.) long, with the tail of the depicted animal sometimes roughened, suggesting a handle of some sort; the objects are fragile and are often found broken in burial accompaniments. Since the incidence of slavery among living Northwestern California Indians was at most confined to slavery to repay a debt and hardly included physical cruelty, the popular term "slave killer" is almost certainly a misnomer.

If these pieces were indeed clubs, the animal effigy shapes better suggest the ceremonial killing of sea lions or other large mammals, perhaps by appointed persons during yearly "first fruit" observances. Surely such great care would not be taken on workaday clubs intended to kill common landed salmon or small sea mammals. Since these well-

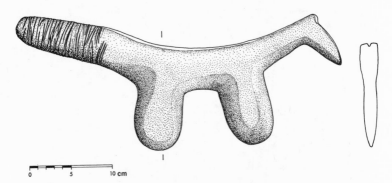

FIGURE 109 Animal effigy of slate, from Northwestern California. (Scale on picture)

smoothed pieces do not show signs of use or wear and are made of a brittle stone, they clearly were not fashioned for any day-to-day use. Probably they were wealth items and had no utilitarian function.

Clay or Stone "Fertility" Figurines

Numbers of figurines of baked clay, clearly representing females, have been found in Central California sites. In Marin County, for example, dozens of complete or fragmentary figures have been recovered from sites dating from the Middle Horizon, or after 1000 B.C. All of them were originally made headless, but show positive representations of human breasts, and sometimes have punctations, seemingly to depict necklaces or perhaps body tattooing. The prominence of the female characteristics suggests some function as a fertility amulet. If Marin County were the center of this usage, influence from there was evidently felt far to the south and the north, although the archaeological finds are spotty. For example, fired clay female figurines of the same general category are abundant in prehistoric sites around Humboldt Bay (fig. 110). In northern San Diego County some apparently crude "female" figurines have been recovered, some with rudimentary heads, but also with bulbous lower terminations, perhaps suggesting pregnancy. They appear to date after A.D. 1500, and thus they are

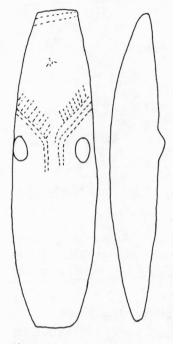

FIGURE 110 Baked clay figurine from Northern California. Length 5 in. [12.7 cm].
From R. F. Heizer and D. M.
Pendergast, *Additional Data
on Fired Clay Human Figurines from California*, 1954)

distantly separated in time from the Central California
figures.

Another baked-clay figurine tradition, from a culture of
southern San Diego County called Hakataya, appears to
have stemmed almost directly from the prehistoric Hoho-
kam culture of the Southwest, at some time after A.D. 1000,
but reaching the San Diego region perhaps as late as A.D.
1400 or 1500. These figures have heads consisting of "coffee
bean" eyes, a nose with small nostrils, and a crudely
punctured mouth (fig. 111). They have no arms or legs,
but may show male genitalia in appliqué, less commonly
female genitalia, or no genitalia at all. They are therefore
less definitely "fertility figurines" than the earlier Central
California pieces.

In Late Horizon Central California (after A.D. 300) a few
bird figurines in baked clay are found, and the Hakataya
tradition also includes some clay mammal figurines. The
most remarkable animal figurines in California, however,

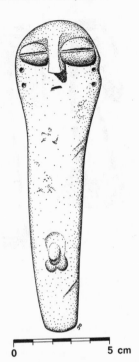

FIGURE 111 "Hakataya" baked clay figurine from Southern California. Length 6 in. [15 cm.]

0   5 cm

are in soapstone and are most commonly found on San Nicolas Island, 60 miles (96 km.) off the Los Angeles coast. These are sometimes accurately wrought sea mammal representations (see fig. 25), often identifiable as to species, although a few abstract forms appear. Some hooklike effigies have been likened to semiabstract depictions of sea birds, probably pelicans (fig. 112). All the San Nicolas Island figures, possibly connected with imitative magic or luck-bringing devices in the sea hunt, are probably dated at about 1000 years ago, and therefore probably correspond with the Canaliño, or ancestral Chumash, culture of the Santa Barbara region to the north.

Some lightly incised slate tablets from southern Monterey County (fig. 113) dating from around the beginning of the Late Horizon in Central California, and some painted stone tablets from Napa County (fig. 114), which probably oc-

FIGURE 112 Steatite hooklike effigies from San Nicolas Island, Southern California coastal region. Length ca. 4 in. [10 cm.].

FIGURE 113 Incised slate tablet from southern Monterey County. Length ca. 2⅜ in. [6 cm.].

curred 1000 years later than the Monterey tablets, also may be suggested as abstract fertility figurines: the characteristic transverse lines may have represented the binding thongs of baby cradle boards, although this is a tenuous extension of the fertility theme.

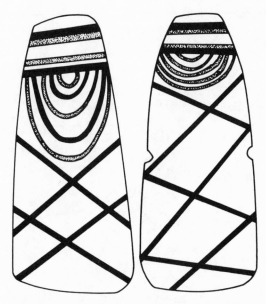

FIGURE 114 Painted stone tablets from Napa County. Length ca. 3 in. [7.5 cm.].

ROCK ART

Surely rock drawings were the most widespread expression of art by California Indians during the prehistoric period. In contrast to the objects already discussed, such as charmstones, animal-form clubs, or clay figurines, which may have had numbers of functions which we can only guess at, there is reasonable evidence from several sources that rock drawings served several specific and identifiable purposes.

Rock art is conventionally divided into two classes: (1) petroglyphs, designs made by engraving, incising, or pecking, and (2) pictographs, paintings made with fingers or brushes. Archaeologists think that the petroglyphs are older than the pictographs, although, since painted elements are likely to weather away more rapidly than engravings, there is no way to prove this. While petroglyphs are known from practically all parts of the state, pictographs are largely concentrated today in the southern half (fig. 115).

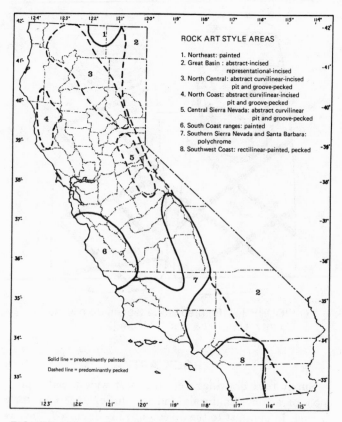

FIGURE 115 Rock art style areas of California.

Petroglyphs

Some scholars believe that the older petroglyph styles, perhaps originating in the Great Basin, were produced in California only during the last 3000 years. It appears that styles of rock art were diffused from one tribe to another, probably as part of a body of ritual, in much the same way as the annual mourning ceremony (chapter 2) spread north out of Southern California up the Sierra Nevada. There is fairly strong presumptive evidence, from the many concentrations of petroglyphs near springs or constricted parts of game trails, that the rock art was linked with hunting magic,

FIGURE 116 Pecked figures (mountain sheep and deer) in petroglyphs in Inyo County. (From R. F. Heizer and W. C. Clewlow, *Prehistoric Rock Art of California*, 1973)

FIGURE 117 "Maze" or "labyrinth" petroglyph in granite, near Hemet, Riverside County. Width ca. 18 in. [45 cm.]. (From J. H. Steward, *Petroglyphs of California and Adjoining States*, 1929)

inherent in the repeated depiction on the rocks of such animals as deer or mountain sheep, or for that matter other symbols or series of symbols that possibly were thought to bring hunting luck (figs. 116, 117).

FIGURE 118 A "rain rock" found in Siskiyou County, now at Fort Jones Museum, Siskiyou County.

Another style of petroglyph, which can best be described merely as agglomerations of pits and grooves carved or pecked, usually in soft rock such as soapstone, has been reported most frequently in Northern California, though some examples exist in the south as well. This style is thought to date from about A.D. 1000, and good evidence has been offered by living Indians that such rocks were "baby rocks" or "rain rocks," that is, they were associated with ideas of human fertility or weather control (fig. 118). Among the Pomo, for example, a woman wanting a baby would visit a "baby rock" and scrape dust from a groove made with a piece of flint. She believed that by mixing the rock dust in water and drinking it would help her to become pregnant.

Pictographs

From several lines of evidence it has been inferred that the pictographs, or rock paintings, of California date from about A.D. 500. We have already mentioned the evidence for the introduction of the bow and arrow, which was probably about or a little before A.D. 300 (chapter 7). The transition from throwing stick (atlatl) to bow is reflected in the rock art: atlatls are depicted in some petroglyphs, and the later bow is associated with pictographs. Although most pictographs are predominantly abstract, often with only crude representations of men or of animals rarely identifiable as to species, there appear on some painted friezes obvious figures of human beings mounted on animals that almost certainly were intended to be horses. The Indians acquired horses from the Spanish intruders, probably in the eighteenth century.

Beyond the evidence from bow and arrow and horse depictions, one other indication of the relative lateness in time of the pictographs lies in good ethnographic records of the association between a certain style of geometric pictographs in Southwestern California and the girls' puberty rites, which were another manifestation of the wish for increased fertility in the society. Among the Luiseño, for example, during the girls' puberty ceremony (an initiation into adult womanhood), the participating girls raced to a certain rock where relatives awaited them with red paint. The girls then painted on the rock diamond-shaped designs representing the rattlesnake, a phallic symbol.

In a geographic band extending approximately from the Santa Barbara coast to the southern Sierra Nevada occurs one of the greatest concentrations of abstract polychrome pictographs in California (fig. 119; plates 19, 20). These examples are usually found in remote mountainous areas and are not associated with villages or game trails. Because of their remoteness, few have been wantonly destroyed by vandals, and it has been possible to observe roughly the normal rate of weathering on some of them during about the last hundred years. Again we see evidence that they were painted in fairly recent times, for even during the past century deterioration from largely natural causes has been considerable. Some of these remarkable examples may have been executed not long before, or even after, the coming of the Spanish. Perhaps we can attribute these pictographs to shamanistic practices, probably in connection with healing or with promoting the general welfare of the local group.

FIGURE 119 Pictographs at the "Painted Cave," near Santa Barbara, in "Santa Barbara Polychrome" style. Large wheel, probably representing the sun, at upper right, is 18 in. [45 cm.] in diameter. (Courtesy of the R. H. Lowie Museum of Anthropology)

We can be sure that they had no frivolous purpose; they must have contributed something of importance to the survival of their makers and their clients. Because the Chumash and the southern Valley Yokuts are known to have taken the hallucinogenic juice of the *Datura* plant, it has been suggested that these elaborate painted designs were made by persons who were under the influence of this drug. However, there is not the slightest evidence that such was the case.

The earliest recording by Euro-Americans of prehistoric petroglyphs in California was done in 1850 by J. Goldsborough Bruff in Lassen County, when he came to mine gold in the newly discovered Sierra Nevada placers (fig. 120). Bruff was interested in these inscriptions and suggested that they were related to Egyptian hieroglyphs, a proposal we now know to be wholly without foundation.

FIGURE 120 "Ancient hieroglyphics" in Lassen County, from a drawing by J. G. Bruff, 1850. These petroglyphs were executed in a style characteristic of Indians that occupied the Great Basin in California and Nevada.

Large Effigies

There is one other form of rock art, which falls slightly outside the field of petroglyphs and pictographs. It is probably best called "earth art," and includes large gravel effigies and rock alignments, which occur in several places in the desert regions of Southeastern California. The alignments are seen in numerous long and straight or curving windrows, sometimes up to 500 feet (152 m.) in length, or looping designs ranging over flat places and sometimes over ridges. Some of the looped designs are comparable to the motifs interpreted as fertility symbols in local petroglyphs. The gravel effigies were formed by raking or scraping aside gravel or small cobbles of the rocky desert cover ("desert pavement"), leaving rimmed clearings in the desired form. Some of these so-called effigies are abstract figures, while others represent human beings or animals of grotesque form. Some are realistic, and to this category belongs one of the best-known series, found near Blythe along the Colorado River (figs. 121, 122). This series depicts pairings of

FIGURE 121 "Giant Desert Figures," near Blythe, California. These form "Group B," one of several sets of similar figures in the vicinity. Human figure is 75 ft. [23 m.] long and points to the north. (Photograph 1932, courtesy of the San Bernardino County Museum, Redlands, Calif.)

FIGURE 122 "Giant Desert Figures" (Group A), near Blythe, California. Here the human figure's head points to the southeast; the entire figure is about 170 ft. [52 m.] long. Note vandalism in form of circles made by wheels of automotive vehicles, and the recently erected protective fences. (Photograph Sherilee von Werlhof, 1977, courtesy of the Imperial Valley College Museum, El Centro, California)

a man and a quadruped animal, which may have been intended as a horse; one of the human effigies here is about 170 feet (52 m.) long.

The figures and alignments were made as if they were intended to be seen primarily from the sky, and thus they resemble other mysterious giant figures on arid flat or floor lands in other parts of North America, in aboriginal Australia, and in ancient Peru. Barring acceptance of the possibility of "ancient astronauts" or balloons or flying machines as part of the prehistoric technology of the Colorado River tribes, we must conclude that these figures were made to be viewed from a low-level perspective, that is, by humans standing on the ground. Why the figures were made so large, we do not know. Their general context suggests that the reason for their having been made is related to the reason for the petroglyphs in the desert region or the sand paintings of the Southwest. The latter were also an element in the boys' puberty ceremonies among the Diegueño and Luiseño tribes near the coast (chapter 2). It has not been possible to date the effigies and aligned figures accurately. No doubt some are ancient, although the representational examples may be late in time and may even relate to the coming of the Spanish.

9. WORLD VIEW
OF CALIFORNIA INDIANS

The great majority of people who live today in California are, by origin, alien to the land and even to the continent. They are the conquerors, and the remnants of the original inhabitants are one of the smallest minorities in the state. Today not more than 1 person in 20,000 in California is an Indian; little more than 200 years ago their ancestors were the only humans in the state. Since Indians occupied California for perhaps 10,000 years, they can be looked on as the ancient custodians of the land, which, from the late eighteenth century on was handed over, however unwillingly, to foreigners. Since California was at that time well forested, had clean air, and was full of game and unspoiled land, it may be interesting for us to examine the Indian world view, a term meaning how people conceive of themselves, of nature, and of society. That is, world view is a people's vision of the world they live in and how they relate to the environment, to others, and to the cosmos. Thus does world view form a people's pattern of day-to-day living.

We are so far removed from the pristine, wholly aboriginal pre-white times and native way of life and belief that we can get only glimpses of the Indian world view. Most anthropologists in the early part of the century were either unaware of or uninterested in such matters, and it is difficult to draw a coherent picture from the bits and pieces of information that were recorded. Probably in 1750, before any white settlement had occurred, there were five hundred quite separate tribelet societies, and five hundred world views, though these last could perhaps be condensed into a half-dozen regional world views.

The world view of Americans in the late twentieth century is a complex one, but many aspects of it make us peculiarly unequipped to understand the Indian view of life. Americans are masters at "subduing" nature. Ideally, they are inventive, resourceful, pioneering, democratic, hard-working. In practice, they have constructed an industrial society which can drive railroad tunnels through the Sierra Nevada, dam almost any river you can name, transport oil from Alaska or natural gas from Texas, and create artificial rivers carrying water from the northern end of California to Los Angeles. Americans believe they can do almost anything they want to with nature, including the creation of rain by cloud seeding from airplanes. All of these activities would seem mystifying, and in some cases unnatural, to an aboriginal California Indian—who would not be surprised that pipelines leak, that nuclear reactors threaten to melt down, and that strip-mining to produce electricity results in enormous pollution of air and water. It is virtually impossible to compare California in 1980 with the Indian California of 1770. The United States today is a country of specialists who are highly trained to do certain tasks, and any desire to live an uncomplicated way of life is beset by restrictions of codified law, housing codes, police regulations, hunting and fishing seasons, taxes, and the like. The California Indians, for all their lack of movies, automobiles, TV, and supermarkets, may really have been better off than we realize.

We must keep in mind the extraordinary localism of California Indians in pre-white times. An ordinary person in his whole life probably did not travel more than 10 or 15 miles away from the spot where he was born, lived, would die, and be buried. During their lives many Indians probably did not regularly converse with over one or two hundred other persons. This restricted experience undoubtedly was an important factor in shaping the world outlook of individuals. There were many exceptions, of course; the Chumash lived in towns of over a thousand inhabitants, as did some of the Sacramento River Patwin. But except for the few such densely populated areas, most native Californians lived in small tribelet societies which numbered a few hundred persons. Under such a limited life experience the individual's horizon of thinking must also have been extraordinarily restricted. But there were compensations. Theft, for example, was unknown. Not only was there little to steal, but everything a thief owned was known, and what he had purloined would immediately be recognized as belonging to another person. Also, the lack of experience with a wider world made each person's own environs familiar, safe, and secure because he or she did not know it was so limited. Strangers who spoke an unfamiliar tongue were to be avoided, not necessarily because one feared them physically, but because they were different and not known. If they were not aiming at some mischief, then why did they not stay at home among their own people? Thus the appearance of strangers was automatically viewed with apprehension.

Still another illustration of the closed nature of Californian native societies is seen in the common practice of teaching the children of the group the boundary markers of the tribelet territory in the greatest detail. Stephen Powers in the early 1870s wrote that

the boundaries of all tribes are marked out with the greatest precision, being defined by certain creeks, canyons, boulders, conspicuous trees, springs, etc., each of which has its individual name. . . . [The mothers] teach these things to their children. . . . Over and over, time and again they rehearse all these boundaries, describing each minutely and by name, with its surroundings. . . . If any Indian knows but little of this great world more than pertains to boundary bush and boulder, he knows his own small fighting ground intimately better than any topographical engineer can learn it.

In 1918, E. W. Gifford interviewed a Northfolk Mono (Monache) woman named Wiinu, who was believed at the time to be about 95 years old. Except for one winter spent, when she was 7 or 8, across the Sierra among the Mono Paiute, she had lived all her life within her tribal territory (in present-day Madera County). During her life, she listed fourteen separate villages in which she had lived for periods ranging from one summer to a number of years. Her reasons for shifting residence twenty-three times (fig. 123) were varied, and included her marriage, the birth of a son, the death of her husband, the death of her son, and reunion with

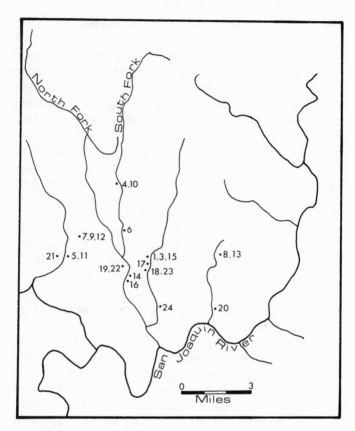

FIGURE 123 The Northfork Mono villages in which Wiinu lived during her lifetime. The numbers indicate the chronological sequence of her moves. (From E. W. Gifford, *The Northfork Mono*, 1932)

her own relatives. But the usual reason Wiinu gave for shifting residence was "just to keep moving." Life may have been so uneventful (the Northfolk Mono villages usually held only four or five family houses) that it encouraged moving about. Her whole life, except for the one winter among the Mono Paiute, was spent in an area measuring no more than 6 by 7.5 miles. Her example was probably fairly typical of most California Indians.

CONTRASTING WORLD VIEWS

There are several strongly contrasting California Indian world views that we can recognize. The Yurok and their close neighbors in the northwestern corner of the State (Tolowa, Wiyot, Hupa, and Karok) illustrate one of these. The Yurok with their fixation on securing and holding wealth have been characterized as an inwardly fearful people, cautious and placatory, suspicious of the motives of others, quick to become jealous, and given to envy. They were sensitive to shaming, touchy about slights, prone to anger, prideful, and slow to forgive. Their system of law made them quick to sue and resourceful in finding causes. Acquiring and retaining wealth (in the form of large chipped obsidian blades, either black or red; curved tubular mollusk shells of *Dentalium*; skins of albino deer; red scalps of the woodpecker) were paramount motivations. Wealth lay in those rare objects of nature, such as skins, obsidian, and shells, which usually came from distant sources and on which the hand of man had been exercised through tanning or chipping or intertribal barter to amplify their value. Food, such as eels, salmon, and acorns, was never sold.

The world of each Northwestern tribe was small, closed, and stable. The Hupa might visit the neighboring Yurok to attend a ceremony, but each tribe generally stayed at home. Each tribal territory yielded the essentials of life, such as flint, deer, salmon, acorns, berries, and the like. Beyond these there were items that could be gotten only through barter with a neighboring people who were one link in a tribal chain that might stretch for hundreds of miles. Precious black volcanic glass (obsidian) came down the Klamath River via the Shasta and the Karok from the Achomawi, who got it at Medicine Lake; dried seaweed (eaten for salt and as a condiment) traveled up the Klamath River, and *Dentalium* shells, taken from deepwater beds on the north end of Vancouver Island, were passed down the coasts of Washington and Oregon to the Tolowa and then to the Yurok. Big round-bottomed redwood canoes were made by the Yurok, who owned large parts of the *Sequoia* tree coastal belt and had the technical knowledge to manufacture the boats, which were traded to the Wiyot in the south, the Hupa upriver, and the Tolowa up the coast.

Beliefs can influence the structure of society. One example will illustrate native thought processes. The Yurok smoked, in tubular wooden pipes with stone bowls, the leaves of the local wild species of tobacco (*Nicotiana bigelovii*). They never used the wild-growing tobacco but used only plants which they had sowed and tended. When asked why, they answered that the wild tobacco might be "poisonous" because it might have grown in a grave. Tobacco is a ruderal plant, one that volunteers readily in disturbed soil—and the soil of a grave is precisely that. Two things are involved here: the native belief in the danger of ingesting contaminated material, and the observation the Yurok made that tobacco often did volunteer in graveyard areas. Botany, magical belief, and a cultural practice came together here.

A second example from the Yurok will suffice. Humans never drank the water from the Klamath River, because they thought it *might* be contaminated by someone's having thrown a dead dog or an aborted fetus in the stream. Such impurity could also cause illness or death through magical contamination.

If we move all the way from the Yurok to the Mohave of the Colorado River, we shall see a quite different tribal psychology. Kroeber, who lived among the Mohave and came to understand their ways, characterized them as amiably obstinate, at times sulky, given to outbursts of temper, frank, inquisitive, and confiding. They were careless of property and spent freely—the very opposite of the Yurok. The Mohave were friendly and smiled generously. Their national pastime was warfare, carried out by a warrior class that lived only to fight. Fighting men exhibited a kind of fatalism, which we cannot clearly understand because its development lies back hundreds of years. In 1903 Kroeber recorded the following from an old Mohave warrior who was speaking of a council of 1850 where the Mohave are discussing fighting the whites, who were appearing in increasing numbers in their land:

In the afternoon the other Mohave [who had held out against the war] said: "I have heard that these whites are everywhere on all sides. You have heard that too. Nevertheless you want to fight them. Well, we will follow your counsel—we will go to fight. That is what we want. We are not like mountains; we do not stay forever. We are not like the sky, always there; not like the sun or moon—we die. Perhaps in a year, in a month, in two or three days. I want to die fighting. Well, how many times do you expect to die? You die once and do not come alive again. We will fight with you and die too. No one likes to die. If you like it, why not tie your hands and feet together and jump into the river? No one does that way; that is killing yourself. So you say you want to die soon? Well, good, we will go along and help you."

The Central California temperament seems to have been much more placid and easygoing than that of Northwestern Californians or the Colorado River people. Louis Choris, a member of the Russian explorer Kotzebue's expedition, wrote in 1816 of the Costanoans he saw at San Francisco Mission, "I have never seen one laugh. I have never seen one look one in the face." This withdrawal and lack of spontaneous humor may very well have been induced by the treatment the Costanoans had received in the mission, where their emotions were repressed. But we think we can read the same in what Captain George Vancouver wrote about the Indians he saw in the village next to Santa Clara Mission in 1792:

Their passions are calm; and regardless of reputation as men, or renown as a people, they are stimulated neither to the obtaining of consequence amongst themselves by any peaceful arts, nor superiority over their neighbours by warlike achievements, so common amongst the generality of Indian tribes. All the operations and functions both of body and mind, appeared to be carried on with a mechanical, lifeless, careless indifference; and as the Spaniards assert they found them in the same state of inactivity and ignorance on their earliest visits, this disposition is probably inherited from their forefathers.

Elsewhere among Central California tribes something quite like the apathy or reticence observed by Choris seems to have prevailed, which cannot have been wholly ascribable to the harsh effects of Franciscan missionization or to the depressive effects of the American invasion in 1849. It seems that the Central California temperament was lower keyed and less sharply defined than that of, say, the Yurok and the Mohave. We may even characterize the standard Central California personality as phlegmatic, peaceable, and reticent.

The Pomo tended to be aloof, suspicious, and fearful of close relations. Taboos were abundant and were strictly observed by persons wishing to protect themselves from malevolent humans or ill-wishing supernatural powers. The Pomo apparently saw all persons outside the immediate family as potentially dangerous and to be feared. To mitigate the threat of illness or death from these others, it was best to avoid them or to be as polite as possible and to generate no cause for hostility. If the Pomo thought that other humans were aggressive and hostile, it can easily be believed that they themselves might sometimes practice on non-relatives a kind of magical "poisoning" (their word) that caused illness.

Chiefs, who had no real power in most of native California beyond that of offering good advice in a persuasive manner, helped to keep life moving along with a minimum of friction. Speeches of chiefs, often delivered to their fellow villagers early in the morning, took a moralistic tone. For example, a Wintu chief advised his village members, "Do right; don't get into trouble; help your neighbor." An Atsugewi chief said, "Get up and do something for your living! Be on your guard [for the Paiute slave raiders]! You have to work hard for your living. There may be a long winter, so put away all the food you can."

Indians not only lived in nature but saw themselves as an integral part of it. In native belief, animals had an intelligence equal to man's, as well as human qualities and emotions; and in many mythologies, animals were said to have occupied the earth before man and to have gotten the world ready for humans. The animals were often seen as providers for man, securing for humans the first acorns, salmon, and fire, as well as instituting fearful events, such as death. Among the Pomo and many other Californian tribes, all plants, animals, and natural features (stones, springs)

were believed to have thought and feeling. A Nomlaki
Indian told one ethnographer, "Everything in this world
talks, just as we are [talking] now—the trees, rocks, everything. But we cannot understand them, just as the white
people do not understand Indians."

An old Wintu woman told the ethnographer Dorothy
Demetrocopoulou in 1930:

The white people never cared for land or deer or bear. When we
Indians kill meat we eat it all up. When we dig roots we make little
holes. When we build houses we make little holes. When we burn
grass for grasshoppers we don't ruin things. We shake down acorns
and pine nuts. We don't chop down the trees. We use only dead
wood. But the white people plow up the ground, pull up the trees,
kill everything. The tree says, "Don't. I am sore. Don't hurt me."
But they chop it down and cut it up. The spirit of the land hates
them. They blast out trees and stir it up to its depths. They saw up
the trees. That hurts them. The Indians never hurt anything, but
the white people destroy all. They blast rocks and scatter them on
the earth. The rock says, "Don't. You are hurting me. . . ." The
water, it can't be hurt. The white people go to the river and turn it
into dry land. The water says, "I don't care. I am water. You can
use me all you wish. I am always the same. I can't be used up. Use
me. I am water. You can't hurt me." The white people use the water
of sacred springs in their houses. The water says, "That is all right.
You can use me but you can't overcome me." All that is water says
this, "Wherever you put me I'll be in my home. I am awfully smart.
Lead me out of my springs, lead me from my rivers, but I came
from the ocean and I shall go back into the ocean. You can dig a
ditch and put me in it, but I go only so far and I am out of sight. I
am awfully smart. When I am out of sight I am on my way home."

All of nature was thought to be interconnected, so that
anything humans did had to be considered in terms of what
effects and reaction might follow from other elements of
nature. Man was seen not as dominating nature but rather
as sharing creation and life with the plant and animal forms
around him. In search for food a sense of responsibility was
felt for the plants and animals collected to eat, and a
solicitousness of their feelings and welfare. There existed a
kind of "land etiquette" in relations between man and
nature. Each form of plant and animal life had a soul, or
spirit, rather like that of man's, so that there was believed to
be a sharing of intelligence and feeling where each had a role

to play. The animal's role was to supply food for men; the plant's role was to nourish both men and animals; and the human role was to gather plants and hunt animals as necessary for food.

Demetrocopoulou says that the Wintu's relationship with nature was "one of intimacy and mutual courtesy. He kills for a deer only when he needs it for his livelihood, and utilizes every part of it, hoof and marrow and hide and sinew and flesh; waste is abhorrent to him, not because he believes in the intrinsic virtue of thrift, but because the deer had died for him."

All over California rituals of supplication, appreciation, and condolence were made in connection with hunting or plant-food gathering, an acknowledgment by man of the crucial help he had received. These feelings were given tacit expression in rituals such as the first-salmon ceremony among the Yurok Indians of Northwestern California. The ritual was designed to assure a constant and adequate supply of salmon, even for tribes living above the Yurok on the Klamath River. Hunters had to be physically clean if deer were to allow themselves to be shot, and so the hunter bathed, stood in fragrant smoke, avoided sexual contact for a certain period before he hunted, and thought pure thoughts. Where some, today, might say that a hunter purified himself to remove the human odor, which would alarm the deer, Indians would have said that that was the way the deer wished it if they were to permit themselves to be shot. A Wintu hunter had to possess two things. First was skill in stalking deer and the ability to use his bow. Second was what was called "luck," by which was meant ensuring that the spirit of the deer was not offended by the failure of the hunter to go through the proper ritual preparation. A Wintu hunter who had lost his luck—that is, could not succeed in killing a deer—did not say, "I cannot kill deer any more"; he said, "Deer don't want to die for me."

Some tribes believed in transmigration—that humans turned into animals when they died. The Sierra Miwok believed that ghosts of the good dead turned into great horned owls and that ghosts of bad people became barn owls, meadowlarks, coyotes, or gray foxes. The Southern

Maidu (Nisenan) thought that when a person died his spirit entered a coyote, an owl, a snake, or a lizard, or it might become a whirlwind.

Thus it can be seen that the Indian lived in two worlds at the same time. One was the practical, everyday world where you were hungry, your wife was sulky, you stubbed your toe on a rock, and you got into a quarrel with your neighbor who had thrown a sharp deer bone out his door, which you stepped on. The other was the very real supernatural world where trees, animals, springs, caves, and mountains contained souls, or spirits, which had to be treated with respect. For this reason, taking a part of any tree, killing an animal, using a spring, or entering a cave was prefaced by some kind of ritual, however simple, in the form of a request or an acknowledgment.

Even the visible world was seen as combining concrete features, such as streams, mountains, and the sky, but in Indian terms of reality there were supernatural features also present. A good illustration of this is the world map of the Yurok (fig. 124) as diagramed by the anthropologist T. T. Waterman. The whole formation of land, sea, and sky was called *kiwesona*, "that which exists." Solid land, the earth, was entirely surrounded by the ocean on which it floated. The sky was formed by a great net knotted by a mythic person called "world-maker" or "sky-possessor," who had made the net and then tossed it into the air, where it became a dome arching over all. Above the ocean was the "sky country," which was also solid land and whose outer edge formed the ultimate boundary of the universe. It was perforated at one point by a "sky hole," which was used by migrating waterfowl (especially geese) as they flew to and from the Northwest on their annual migrations. The edge of the sky rose and fell into the ocean at regular intervals, causing the breakers that pounded on the shore. Mythic characters could reach the sky country by traveling in a boat across the ocean to where the sky edge met the water, and by carefully counting off, they could slip under the edge of the sky while it was rising. Parts of the sky country were apportioned to important mythic characters such as the

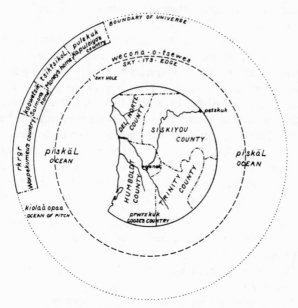

FIGURE 124   Diagrams of the Yurok idea of the
world. (From T. T. Waterman, *Yurok Geography*,
1920)

culture hero Woxpekemeu, the salmon, the Dentalium, and
an important mythic person, Kapuloiyo. There is no deny-
ing the fact that the Yurok world map made a neat and
logical package that contained the essential parts of the
palpable world and the supernatural one, which was peopled
by spirits. Since the earth, the sky, the ocean, the salmon
runs, and the geese migrations were timeless features, they
could be taken as demonstrations that the scheme was
correct.

SONGS

Indian songs were composed and sung for all sorts of
occasions. There were dance songs, gambling luck songs,
hunting luck songs, girls' puberty-rite songs, and many
more. Allusions to nature, nature spirits, animals, and

flowers are common in them. Here are a few examples from the Wintu.

Numbers 1-4 are songs from Dream Dances; that is, they are songs in which instructions on the rules and paraphernalia of the dance were received by a special person through dreams. Number 5 is a song of unrequited love. Number 6 is a derisive song of a McCloud River woman, raised on juicy salmon and married to a Stillwater district husband who can provide her with only grasshoppers and minnows. Number 7 is a love song composed by a lover who was rejected because he was poverty-striken. He later finds his old love (the beautiful bear) in reduced circumstances and living on a diet of clover.

1. Above the place where the minnow maiden sleeps
   while her fins move gently in the water,
   Flowers droop,
   Flowers raise back again.
2. Above shall go
   The spirits of people, swaying rhythmically,
   Swaying with the dandelion puffs in their hands.
3. There above, there above,
   At the mythical earthlodge of the south,
   Spirits are wafted along the roof and fall,
   Flowers bend heavily on their stems.
4. Daybreak people [sparrows] have been chirping
   Above on the roof [of the earthlodge]
   Alighting they chirp.
5. Long ago I wept for you,
   But now I weep for him who lives west, farther west.
   I weep for him who dwells in the west
   Under the sharp pinnacles of Lime Rock.
6. Of course,
   If I went to the McCloud
   I might choke on a salmon bone.
7. Down in the west lying down,
   Down in the west lying down,
   A beautiful bear I found
   Tearing up clover in fistfuls.

A Maidu song, recorded over a century ago by Stephen Powers, goes:

> I am the Red Cloud;
> My father formed me out of the sky.
> I sing among the mountain flowers.
> I sing among the flowering chamise of the mountains.
> I sing in the mountains like the prairie falcon.
> In the morning I cry in the mountains.
> In the morning I walk the path.
> I cry to the morning stars.

And finally, a Maidu acorn song sung in a ceremony asking for the blessings of the spirits for the tribe:

> The acorns come down from heaven.
> I plant the short acorns in the valley.
> I plant the long acorns in the valley.
> I sprout, I, the black acorn, sprout, I sprout.

We know that such songs must have been highly evocative, though songs and poetry (of whatever origin) unfortunately lose in translation most of their linguistic music. And we are dealing here with expressions of a culture even harder for us to grasp than, say, that of the ancient Greeks, which left us such tantalizing fragments of Sappho's poetry. Conditioned as we are by our twentieth-century industrialized life, we can only guess at the resonance and emotional effect these songs must have had for the people who composed them, remembered them, and passed them on to their descendants.

MYTHS

Myths were of great importance in the Indian world view. They were the oral literature of peoples who did not have writing, and they constituted what was the history of the world and what it held, however imaginary. The emphases or themes in myths vary from tribe to tribe and area to area. The characters or actors in myths were usually animals who had human emotions, temperaments, and intelligence and who used human speech. These animals did all sorts of human things. They hunted, wove baskets, collected seeds, got hungry, cheated, fell in love, lied, gambled, got angry, quarreled and fought, and killed—in short, they exhibited the gamut of human emotions and activities. They did ordinary things as ordinary humans do, but some mythic characters were capable of performing remarkable feats, which could only be called magical. Reality was often introduced into these tales through reference to a geographical feature that was familiar to every listener—a prominent mountain peak, a cave, an unusual cleft rock, a line of trees along a stream.

Many myths were explanatory and accounted for the existence of things familiar to those listening to the tale. Such explanations included how the world was created, why the sun and moon have their form, what the constellations are and how they came into existence, how man got fire, salmon, acorns, or pine nuts, how death came to be, and why there are both men and women instead of sexless humans. Some Indian myths were recounted in a religious context, but usually they were told for entertainment and were the functional equivalents of the history, science, and philosophy of today.

Here are a few, much-abbreviated plots of some California myths:

1. Southern Sierra Miwok tale of the beginning of the world: Before there were people, there was only water. Coyote looked among the ducks and sent one particular kind to dive. It went down, reached the bottom, bit the earth, and came up to the surface. Coyote took the earth and sent the duck to dive for seeds. He mixed the earth and seeds into a ball, which swelled until the water disappeared and the earth came into existence.

2. Yurok tale of how some sea mammals got their characteristics: Sea Otter woman was dancing at Omenoku [a town on a small lake or pond just north of the mouth of the Klamath River], learning to become a doctor. Kingfisher was to marry her, but the bride price was so large that he was traveling all around the world to collect the amount. Seal and Sea Lion were in the Omenoku sweathouse singing "Kingfisher is going all around the world to collect his bride price. I hope he dies." Suddenly Kingfisher's boat, made of obsidian, landed. He heard them, was angry, and in revenge set the sweathouse on fire. Seal and Sea Lion had their

arms burned off short, and that is why they have flippers and why Sea Lion is black on the shoulders. Sea Otter was burned a little and that is why her arms are short. She rushed into the river and swam out to sea.

3. Kato story of the creation: The old sky was made of sandstone stock, but it began to wear out. Nagaitcho [the creator] and Thunder made a new sky with portals and trails for the summer and winter sun to travel on. They burned the uplands to make clouds, and fired the creek bottoms to make mist. Thunder then made the first man of grass and clay; blood he made of red ochre. Then it rained for a long time incessantly and water covered the earth.

People [in animal form] came into being. Whale became a human woman, and that is why women are so fat. Blue Lizard was thrown [by Nagaitcho] in the water and became the sucker fish. Bull Snake was thrown in the water and became the hookbill salmon. Grass Snake was thrown in the water and became the steelhead. Lizard was thrown in the water and became the trout. Salt was made of ocean foam so that people could eat clover with it. Redwoods, firs, chestnuts, and oaks, and pines were put in different places. Creeks were made by Nagaitcho dragging his foot.

Nagaitcho said, "There will be brush on this mountain," and he made manzanita and whitethorn grow there. "Here there will be many deer," he said. "There will be many grizzly bears at this place. Here a mountain will stand. Many rattlesnakes, bull snakes, and water snakes will be in this place. Here will be good land. It shall be a valley." And in this way the earth and everything in it was made.

4. Yurok tale about animals: None of the animals in the beginning had fur or feathers or tails. A great eagle who lived on the top of Shelton Butte [on the Yurok-Karok boundary] had all the feathers. Everybody came to the Butte to shoot at the eagle to get his feathers, but all failed because the Butte was so lofty. Coyote came downstream with an otterskin quiver of arrows. He shot all his arrows at the eagle but did not hit him. The next day he shot again and at last killed the eagle, who fell and rolled down almost to the river. Coyote said, "We will go there in the morning and get the feathers. The rich will get the best feathers, and the poor the small feathers."

Coyote thought he would get up before anyone else and get the best feathers, but when he awoke he found that all the others had gone. They took all the hair and feathers from the eagle and distributed them, leaving Coyote only one worn old tail feather. Coyote took the feather and stuck it on his back. This became Coyote's tail.

5. Yokuts story of the making of the Sierra Nevada and the Coast Range: Falcon and Crow [in other versions Coyote and Eagle] took some of the earth brought up by Duck from the mud

beneath the primeval floodwaters [see myth 1]. The water was so deep that the trip down to the bottom and back to the surface had taken Duck a day and a half. Carrying some of the earth, Falcon flew west and Crow flew east, and as they flew they scattered grains of soil and told them to become mountains. Falcon and Crow met in the south at Tehachapi Pass. Crow, who had built the Sierras, asked Falcon, "Why didn't you put up bigger hills?" Falcon answered, "Because you had more dirt than I."

6. Yokuts story of the theft of fire: In the myth days Coyote wanted his food cooked, but there was no fire. Falcon reported that a cannibal, Wainus, who lived to the north, had fire. Falcon told Coyote to take a stick and go with Roadrunner to get fire from Wainus. Coyote got the stick glowing in the fire, but he was discovered and pursued by the cannibal and in order to escape threw the stick down. Roadrunner picked it up and ran, but Wainus made rain to extinguish the coals. Roadrunner put the coals under the feathers on either side of his head to keep them dry, and reached home safely. That is why Roadrunner today has red spots on each side of his head.

7. Yokuts tale of war between the foothill and the plains people: The birds and animals of the mountains went to war with the valley animals of Tulare Lake. Coyote, with the mountain party, had a big quiver full of arrows, and he led the way. Alongside him was Hummingbird. Also with the party were three Owls, one carrying stone arrowpoints, another carrying sinew [for wrapping], and the third carrying feathers for arrowshafts. As the arrows of Coyote were used up the Owls made new ones from the material they carried. The mountain people won over the plains people except for two they could not kill—Fish and Turtle. One was too slippery to hit, and the other had a hard shell off which the arrows glanced. Then Coyote broke his own leg, took out a sharp bone splinter, put it on the end of his arrow, and shot Fish in the neck and Turtle through the neck opening in the shell.

Eagle, chief of all the animals, told the victorious mountain people that they could not remain on the plains and asked them where they wished to go. Eagle said, "What are you going to become? What will you be? I myself am going to fly high up in the air and live on squirrels and sometimes on deer." Dog said, "I will stay with people and be their friend. I will follow them, and perhaps I will get something to eat in that way." Buzzard said, "When something dies I will smell it. I will go there and eat it." Crow said, "When I see something lying dead, I will pick out its eyes." Coyote said, "I will go about killing grasshoppers. That is how I will live." Hummingbird said, "I will go to the flowers and get my food from them." Condor said, "I will not stay here. I will go far off into the mountains. Perhaps I will find something to eat there." Woodpecker said, "I will get acorns and make holes in the trees [to store them in]." Bluejay said, "I am going to make trees grow over the hills. I will work." Rat said, "I will go where there are old trees and make my house in them." Mouse said, "I will run here, there, and everywhere. I shall have holes, and perhaps I can live in that way." Trout said, "I will live in the water and perhaps I can find something to eat there."

That was the time they stopped being like us [i.e., humans] and scattered.

8. The Cahuilla, who ate the bitter acorns of the Black or Kellogg Oak, Coast Live Oak, Scrub Oak (*Quercus dumosa*), and Golden Cup Oak, have a myth in which it is told that in ancient times acorns were sweet, but that when the creator, Mukat, became angry with his people he turned the acorns bitter. One may wonder whether this myth did not occur to some Cahuilla woman after she had spent about thirty years of her life heating water to leach bitter acorns. The tale can be interpreted as describing man's fall from grace.

To the Indian these tales were not merely stories, but rather explanations of how things came to be as they are. There probably seemed nothing remarkable to the Indian about these fictional tales in which animals once had human form, since scientific explanations were unknown to them. The real world of people, houses, trees, sunlight, animals, and mountains was seen and understood by Indians for what it was. But there was also the supernatural or mythic world in which animals talked, performed all sorts of actions similar to those of living men and women, and expressed human emotions such as anger, greed, and fear. These worlds, the natural and the supernatural, were not separate realities but were inextricably linked together, so that any human act might involve supernatural spirits. The hunter who failed to kill an animal did so because of supernatural intervention caused by the man's failure to observe some taboo or his committing of some act that displeased the animal's spirit. The network of life, as conceived by the Indian, was one that involved both spirits and the mundane world. The world had its own order and system, and man was only one element in it. This belief created a feeling of the relative unimportance of any particular human and his fate in the large scheme of life. It was this attitude which led the Mohave warriors to say, "We are not like the sky, always there; not like the sun or moon—we die," or "I am a man and cannot live forever. A mountain lives on, and the river; the night and the sun keep coming on to us forever, every day. But any man whom you see dies; I will die too." The human saw himself as a temporary element in unchanging Nature, whose unseen, but real, creators and directors were ever ready to punish man for any nonconformity.

In the native peoples of California, who lived here for so very long before the whites appeared, we can see the true ecological man—people who were truly a part of the land and the water and the mountains and valleys in which they lived. The environmentalists and conservationists of today feel a kinship with the Indians in their respect for nature, a feeling which at times rises to that of the sanctity of the natural world.

10. THE INDIANS
IN THE HISTORIC PERIOD

For half a century after the discovery of the New World by Columbus in 1492, the Spanish were much occupied with consolidating their conquests of the native peoples. Once the peoples of Mexico, Central America, and western South America had been brought under the Spanish yoke, a search was begun for new lands to exploit.

SPANISH EXPLORATION

Pedro de Alvarado, one of the lieutenants of Cortés, had been given the assignment of the conquest of Guatemala, a task which he accomplished with efficiency and ruthlessness. One of Alvarado's aides in this enterprise was a Portuguese, Juan Rodriguez Cabrillo, who had taken part in the conquest of Mexico, commanding a company of crossbowmen in Cortés' army. A fleet of ships built in Guatemala by Alvarado was placed under the command of Cabrillo and sailed to Puerto de Navidad (near present-day Manzanillo, Colima, on the west coast of Mexico), where it was provisioned for exploration of the Pacific Ocean. Alvarado, who was in overall command, was killed there during a battle with the Indians. The fleet was then divided, one part being directed to the Philippines, and one part assigned to Cabrillo for the purpose of exploring the shore of the North Pacific, with the hope of finding civilized peoples who had gold or other possessions which the Spanish desired.

Cabrillo sailed north on June 27, 1542, up the west coast of Lower California, and entered San Diego Bay on October 7, to become the European discoverer of California and to take possession of that land for the king of Spain. Cabrillo's description of the Chumash of the Santa Barbara mainland

FIGURE 125 Fragment of an Indian seed-grinding stone, found on Santa Rosa Island in 1901. Incisions, including initials JR suggest that this was the gravestone of Juan Rodriguez Cabrillo, Portuguese navigator who came to Alta California (San Diego) in 1542 and died after a landing accident on one of the Santa Barbara Channel Islands in 1543. The stone is possibly California's oldest historical relic concerning Indian and white contact. (Courtesy of the R. H. Lowie Museum of Anthropology)

is the oldest ethnohistoric document concerning California Indians. He died on one of the Channel Islands in January 1543, as a result of an injury incurred while landing from a small boat to aid some of his men, who had been attacked by Indians. He was buried there, either on Santa Rosa or on San Miguel Island. What is possibly the gravestone of

FIGURE 126 "The Indians Welcome Sir Francis Drake to California in 1579," from an engraving in a book by Johann DeBry, published in Europe in 1599.

Cabrillo (fig. 125) was found on Santa Rosa Island in 1901 by Philip Mills Jones, an archaeologist working for the University of California.

After the Cabrillo voyage, almost forty years passed before any other European visited California, this occasion being the five-week stopover for ship reconditioning by the Englishman Francis Drake in June 1579. Despite various claims, the exact spot or bay where Drake stayed is not known. The only good evidence for the location of Drake's landfall is a short list of Indian words spoken by the people who visited his camp. These prove to be in the tongue of the Coast Miwok tribe, which allows the ethnologist to suggest that the bay where Drake sojourned was one of those within the territory of the Coast Miwok tribe (fig. 126). The words recorded, perhaps imperfectly, and their cognates in recent Coast Miwok are the following:

1579 Record	Modern Coast Miwok
Hioh, hioghe (chief)	Hoipu
Cheepe (bread)	Tcipa
Huchee kecharoh (come into the house)	Hoki kotcato
Nocharo mu (don't touch me)	Notcato mu

In 1595 Sebastián Rodríguez Cermeño, captain of the *San Agustín* sailing back from the Philippines to Acapulco on the west coast of Mexico, landed in what is today called Drake's Bay, about 30 miles north of the Golden Gate. A storm arose, and the ship was thrown on the shore and wrecked. Cermeño and his crew returned to Mexico in a small launch that had been made in the Philippines and carried on the *San Agustín*. The ship's cargo, mainly silks and Ming porcelain, was lost. While we can only imagine the sight of the Coast Miwok Indians of Drake's Bay dressed in valuable Chinese silks, we are more certain that they salvaged the porcelain and used it, because fragments of hundreds of porcelain dishes and bowls (fig. 127) have been excavated from archaeological village sites on the shores of the bay.

The Spanish navigator Sebastián Vizcaíno in 1602 sailed up the coast of California from Mexico and, like Cabrillo, Drake, and Cermeño, left accounts of Indian customs for posterity. There then ensued another long interval when no European visitors reached California. Only in 1769, two and a quarter centuries after Cabrillo's discovery, was the first Spanish settlement made. Spain had come to see that the Pacific was no longer a Spanish ocean, and to prevent occupation of California by Russia or England, decided to colonize the area and thus protect the northwestern frontier of New Spain. At this time California is estimated to have had an Indian population of about 310,000.

THE MISSION PERIOD

The Spanish crown in the eighteenth century considered it a religious duty to reduce heathenism and to bring to as

FIGURE 127 Chinese porcelain vessel found at Drake's Bay Indian occupation site and attributed to Sebastián Rodriguez Cermeño's shipwreck landing at Drake's Bay in 1595. Diameter of vessel at bottom, ca. 5 in. [12.5 cm.]. (From R. K. Beardsley, *Temporal and Areal Relationships in Central California Archaeology*, 1954)

many native peoples as possible the virtues of Catholicism. Only in this way could non-Christians, who were considered immoral and ignorant, be made truly human. The means used to carry out this lofty aim amounted to a near catastrophe for the native peoples.

The Franciscan order was selected to establish the missions of Alta California, or New California. The first mission was founded at San Diego in 1769, and others followed toward the north, the last being Sonoma Mission, established in 1823.

The Indians were friendly and for some years seem to

have entered the missions willingly. Once baptized, they were regarded as neophytes, or new converts, yet in fact were little better than slaves in spirit and in body. In the theory of the mission system, native converts would learn to speak Spanish and to adopt the values of the church and the state and would then "graduate" from the missions to become useful citizens who could practice a, trade in the pueblos, or Spanish towns. But this never happened. Converts spent their lives in the missions (fig. 128) and were not used as tradesmen in the few civilian pueblos that were founded, such as those at San José and Los Angeles.

In the brief span of 65 years of mission operation, extending from the first founding (1769) to the secularization of the missions (1834), 81,000 Indians were baptized in the missions, and 60,600 deaths were recorded. In 1834 there remained about 15,000 resident neophytes in the twenty-one missions, who were then released from the care of the mission fathers. Those released either attached themselves to the great Mexican ranchos as peons or returned to the interior, where native life was still being lived much as it had been in the last thousands of years.

FIGURE 128 Indians gambling at Mission Dolores, San Francisco, ca. 1816, by Louis Choris. Engraving published in Paris in 1822.

During the mission period the death toll was exorbitant. Causes for the high death rate were varied. Foremost among them seen to have been European diseases, such as smallpox, measles, diphtheria, and other ailments, to which the Indians had no natural immunity. Medical knowledge was so deficient that nothing, literally, could be done to cure the sick. The missions were almost entirely self-sufficient. Enough grains could usually be grown to feed the neophytes, but there were frequent periods when food was short, and this scarcity no doubt made the Indians more susceptible to disease. While the labor demanded of the Indians in the mission was steady, it does not seem to have been unduly harsh. The Indians, however, were by their old custom unused to steady work all day every day, and when they malingered they were usually punished with the lash at the order of the priest. Remember that each mission absolutely had to grow the food for the resident group, and this required unremitting attention.

The daily routine in the mission was a simple one. Rising early, the neophytes attended services, had a breakfast of barley mush, and went to work in the shops or fields. The midday meal was a gruel of barley, peas, and beans. Evening services in the mission church were followed by a supper of barley mush. There is conflicting information on how much meat in the form of beef from the mission herds was provided for the neophytes; it seems to have been not very great in quantity nor provided regularly. Each year a neophyte could usually look forward to a "vacation" from the mission, at which time he might visit relatives or friends in distant villages occupied by still unconverted natives. When a mission ran short of stored grain, the neophytes might be sent out into the surrounding area to hunt wild animals and collect edible seeds, roots, and berries.

Many neophytes found life in the mission unbearable. Those brought into the mission from native villages felt their loss of freedom and self-expression. Presumably those born in the mission learned, as they grew up, to accommodate to the regime. For individuals who found mission life intolerable because of culture shock, the scarcity of food, the death of family members, or punishment for minor infractions, the maximum response was to run away. Fugitives were a cause of concern to the missionaries, for they set an example that others might follow. They were regarded as apostates, or defectors, and were not tolerated, because the missionary fathers felt that they had failed in their sacred duty to convert and civilize the heathen. Whenever possible, the small body of soldiers (often only four or five men under the command of a sergeant) attached to each mission was sent out to round up and return the runaways. Although the search parties were often successful, the mission records show that about 10 percent of all neophytes became permanent fugitives. The number of temporary runaways—those who either were recaptured or returned voluntarily—was far larger.

The priests, celibate in accord with their vows, did not have an enlightened view of Indian sexual customs. They considered their native charges to be immoral by nature, and thought it their duty to lead them into a moral way of life. Neophytes in the mission could marry and have a separate house either within or just beyond the mission compound. But they could not divorce, and the normal strains that are common between husband and wife, plus the difficulties of living in the austere mission regime, seem to have led to many unhappy marriages. One hint of this was the practice among married women of abortion and infanticide, which were reported as common by the priests, who seemed powerless to prevent it. Infanticide and the high death rate of infants and children severely reduced the rate of increase of neophytes. As time went on, especially after 1800, the number of available converts was reduced as local village populations were used up, and there were too few soldiers to make regular forays into the back country. When the California missions were secularized and the remaining neophytes released, it came as a kind of reprieve for the mission system itself because, in the simplest and harshest terms, the missions were running out of Indians.

When the mission period ended, there were probably slightly more than 100,000 California Indians still living.

Even a liberal estimate of 150,000 would mean that between 1769 and 1834 the native population had been reduced 50 percent. A devastating epidemic of malaria in the Sacramento and San Joaquin valleys in the early 1830s may have caused about 20,000 deaths, according to a study made by S. F. Cook. The disease was introduced to the Sacramento Valley in 1828 or 1829 by Hudson Bay trappers coming from Fort Vancouver, where malaria had been transmitted by persons coming on trading ships from the Hawaiian Islands. Travelers in 1833 reported that entire villages along the Sacramento River and the lower courses of the feeder rivers flowing from the Sierra had been wiped out. After a few years the disease seems to have run its course.

THE RANCHOS

With Mexican independence from Spain in 1821 and the secularization of the missions in 1834, California settled into a quiet interlude—the calm before the Gold Rush. Large land-grant ranches (ranchos) were easily secured, and these were taken up both by Mexican nationals and by European and American settlers, who had found their way to the Pacific shore either overland or by sea. John A. Sutter, a Swiss, in 1839 became one of these land barons, as did John Wolfskill in Yolo and Solano counties, George Yount in Napa County, Hugo Reid in Los Angeles, and dozens of others.

Each of these rancho owners utilized local Indians for labor in managing cattle herds or in farming operations. These were, for the most part, mere peons who were little better than slaves. In return for their labor they were housed and fed. A visitor, James Clyman, at Sutter's Fort, headquarters for Sutter's land-grant rancho in 1846, describes mealtime for the Indians at the fort:

The Capt. [Sutter] keeps 600 or 800 Indians in a complete state of slavery and [as] I had the mortification of seeing them dine I may give a short description. 10 or 15 troughs 3 or 4 feet long were brought out of the cook room and seated in the broiling sun. All the labourers grate and small ran to the troughs like so many pigs and fed themselves with their hands as long as the troughs contain even a moisture.

During the Mexican period (1821-1846) the Indians living away from the ranchos were not much molested. Indians did engage in cattle and horse stealing, acts which at times led to retaliatory raids; but the natives outnumbered the Mexican ranchers, and as they became increasingly equestrian and learned some basic battle tactics, they were a good match for the Mexicans. Indeed, by the end of the Mexican period there was serious talk of establishing defensive forts in the Coast Range passes to protect the coastal settlements from raids by mounted Indians. It has been suggested that had the Gold Rush not occurred and had California remained a distant frontier outpost of Mexico, the growing aggressiveness of the interior natives would have culminated before long in the elimination or expulsion of the Mexican overlords.

THE GOLD RUSH

California came under American control in 1846 during the war between the United States and Mexico. Until late 1850 California was under military rule, which was not very effective, because of the hordes of gold seekers, the absence of local government, and the scarcity of troops to maintain order. By 1848, when the Gold Rush began, most of the Indians along the coastal section from San Diego to San Francisco were gone. There were pockets of survivors of the Southern California missions around Santa Barbara and at a few other places, but these remnants numbered at most a very few thousand, perhaps only 10 percent of their numbers in the 1770s, when missionization began. The area north of a line running between Bodega Bay and Sacramento, the desert areas south and east of the Sierras, and the Sierra Nevada themselves were beyond the range of Spanish and Mexican penetration, and in these areas, amounting to about four-fifths of the state, the Indian societies in 1848 were operating much as they had for thousands of years.

The swarm of gold miners and settlers moved in huge numbers into the Interior Valley and the gold-bearing regions of the Sierra and the far north. The miners came into abrupt conflict with the natives in an unequal struggle for possession of the land and what it produced in precious metal (which the Indians knew of but had no interest in before 1848) and food (essential to both groups). Armed with guns and holding the opinion that the Indians must be killed to make the area safe, the miners treated the Indians as though they were dangerous animals. Between 1848 and 1870, outright killing—scores of encounters can be correctly classed as massacres—together with starvation and introduced diseases caused a decline in the Indian population of between 50,000 and 70,000. By 1870 the struggle was over, with the white population numbering 560,000 and the Indians from 30,000 to 50,000. The reduction proceeded until 1910, when the Indian population fell to about 20,000 and then began to rise through natural causes and Indian inmigration from other states. The Indian population of California is now between 90,000 and 100,000.

INDIAN TREATIES

The conflict between the Indians and the Americans after 1848 led the federal government to try some ameliorative measures. Three treaty commissioners in 1851-1852 roamed over those parts of the state where they could bring Indians together and entered into a series of eighteen treaties, mainly with former mission tribes in the south and with the Indians in the Sierra and in the northernmost part of the state (fig. 129). But the United States Senate, which had ordered the treaties to be entered into, refused, in 1852, to ratify them, and so the areas intended to be reserved for Indian occupancy were never established, nor were the Indians paid for their lands, which were preempted by the federal government.

The eighteen areas that were to have been reserved in perpetuity for Indian occupancy under the treaties amounted to 7,500,000 acres. California citizens and their senators

FIGURE 129 Reservation areas (stippled), proposed in the 1851-52 treaties and supposed land cessions to whites (blank) west of the Sierra Nevada.

argued that California belonged to the Americans by right of conquest and that the proposed reservation areas were too useful and valuable to whites to be allotted to Indians. The Senate, by its act of rejecting the treaties, automatically denied the longheld principle of Indian land tenure and the moral requirement that title to Indian land be extinguished through treaties.

California's Indians became a dispossessed population,

with no rights of citizenship or recourse to the law. In 1850, immediately following the admission of California to the Union, the state legislature enacted the civil and criminal statutes by which the state was to operate. Indians were denied the right to vote and to possess firearms, and were barred from giving testimony against whites. In addition, the legislature passed the Act for the Government and Protection of Indians, which was a thinly disguised legalization of slavery. By this act, which was not repealed until 1863, when Lincoln's Emancipation Proclamation made repeal necessary, any white having possession of an Indian minor could "indenture" that child, a minor male until he was eighteen and a minor female until she was fifteen. In 1860 the age of majority for such indentured servants (some records show that infants as young as two were indentured) was extended for males to twenty-five and for females to twenty-one if they had been indentured before they were fourteen. Indians who were between fourteen and twenty-one years of age could be held until they were thirty (if male) and twenty-five (if female). Numbers (perhaps thousands) of very young children, aged from five to twelve, indentured in Humboldt County were described as "prisoners of war," meaning that they had been collected from native villages attacked by whites and that their parents had been killed in the attacks.

Several generations later, the federal government permitted the Indians of California to sue for compensation for their lost lands, and in 1944 they secured a judgment of $17,053,941 on the basis of $1.25 per acre for the reserved areas that had been promised in the unratified treaties of 1851-1852. From this was deducted $12,029,099, the sum that had been spent by the federal government on Indians after 1850. The amount the Indians actually realized from the suit was $5,024,842. A second claims case was allowed in 1946, from which a judgment of $29,100,000 was secured in 1968. This settlement was based on a calculation of 47 cents an acre for land recognized by the Indian Claims Commission as belonging to the Indians as of March 3, 1853, and later taken from them without payment.

In 1852, immediately after the U.S. Senate refused to ratify the eighteen treaties, a series of reservations was established and operated by the army. These were on lands belonging to the Indians in the first place and now set aside for the Indians' exclusive use. In some cases the Indians were compelled to live on the reservations. The complicated history of lands allotted to Indians since 1852 can be followed in Sutton (1975) and Dale (1949). Frequently the reservations were badly planned and worse managed. Food always seemed to be scarce, Indians were inadequately protected by the soldiers, and federal funds intended for the benefit of the Indians were often diverted to the agents and their cronies.

In about 1880, largely through the reports of special investigators and the books of Helen Hunt Jackson, such as *Ramona*, published in 1884, the public conscience was aroused, and the government was compelled by popular opinion to be more considerate of Indian needs.

The present grand total of Indian Trust Lands in California, mainly reservation areas, amounts to 540,473 acres, which is roughly 0.54 percent of the total area of California (fig. 130). In 1976, according to the State of California Department of Housing and Community Development, there were about 20,200 Indians living on Trust Lands. Most of this land is poor and stony, and much of it is waterless. With a few exceptions, it is land that nobody else ever wanted because it appeared to be useless. On the reservations generally, housing is substandard, sanitation facilities are inadequate, and roads are unimproved. The Trust Lands are a far cry, indeed, from the kind of land the Native Californians once used for their livelihood.

Thirty-three counties in California contain a total of 117 reservations whose size varies from 1 acre (Strawberry Valley, Yuba County) to 87,497 acres (Hoopa Valley Reservations, Humboldt County). Some reservations contain valuable resources, such as farmland (Colorado River Reservation, Riverside County; and Round Valley Reservation, Mendocino County) or timber (Hoopa Valley Reservation and Hoopa Extension; and Tule River Reservation,

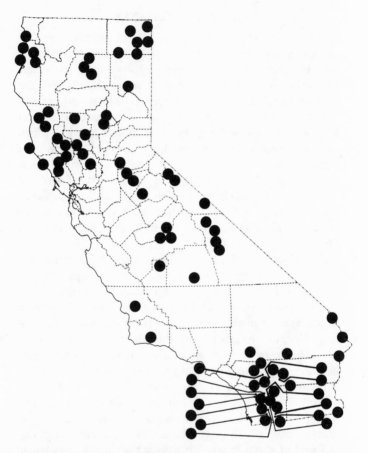

FIGURE 130 Indian Trust Lands in California (540,473 acres = .54 percent of land). Note that circles denote locations only, and are shown much larger, proportionally, than actual size of land represented.

Tulare County). The Palm Springs Cahuilla own some very valuable land from which they secure money from rents and leases.

It can be estimated that about one-half of the American Indians in California are descendants of California Indians; the rest have entered from other states.

CALIFORNIA TODAY

California has been settled by Europeans for over two hundred years, but only since the 1840s has the impact of the whites on the original people, the land and its water, animals, and plants been felt everywhere. Nearly half the land of California is the property of the federal government, most of it about equally divided between the Bureau of Land Management and the U.S. Forest Service, which exercise control over misuse of these lands. The rest of California is subject to few effective controls, with the result that it is rapidly being changed into a product of artificial character. Many of the changes in California's land, plants, and animals since 1850 are permanent and irreversible. All of this has been well documented in R. F. Dasmann's book, *The Destruction of California.*

If the whites and all minorities except the Indians were suddenly to disappear and the erstwhile native people were to possess the state once again, how would they fare? Acorn mush might become once more a standard food; the salmon would again run the rivers (in ever larger numbers as the great Corps of Engineers and Bureau of Reclamation river dams burst from lack of maintenance); the deer would multiply enormously without predators such as the Grizzly Bear and the mountain lion; and there would be amply bearing orchards of introduced fruit ready for the picking. All of this would require a period of relearning for the Indians, not only to forget the habits and devices of "civilization" but also to master once more the ancient knowledge, skills and artifacts of the ancestral people, which have, in little more than a century, been quite lost or forgotten. If the Indians were regranted their patrimony, they might make out rather well.

No person or agency can turn back the clock, but the rush to change environment can surely go too far if it is not accompanied by a view of what future effects may be. The Spanish and the Americans effectively destroyed the hundreds of native societies that lived in the state, just as they hunted the Grizzly Bear and the Timber Wolf out of existence. Most of the state's rivers have been so modified by dams that they are no longer natural streams, but rather captured ones whose flows are controlled for the service of the population. After the total destruction of centuries-old native cultures, elimination of wild species, introduction of new forms, leveling of lands, building of cities, changing of bay shorelines and the like, there must in the end come the point when no more such changes can be made: the environment becomes an artifact that is too complicated to control. If man so alters nature, nature may become a weapon turned against man himself.

APPENDIX 1

PLANTS COMMONLY USED
BY CALIFORNIA INDIANS

Any listing of this kind is an abbreviation; a so-called complete listing would necessarily have to itemize all species used within a given genus and would ideally indicate the locale of the use of the plant. Such locations can be given for a limited number of Indian tribes, since the plant usages of many now extinct or isolated groups were left unrecorded. Some of the plants reported to ethnographers and others have not been identified in modern treatises on botany. Except for a few isolated instances, such as certain fungi, all plants in this summary are described botanically in W.L. Jepson, *A Manual of the Flowering Plants of California* (Berkeley and Los Angeles: University of California Press, 1951 ed.), or P.A. Munz and D.P. Keck, *A California Flora* (Berkeley and Los Angeles: University of California Press, 1968).

In addition to these books the following works were most heavily consulted in the preparation of this Appendix:

Almsted, R.F. Diegueño Curing Practices. San Diego Museum of Man, Paper No. 16. San Diego, 1977.

Balls, E.K. Early Uses of California Plants. California Natural History Guides, No. 10. Berkeley and Los Angeles: University of California Press, 1962.

Barrett, S.A., and E.W. Gifford. Miwok Material Culture. Bulletin of the Milwaukee Public Museum, Vol. 2, No. 4. Milwaukee, 1933. Reprinted by Yosemite Natural History Association, Inc., Yosemite National Park, Calif.

Bean, L.J., and K.S. Saubel. Temalpakh (From the Earth): Cahuilla Indian Knowledge and Usage of Plants. Morongo Indian Reservation, Calif.: Malki Museum Press, 1972.

Chesnut, V.K. Plants Used by the Indians of Mendocino County, California. Contributions of the United States National Herbarium, Vol. 7, No. 3. Washington, D.C., 1902. Reprinted 1974 by Mendocino County Historical Society, Ukiah, Calif.

Gifford, E.W. Ethnographic Notes on the Southwestern Pomo. University of California Anthropological Records, Vol. 25. Berkeley and Los Angeles: University of California Press, 1967.

Kirk, D.R. Wild Edible Plants of the Western United States. Happy Camp, Calif.: Naturegraph Publishers, 1975.

Mead, G.R. The Ethnobotany of the California Indians: A Compendium of the Plants, Their Users, and Their Uses. Occasional Publications in Anthropology, Ethnology Series. Greeley, Colo.: University of Northern Colorado, 1972. Mimeographed; additional volumes forthcoming.

Merrill, Ruth E. Plants Used in Basketry by the California Indians. University of California Publications in American Archaeology and Ethnology, Vol. 20, No. 13. Berkeley and Los Angeles: University of California Press, 1923.

Train, P., J. Henrichs, and W. Archer. Medicinal Uses of Plants by Indian Tribes of Nevada. U.S. Department of Agriculture, Washington, D.C., 1941. Dittoed; includes some plants from the Great Basin in California.

It should be emphasized that the listing below is not to be used as a practical guide to food or medicinal plants. The California Indians were extremely sophisticated in their use of plants and had knowledge and long experience in extracting poisons from food plants like buckeyes or regulating dosages of a number of medicinal plants that contained dangerous toxins. Mere mention of many of the plants thus does not indicate the sometimes elaborate preparatory techniques followed or what parts of the plant were utilized and what rejected.

The list is arranged alphabetically according to genus, followed by common names, where possible, of at least one exemplary species in parentheses. The reader is reminded of the fanciful qualities of such names and will note that several plants of different nature have almost the same common names. Indian uses of the plants are shown in roughly approximate order of importance, and the parts of the plant utilized, when these were reported. In by far the greater number of cases, the native wild species are those used by the Indians before contact with the whites. However, a few heavily used introduced species are included (e.g., Horehound), as well as the three cultivated genera grown in the southeastern part of the state: maize, beans, and squash.

Abies spp. (Fir): Housing (posts, walls), fish spears—wood; meat platters—bark; medicine—bark, needles.

Abronia villosa (Sand Verbena): Medicine—part not reported.

Acacia greggii (Catclaw): Food—pod.

Acer spp. (Maple): Basketry—stems, bark (for rim wrapping); clothing—bark; snowshoe frames, mush paddles—wood; "love medicine"—leaves(?)

Achillea spp. (Common Yarrow): Medicine (tea)—roots, leaves.

Adenostoma fasciculatum (Chamisal, Greasewood): Arrow foreshafts, throwing sticks—wood; food—seeds; medicine—twigs.

Adiantum jordani (Maidenhair Fern): Basketry—stems and outside fibers; for keeping earring holes open and increasing size—stems.

Aesculus californica (California Buckeye): Food—seeds ("nuts"); fish poison—seeds, leaves; arrows, basketry—long shoots; bows, fire drill shafts and hearths—wood.

Agastache urticifolia (Giant Hyssop): Medicine—leaves.

Agave deserti (Desert Agave): Food—"cabbages" and stalks; basketry and cordage—leaf fibers.

Agropyron spp. (Wheat Grass): Food—seeds.

Allenrolfea occidentalis (Iodine Bush): Food—seeds.

Allium spp. (Wild Onion, Wild Garlic): Food—bulbs, seeds, leaves, stalks.

Alnus spp. (Alder): Dye—bark; arrowshafts—shoots; basketry—roots; medicine—leaves, bark.

Amaranthus fimbriatus (Pigweed): Food—seeds, leaves.

Ambrosia artemisifolia (Low Ragweed): Medicine—leaves(?)

Amelanchier spp. (Serviceberry, Sarvisberry): Food—berries; medicine—roots; house thatching, armor—stems; arrowshafts—shoots; basketry— twigs and stems.

Amsinckia menziesii (Fiddleneck): Food—seeds.

Amsonia brevifolia: Cordage—stem(?) fibers.

Anemopsis californica (Yerba Mansa): Medicine—roots.

Angelica spp.: Food—roots, green sprouts; medicine—roots, juice; body "perfume" for hunting—roots.

Antennaria spp. (Cottonweed, Pussytoes): Medicine—blossoms.

Anthemis cotula (Mayweed): Medicine—leaves and flowers.

Apiastrum angustifolium (Wild Celery): Food—stalks.

Apocynum spp. (Wild Hemp, Hemp): Cordage, nets—stems, bark fibers; food—seeds.

Aquilegia spp. (Columbine): Food—seeds; medicine—leaves.

Aralia californica (Elk Clover): Medicine—roots.

Arbutus menziesii (Madrone): Food—berries; medicine—leaves, bark; drinking cups, lodgepoles—wood.

Arceuthobium spp. (Pine Mistletoe): Medicine—leaves, used with pitch of trees.

Arctostaphylos spp. (Manzanita): Food (cider)—berries; bows, housing materials, canes, spoons, mush stirrers, tobacco—wood; medicine—bark, leaves, berries.

Aristolochia californica (Dutchman's Pipe): Medicine—entire plant.

Artemisia spp. (Sagebrush, Mugwort): Food—seeds, shoots; basketry—stems; medicine—bark, leaves, stems; arrowshafts—shoots; granary construction—branches; tattooing (green color)—leaves.

Asarum spp. (Wild Ginger): Medicine—leaves.

Asclepias spp. (Milkweed, Milk Plant): Cordage, nets, aprons—bark, stems; medicine—stalk juice; food (chewing gum)—juice.

Astragalus spp. (Locoweed): Spice—pods.

Atriplex spp. (Salt Bush): Food—seeds; arrow foreshafts—stems.

Avena spp. (Wild Oats): Food—seeds.

Baccharis viminea (Mule Fat): Medicine—leaves; arrow foreshafts—wood.

Balsamorhiza spp. (Balsam Root): Food—seeds, roots; medicine, fumigant—roots.

Berberis spp. (Oregon Grape, Barberry): Dye—roots, bark; food—berries; medicine—roots.

Betula occidentalis (Water Birch): Bows—wood.

Blennosperma nanmum: Food—seeds.

Bloomeria spp. (Golden Stars): Food—bulbs.

Boisduvalia spp. (Dense-Flowered Evening Primrose): Food—bulbs, seeds.

Boletus spp. (Mushroom): Food—stems, heads.

Boschniakia hookeri (Cancer Root): Food—roots.

Boykinia elata: Medicine—roots.

Brassica spp. (Mustard): Food—stems and leaves.

Brodiaea spp. (Grass Nuts, Indian Potato): Food—roots, bulbs; adhesives and paint binders when used on bows—juice.

Bromus spp. (Wild Grass): Food—seeds.

Bursera microphylla (Elephant Tree): Medicine—sap.

Calamagrostis nutkaensis (Reed Grass): Food—seeds.

Calandrinia spp. (Red Maids): Food—seeds, flowers, leaves.

Calocedrus decurrens (Incense Cedar): Slabs for house construction—wood.

Calochortus spp. (Beaver-Tail Grass Nut, Yellow Mariposa Lily): Food—bulbs.

Calycadenia multiglandulosa (Rosin Weed): Medicine—seeds.

Calycanthus occidentalis (Spice Bush, Sweet Shrub): Arrow-shafts—young shoots; basketry—stems, bark; medicine—bark.

Camassia quamash (Camas): Food—bulbs.

Carduus spp. (Thistle): Food—buds.

Carex spp. (Sedge): Basketry—roots, leaves.

Castanopsis chrysophylla (Giant Chinquapin): Food—nuts.

Castilleja spp. (Painted Cup): Food—seeds.

Caucalis microcarpa (California Hedge Parsley): Food, medicine—roots.

Caulanthus crassicaulis (Wild Cabbage): Food—leaves and stems.

Ceanothus spp. (Buckbrush, Wild Lilac): Acorn granaries—stems; mush stirrers, digging sticks—wood; medicine—leaves, bark, roots, twigs; food—berries, seeds; basketry—stems, shoots; fish dams—branches.

Centaurium spp. (Centaury): Medicine—stems, leaves.

Cercidium floridum (Palo Verde): Food—slender beans.

Cercis occidentalis (Redbud): Basketry—bark, sapwood, stems.

Cercocarpus spp. (Mountain Mahogany): Spears, clubs, digging sticks, wedges for plank splitting, house construction, harpoons, bows, stick armor—wood; red dye—bark and roots.

Cereus giganteus (Saguaro): Food—fruit, seeds, flowers.

Chaenactis spp. (Pincushion): Food—seeds; medicine—leaves.

Chamaebatia foliolosa (Mountain Misery): Medicine—leaves.

Chamaecyparis lawsoniana (Port Orford Cedar): Planks, headrests—wood; brooms—branches.

Chenopodium spp. (Goosefoot, Pigweed): Food—seeds, leaves, stems; medicine—leaves; soap—roots.

Chilopsis linearis (Desert Willow): Food—blossoms, seed pods; framing, bows—wood; clothing—bark.

Chimaphila umbellata (Prince's Pine, Pipsissewa): Medicine—leaves.

Chlorogalum pomeridianum (Soaproot): Soap, brushes—roots; food—roots, shoots; basketry—roots, juice (to make baskets seedproof); fish poison, glue—juice; medicine—roots; tattoo paint—green leaves.

Chrysothamnus spp. (Rabbit Brush): Medicine—twigs; food (chewing gum)—roots.

Cinna latifolia (Wood Reedgrass): Basketry—stems.

Cirsium spp. (Thistle, Sunflower): Food—buds, roots, peeled stems, stalks.

Cladium mariscus (Saw Grass): Basketry—roots.

Clarkia amoena (Summer's Darling, Farewell-to-Spring): Food—seeds.

Clematis lasiantha (Clematis, Coyote's Rope, Pipestem): Medicine—stems, bark.

Cneoridium dumosum (Bush Rue): Medicine—part not reported.

Condalia parryi (Crucillo, Wild Plum): Food—fruit (berries).

Convolvulus spp. (Bindweed): Medicine—leaves and stems.

Conyza canadensis (Horseweed): Food—leaves and tops.

Cornus spp. (Dogwood): Bows, arrowshafts—wood; basketry—long shoots; medicine—roots, bark; food—berries.

Corylus cornuta (Hazelnut): Food—nuts; basketry—stems; arrowshafts, frames for snowshoes—wood; fish traps—twigs.

Crepis spp. (Hawksbeard): Food—stems, leaves.

Croton californicus (Croton): Medicine—stems, leaves.

Curcurbita spp. Includes *C. foetidissima* (Calabazillo, Wild Squash) and *C. pepo* (cultivated): Food—seeds, fruit pulp; medicine—roots, fruit; soap—fruit; ladles—gourds; dye—blossoms.

Cynoglossum grande (Hound's Tongue): Food, medicine—roots.

Cyperus erythrorhizos (Umbrella Sedge): Food—seeds.

Dalea spp. (Indigo Bush, Parosela): Dye—stems; medicine—part not reported; food—roots, seeds; basketry—stalks.

Datura meteloides (Jimsonweed): Narcotic—juice of roots, whole plant; medicine—roots.

Daucus spp. (Wild Carrot, Rattlesnake Weed): Food—roots; medicine—roots(?)

Delphinium decorum (Larkspur): Paint (blue) for bows—flowers; food—leaves, flowers.

Descurainia spp. (Pepper Grass, Tansy Mustard): Food—seeds.

Distichlis spicata (Salt Grass): Food (salt)—leaves and stems.

Dodecatheon hendersonii (Shooting Star) Food—roots and leaves.

Dudleya spp. (Hen and Chickens): Food—juice of leaves, leaves themselves.

Echinocactus spp. (Devil's Pincushion): Food—fruit; basketry awls—spines.

Eleocharis spp. (Spike Rush): Food—bulbs.

Elymus spp. (Rye Grass): Food—seeds; arrowshafts—stems; house thatching—entire plant.

Encelia farinosa (Brittlebush): Medicine—blossoms, leaves, stems.

Ephedra spp. (Mormon Tea; Joint Pine): Food—seeds; medicine (tea)—twigs, leaves, blossoms.

Equisetum spp. (Horsetail Rush): Abrasive (e.g., for polishing arrows)—stalks; medicine—stems (pulp).

Eremocarpus setigerus (Turkey Mullein): Fish poison—leaves; medicine—leaves.

Erigeron spp. (Fleabane): Medicine—roots.

Eriodictyon spp. (Yerba Santa): Medicine—leaves, stems, flowers.

Eriogonum sp. (Wild Buckwheat, Sour Grass): Medicine—leaves, stems, roots; food—stems.

Eriophyllum lanatum (Golden Yarrow): Medicine—leaves.

Eschscholzia californica (California Poppy): Food—leaves, flowers; medicine—roots.

Euphorbia spp. (Spurge, Rattlesnake Weed): Medicine—leaves.

Evernia spp. (Wolf Moss): Dye, bedding material, medicine; arrow tip poison(?)—thalli (whole plants) used for all listed purposes.

Fouquieria splendens (Ocotillo): Food—blossoms and fruit.

Fragaria californica (Wild Strawberry): Food—berries.

Fraxinus latifolia (Oregon Ash): Tobacco pipes, canes, harpoon shafts—wood; medicine—roots.

Fremontodendron californicum (Fremontia): Cordage—bark; cradle frames—stems; hoops for games—bark wrapped with buckskin.

Fritillaria spp. (Fritillary): Food—roots.

Fucus spp. (Edible Seaweed): Food—thalli.

Galium triflorum (Sweet Bedstraw): Medicine, including "love medicine"—seeds(?)

Garrya spp. (Bear Brush): Pry bars for mussels—wood; medicine—leaves.

Gaultheria shallon (Salal): Food—berries.

Geranium oreganum (Incised Cranesbill): Medicine—roots.

Gilia spp. (Cushion Gilia): Food—seeds; medicine (tea)—whole plant(?)

Gnaphalium spp. (California Everlasting): Medicine—leaves, flowers; as disguise in hunting deer—whole plant.

Grindelia spp. (Gum Plant): Medicine—whole plant; food—leaves, stems; shampoo—roots.

Gutierrezia microcephala (Matchweed, Snakeweed): Medicine—whole plant(?)

Haplopappus spp. (Tree Haplopappus): Medicine—leaves; food—seeds, stems.

Helenium puberulum (Sneezeweed): Medicine—whole plant.

Helianthella californica: Food—flowers.

Helianthus spp. (Wild Sunflower): Food—seeds; medicine—roots.

Heliotropium curassavicum (Wild Heliotrope): Food—seeds; medicine—roots.

Hemizonia spp. (Spikeweed, Tarweed): Food—seeds.

Heracleum lanatum (Cow Parsnip): Food—shoots, leaves, flowerstalks; dye—leaves; medicine—roots.

Hesperocallis undulata (Desert Lily): Food—bulbs.

Heteromeles arbutifolia (Toyon): Food—berries; medicine—leaves and bark.

Heterotheca grandiflora (Telegraph Weed): Arrowshafts—stems.

Heuchera spp. (Alum Root): Food—leaves.

Hierochloe occidentalis (Vanilla Grass): Medicine—stems(?)

Holocarpha virgata (Tarweed): External medicine—leaves, stems.

Holodiscus discolor (Cream Bush): Food—small fruit; arrowshafts, gambling sticks, armor—stems (twigs).

Hordeum spp. (Wild Barley): Food—seeds.

Hypericum spp. (St. John's Wort): Medicine—whole plant(?); food—bulbs.

Hyptis emoryi (Desert Lavender): Medicine—leaves, blossoms.

Ibicella lutea (Devil's Horns): Basketry—seed pods.

Iris spp. (Wild Iris): Cordage (especially for nets), basketry—leaves; medicine—roots.

Isomeris arborea (Bladder Pod): Food—pods.

Juncus spp. (Rush): Basketry, clothing—leaves, stalks; food—shoots, seeds.

Juniperus spp. (Juniper): Food, beverages—berries; medicine—twigs, branches; basketry—roots; bows—wood; cradle mattresses—bark.

Larrea tridentata (Creosote Bush): Medicine—leaves, stems; body deodorizer—leaves; shampoo—whole plant(?)

Lasthenia chrysostoma (Goldfields): Food-seeds.

Lathryus spp. (Wild Pea): Food—seeds, leaves; medicine—whole plant(?)

Layia platyglossa (Tidytips): Food—seeds.

Lepechinia calycina (Pitcher Sage): Medicine—leaves.

Lepidium spp. (Pepper Grass): Food—seeds, leaves.

Lewisia rediviva (Bitterroot): Food—roots.

Ligusticum spp. (Lovage): Medicine, fish poison—roots; food—leaves.

Lilium pardalinum (Tiger Lily): Food—bulbs, seedlike portions.

Linanthus spp: Medicine—whole plant(?)

Lithocarpus densiflora (Tanbark Oak, Tan Oak): Food—acorns (usually most preferred of California acorns).

Lolium temulentum (Darnel): Food—seeds.

Lomatium spp. (Incense Root, Indian Balsam): Food—shoots, roots, stems, leaves; smoking material, medicine—roots.

Lonicera spp. (California Honeysuckle): Basketry—stems; medicine—leaves.

Lotus spp. (Hill Lotus, Spanish Clover): Medicine—whole plant; food—leaves; thatching for houses—stems(?)

Lupinus spp. (Lupine): Food—leaves, flowers; medicine—whole plant; cordage—roots.

Lycium spp. (Boxthorn): Food—berries.

Lycoperdon spp. (Common Puffball, a fungus): Medicine—spores; food—heads.

Macrocystis spp. (Kelp): Salt, food (for flavor)—thalli; medicine—ashes.

Madia spp. (Tarweed): Food—seeds.

Malva parviflora (Cheeseweed, a native of Eurasia): Medicine—leaves and stems.

Marah spp. (Manroot): Food—"nuts"; fish poison—roots, seeds; red paint—seeds; medicine—roots.

Marrubium vulgare (Horehound, naturalized from Europe): Medicine—leaves, flowering tips.

Matricaria matricarioides (Pineapple Weed): Medicine—leaves and flowers.

Melica bulbosa (Melic Grass): Food—corms.

Mentha spp. (Horse Mint): Medicine (tea)—leaves, stems; perfume—leaves.

Mentzelia spp. (Blazing Star, Buena Mujer): Food, medicine—seeds.

Mesembryanthemum chilense (Sea Fig): Food—fruit.

Mimulus moschatus (Monkey Flower, Musk Plant): Medicine—whole plant; food (salt from ashes)—leaves.

Mirabilis spp. (Four-o'Clock): Medicine—leaves.

Monardella villosa (Coyote Mint): Food, beverage—leaves, stalks, flower heads; medicine (tea)—leaves, upper stems, flowers; perfume—leaves, flowers.

Montia perfoliata (Miner's Lettuce): Food—stems, leaves, blossoms.

Muhlenbergia rigens (Deer Grass): Basketry—stalks.

Nasturtium officiniale (Water Cress, naturalized from Europe): Food, medicine—green tops.

Navarretia cotulaefolia (Potela): Medicine—whole plant(?)

Nicotiana spp. (Tobacco): Smoked, chewed, taken as medicine—leaves.

Nuphar polysepalum (Pond Lily): Food—seeds, roots.

Oenothera clavaeformis (Evening Primrose): Food—leaves.

Olneya tesota (Ironwood): Food—pods, seeds; throwing sticks, clubs—wood.

Opuntia acanthocarpa (Buckhorn Cholla): Food—fruit buds, joints or "pads," stalks, seeds; medicine—fruit.

Orobanche ludoviciana (Broom Rape): Food—roots.

Oryzopsis spp. (Rice Grass, Sand Grass): Food—seeds.

Osmorhiza spp. (Sweet Cicely, Snakeroot): Food—leaves; medicine—roots.

Oxalis oregana (Redwood Sorrel): Medicine—whole plant; charm—part not recorded.

Paeonia brownii (Peony): Medicine—roots, seeds.

Palafoxia linearis (Spanish Needles): Dye—leaves(?)

Panicum urvilleanum (Panic Grass): Food—seeds.

Paxistima myrsinites (Oregon Boxwood): Food—berries.

Pectis papposa (Chinchweed): Flavoring—flowers; dye—leaves(?)

Pedicularis attollens (Little Elephant's-Head): Medicine—leaves.

Pellaea ornithopus (Bird's-Foot Fern): Medicine—whole plant(?)

Peltiphyllum peltatum (Indian Rhubarb): Food—young shoots; medicine—roots.

Penstemon spp. (Small-Flowered Beard Tongue): Medicine—roots, stems, leaves.

Perezia microcephala (Sacapellote): Medicine—leaves(?)

Perideridia gairdneri (Squawroot): Food—roots; medicine—flowers.

Petasites palmatus (Sweet Colt's-Foot): Medicine—roots; food (salt)—stems, leaves.

Phacelia heterophylla (Various-leaved Bluebell): Medicine—whole plant(?)

Phaseolus spp. (cultivated species: Beans): Food—beans.

Philadelphus spp. (Mock Orange, Syringa): Tobacco pipes—wood; arrowshafts—stems.

Phlox longifolia (Wild Phlox): Medicine—roots, stems, leaves.

Phoenicaulis cheiranthoides (Dagger Pod): Medicine—roots.

Phoradendron spp. (Mistletoe): Food—berries; medicine (tea); dye—leaves.

Phragmites communis (Common Reed): House thatching, arrowshafts, flutes—stems; cordage, nets—stem fibers.

Physaria chambersii (Twin Pod): Medicine—leaves, roots.

Physocarpus capitatus (Ninebark): Food—berries; arrowshafts—stems.

Pinus spp. (Pine): Food—seeds ("nuts"); adhesive or sealant—pitch; basketry—needles, roots; house roofing—wood.

Plagiobothrys campestris (Popcorn Flower): Food—shoots, flowers.

Platanus racemosa (Western Sycamore): House construction, bowls—wood.

Platystemon californicus (Creamcups): Food—leaves.

Pluchea sericea (Arrowweed): Food—roots; house construction, granaries, arrowshafts—stems.

Pogogyne parviflora (Pennyroyal): Food—seeds; medicine—leaves; insect repellent—whole plant.

Polygala cornuta (Horned Milkwort): Medicine—whole plant(?)

Polygonum spp. (Knotweed, Smartweed): Food—seeds; medicine—roots.

Polypodium californicum (Polypody): Medicine—roots.

Polyporus spp. (Bracket Fungus): Food—whole plant.

Polystichum munitum (Sword Fern): Lining for acorn-leaching basins—fronds.

Populus spp. (Cottonwood): Implements (including mortars), house posts—wood; medicine—leaves, bark.

Porphyra spp. (Seaweed, Laver): Food (salt)—"fronds."

Postelsia palmaeformis (Sea Palm): Food—stalks.

Proboscidea althaeafolia (Unicorn Plant, Devil's Claw): Basketry—thorns ("claws"); food—seeds.

Prosopis spp. (Honey Mesquite, Screwbean Mesquite, Tornillo): Food—blossoms, pods; mortars, arrowshafts, house posts—wood; baby diapers, clothing, nets—bark; medicine, adhesive—sap.

Prunus spp. ("stone fruits"; Holly-leaved Cherry, Desert Peach, Chokecherry): Food—fruits, kernels; medicine—bark.

Psathyrotes spp. (Turtleback): Medicine—whole plant.

Pseudotsuga menziesii (Douglas Fir): Basketry—wood; medicine, beverage—needles; house planks, harpoon shafts, dipnet poles—wood.

Psoralea macrostachya (Leatherroot): Dye—roots; cordage—bark, roots.

Pteridium aquilinum (Brake, Bracken): Food—shoots; basketry—underground runners.

Purshia tridentata (Antelope Bush): Medicine (tea)—stems and leaves(?)

Pycnanthemum californicum (Mountain Mint): Medicine (tea)—whole plant.

Pyrola asarifolia (Shin Leaf): Medicine—whole plant.

Quercus spp. (Oak): Food—acorns; medicine—ashes, "oak galls" (a fungus); dye—bark; mortars, bowls—wood.

Ranunculus occidentalis (Buttercup): Food—seeds.

Rhamnus spp. (Coffeeberry, Buckthorn): Medicine—berries, bark; food—berries.

Rhus spp. (Sumac, Poison Oak): Basketry—stems; food (also beverages)—berries; medicine (tea)—leaves, roots.

Ribes spp. (Currant, Gooseberry): Food—berries.

Romneya coulteri (Matilija Poppy): Beverage—watery substance (in desert regions).

Rosa spp. (Wild Rose): Food (also beverage)—buds and blossoms; medicine—blossoms.

Rubus spp. (Blackberry, Raspberry, Thimbleberry): Food—berries; medicine—roots(?)

Rumex spp. (Dock, Sorrel): Food—leaves, seeds; medicine—roots; tanning hides—roots.

Sagittaria latifolia (Wappato, Tule): Food—tuber.

Salix spp. (Willow): Basketry—small branches; bows—wood; medicine—leaves.

Salvia spp. (Sage): Food—seeds; medicine—seeds, leaves.

Sambucus spp. (Elderberry): Food—berries; medicine—blossoms, roots; dye—berries, stems; whistles—stems or "twigs."

Sanicula bipinnata (Poison Sanicle): Food—leaves; medicine—roots.

Sarcobatus vermiculatus (Greasewood): Arrow foreshafts—stems; medicine—whole plant (ashes).

Sarcodes sanguinea (Snow Plant): Medicine—stems, leaves(?)

Satureja douglasii (Yerba Buena): Medicine—stems, leaves.

Schoenolirion album: Food—leaves(?)

Scirpus spp. (Bulrush, Tule): Food—roots, seeds; mats, roofing, basketry, balsas (boats)—stalks.

Scrophularia californica (Bee Plant): Medicine—leaves.

Scutellaria spp. (Skullcap): Medicine—leaves, stems(?)

Sequoia sempervirens (Coast Redwood): Boats, house planks, stools—wood.

Sidalcea malvaeflora (Checker): Food—part not reported.

Silene campanulata (Catchfly, Campion): Medicine—part not reported.

Simmondsia chinensis (Goatnut, Jojoba): Food (beverage also)—fruit, seeds.

Sisymbrium irio (London Rocket): Food—leaves.

Sitanion spp. (Squirreltail, Wild Rye): Medicine—whole plant.

Smilacina stellata (False Solomon's Seal): Medicine—roots, leaves.

Smilax californica (Greenbrier): Basketry—"trailing limbs."

Solanum spp. (Nightshade): Medicine—berries (juice).

Solidago californica (California Goldenrod): Food—young leaves; medicine—leaves.

Sphaeralcea munroana (Globe Mallow): Medicine—roots.

Sphenosciadium capitellatum (Ranger's Buttons, Whiteheads): Medicine—roots.

Sporobolus airoides (Alkali Sacaton, Dropseed): Food—seeds.

Stanleya pinnata (Prince's Plume): Medicine—roots.

Suaeda spp. (Sea Blite, Seepweed): Food—seeds, leaves; dye—leaves; soap—part not reported.

Symphoricarpos spp. (Snowberry): Medicine—roots.

Taraxacum californicum (Dandelion): Food—stems, leaves.

Taxus brevifolia (Western Yew): Bows, tobacco pipes—wood; medicine—bark; food—berries.

Tetradymia canescens (Horsebrush): Medicine—stems, leaves.

Thalictrum fendleri (Meadow Rue): Medicine—roots, stems, leaves.

Thamnosma montana (Turpentine Broom): Medicine—stems.

Thermopsis macrophylla (False Lupine): Medicine—leaves.

Therofron elatum: Medicine—roots.

Thysanocarpus curvipes (Lacepod): Food, medicine—seeds.

Torreya californica (California Nutmeg): Food—nuts; basketry—roots.

Trichostema spp. (Blue Curls, Camphorweed): Medicine—leaves, flowers; flea repellent, fish poison—whole plant.

Trifolium spp. (Clover): Food—leaves, seeds.

Trillium chloropetalum (Wake Robin): Medicine—leaves, roots.

Typha latifolia (Common Cattail, Soft Flag): Food—roots, pollen; medicine—roots; bedding material, house construction material—stalks.

Umbellularia californica (California Bay, California Laurel): Food—berries; medicine—leaves.

Urtica spp. (Nettle): Food—leaves; basketry, medicine, cordage, bowstrings—stems.

Usnea spp. (Lichen, Spanish Moss): Bedding material, diapers for babies—thalli.

Vaccinium ovatum (Huckleberry, Blueberry): Food—berries.

Veratrum californicum (False Hellebore, Skunk Cabbage): Contraceptive, medicine—roots.

Verbena hastata (Verbena, Verrain): Food—seeds.

Vicia americana (Vetch, Tare): Food—stems, leaves; tying materials—roots.

Vitis californica (Wild Grape): Food—fruit; withes—vines.

Washingtonia filifera (California Fan Palm): Food—fruit, pith, young leaf base; housing material—fronds; basketry, sandals—leaves; bows—stems; kindling—fruit stems.

Woodwardia radicans (Chain Fern): Basketry—stems.

Wyethia glabra (Mule Ears): Medicine—roots, leaves; food—leaves, stems, seeds.

Xerophyllum tenax (Bear Grass): Food—roots; basketry, cordage—stems, leaves.

Yucca spp. (Spanish Bayonet, Yucca): Food—flower stalks, blossoms, fruit pods; soap—roots; cordage, bowstrings, netting, brushes, basketry, sandals—leaves; dye—rootlets.

Zauschneria californica (California Fuchsia): Medicine—leaves.

Zea mays (Indian corn, cultivated species): Food—kernels.

Zigadenus venenosus (Death Camas, Zygadene): Medicine (external)—bulbs.

APPENDIX 2

MUSEUMS, LIBRARIES, AND OTHER PLACES IN CALIFORNIA WITH COLLECTIONS OR DISPLAYS ON CALIFORNIA INDIANS

There are more than one hundred museums in the state that are open to the public and devoted, either in part or entirely, to depictions of Indian life. The museums are arranged below in alphabetical order, by town in or near which they are located. Many of these are represented by a diversity of archaeological specimens, consisting of such things as stone mortars or arrowpoints excavated by farmers or amateurs. Some have excellent collections of locally made Indian baskets; Indian relics in smaller museums are usually presented in connection with local white history. The institutions marked with an asterisk have large collections of Indian artifacts or books on Indians and occasional or permanent exhibits of portions of these materials.

Amador City: Gold Rush Museum
Avalon, Catalina Island: Catalina Island Museum Society
*Bakersfield: Kern County Museum
*Banning: Malki Museum, Morongo Indian Reservation
Berkeley, University of California
  *Bancroft Library
  *R.H. Lowie Museum of Anthropology
Blairsden: Plumas-Eureka State Park
Carmel: Carmel Mission
Carpinteria: Carpinteria Valley Historical Society
Cathedral City: Museum of Antiquities and Art
Columbia: Columbia State Historic Park
Death Valley: Death Valley National Monument Museum
Desert Hot Springs: Landmark Conservators
El Centro: Imperial Valley College Museum
El Monte: El Monte Historical Museum
Essex: Mitchell's Caverns State Reserve
Eureka: Clarke Memorial Museum
  Indian Action Library
Fall River Mills: Fort Crook Historical Museum
Fort Jones: Fort Jones Museum

Fremont: Coyote Hills (East Bay) Regional Park: Archaeological site (appointment only)

Fresno: Fresno Museum of Natural History and Junior Museum

*Highland Park: Southwest Museum

Independence: Eastern California Museum

Jackson: Amador County Museum
    Amador—Livermore Valley Historical Society Museum

Jolon: San Antonio Mission

Julian: Cuyamaca Rancho State Park Museum

Lakeport: Lake County Museum

La Puente: La Puente Valley Historical Society

Lodi: San Joaquin County Historical Museum

Lompoc: La Purisima Mission State Historic Park
    Lompoc Museum

Long Beach: La Casa de Rancho Los Cerritos

Los Angeles: Lummis Home, El Alisal
    *Natural History Museum of Los Angeles County

Los Banos: Ralph LeRoy Milliken Museum
    Bureau of Reclamation (San Luis Dam Site): Interpretive exhibit

Los Gatos: Los Gatos Museum

Madera: Madera County Historical Society

Mariposa: Mariposa County Historical Society

Mineral: Loomis Museum, Lassen Volcanic National Park

Mission Hills: San Fernando Valley Historical Society

Monterey: Monterey State Historic Park (Pacific Bldg.)
    Presidio of Monterey Museum

Morro Bay: Morro Bay State Park Museum of Natural History

Murphys: Old Timers' Museum

National City: Museum of American Treasures

New Almaden: New Almaden Museum

Newhall: William S. Hart County Park

Novato: Novato Prehistory Museum

*Oakland: Oakland Museum

Oceanside: San Luis Rey Historical Society

Orick: Patrick's Point State Park Museum

Oroville: Lake Oroville State Recreational Area (Kelley Ridge Visitor Center)

Pacifica: Sanchez Adobe

Pacific Grove: Pacific Grove Museum of Natural History

Pacific Palisades: Will Rogers State Historic Park

*Palm Springs: Palm Springs Desert Museum

Palo Alto: Palo Alto Junior Museum

Placerville: El Dorado County Historical Society Museum
Pomona: Adobe de Palomares
Porterville: Porterville Museum
Quincy: Plumas County Museum
Randsburg: Desert Museum
Red Bluff: Kelly-Griggs House Museum
Redding: Redding Museum and Art Center
    Shasta College Museum and Research Center
Redlands: Asistencia de San Gabriel
    San Bernardino County Museum
Ridgecrest: Maturango Museum of Indian Wells Valley
Riverside: Jurupa Mountains Cultural Center
    Riverside Municipal Museum
Rosamond: Kern-Antelope Historical Society Museum
*Sacramento: California State Indian Museum
San Andreas: Calaveras County Historical Museum
San Diego: Mission San Diego de Alcalá
    San Diego Historical Society
    *San Diego Museum of Man
San Francisco: California Academy of Sciences
    *California Historical Society
    Fine Arts Museums of San Francisco (DeYoung Museum)
    Josephine D. Randall Junior Museum
San Gabriel: San Gabriel Mission Museum
San Jacinto: San Jacinto Museum
San Juan Bautista: Old Mission San Juan Bautista
San Luis Obispo: Mission San Luis de Tolosa
    San Luis Obispo County Historical Museum
*San Marino: Huntington Library
San Mateo: San Mateo County Historical Association
San Miguel: Mission San Miguel
San Rafael: Marin Museum of Natural Science
Santa Ana: Charles W. Bowers Memorial Museum
*Santa Barbara: Santa Barbara Museum of Natural History
    University Art Galleries, University of California
Santa Cruz: Santa Cruz Museum
Santa Maria: Santa Maria Valley Historical Society
Santa Rosa: Jesse Peters Memorial Museum
Shasta: Shasta State Historic Park
Sonoma: Sonoma Valley Historical Society
Stanford: Stanford University Museum and Art Gallery
Stockton: Pioneer Museum and Haggin Galleries
Thousand Oaks: Stagecoach Inn Museum

Three Rivers: Sequoia and Kings Canyon National Parks
(Museum and Visitor Center)
Truckee: Donner State Park Museum
Tule Lake: Lava Beds National Monument
Ukiah: Held-Poage Memorial Home and Research Library
Upland: Chaffey Communities Cultural Center
Ventura: San Buenaventura Mission Museum
    Ventura County Historical Museum
Visalia: Tulare County Museum
Volcano: Indian Grinding Rock State Historical Monument
Walnut Creek: Alexander Lindsay Junior Museum
Weaverville: J.J. Jackson Memorial Museum
Williams: Sacramento Valley Museum Association
Willits: Mendocino County Museum
Yosemite: Yosemite National Park Museum
Yreka: Siskiyou County Museum
Yucaipa: Mousley Museum of Natural History
Yucca Valley: Hi Desert Nature Museum

APPENDIX 3

Pronunciation of California Indian Tribal Names

Linguistic stock names:

Algonkian	Al-gon'-kee-an
Athabascan	Ath-a-bas'-can
Hokan	Ho'-kan
Penutian	Pee-noo'-shee-an
Uto-Aztekan	Yoo'-to-Az-take'-an

Tribal names:

Achomawi	Ah-cho-mah'wee
Alliklik	Al-lik'-lik
Atsugewi	At-su-gay'-wee
Cahuilla	Kah-wee'-yah
Chemehuevi	Chem-eh-way'-vee
Chilula	Chil-lu'-lah
Chimariko	Chih-mair'-ih-ko
Chumash	Choo'-mash
Costanoan	Cost'-an-no'-an
Cupeño	Coo-pay'-nyo
Diegueño	Dee-eh-gay'-nyo
Esselen	Ess'-sel-len
Fernandeño	Fer-nen-day'-nyo
Gabrielino	Gab-ree-al-ee'-no
Halchidhoma	Hal-chid'-do-mah
Huchnom	Hooch'-nome
Hupa	Hoo'-pah
Juaneño	Wahn-ayn'-nyo
Kamia	Kah'-mee-ya
Karok	Kah'-rock
Kato	Kah'-to
Kaweah	Kah-wee'-yah
Kawaiisu	Kah-wy'-ih-soo
Kitanemuk	Kih-tan'-nee-muk
Konomihu	Ko-no'-mee-hoo
Koso	Ko'-so
Lassik	Las'-sik
Luiseño	Loo-is-ay'-nyo
Maidu	My'-doo

Mattole	Mat-toal'
Miwok	Mee'-wock
Modoc	Mo'-dock
Mohave	Mo-hah'-vee
Monache	Mo-nah-chee
Nomlaki	Noam'-lah-kee
Nongatl	Non'-gatl
Okwanuchu	Oke-wah-noo'-choo
Paiute	Pie-yoot'
Patwin	Pat'-win
Pomo	Po'-mo
Salinan	Sal-leen'-nan
Serrano	Ser-rah'-no
Shasta	Shas'-ta
Sinkyone	Sink'-yoan
Tolowa	Toe'-lo-wah
Tübatulabal	Too-bah'-too-lah'-bal
Vanyume	Van-yoo'-mee
Wailaki	Wy'-lak-kee
Wappo	Wahp'-po
Washo	Wah'-sho
Whilkut	Whil'-koot
Wintun	Win-toon'
Wiyot	Wee'-yot
Yahi	Yah'-hee
Yana	Yah'-nah
Yokuts	Yo'-koots
Yuki	Yoo'-kee
Yuma	Yoo'-mah
Yurok	Yur'-ock

SELECTED REFERENCES

There is a voluminous literature dealing with California Indians. Two bibliographical compilations will be helpful in providing references to particular tribes and subjects. These are:

Murdock, G.P., and T.J. O'Leary. Ethnographic Bibliography of North America, Vol. 1, pp. 87-105; Vol. 3, pp. 93-172. New Haven, Conn.: Human Relations Area Files Press, 1975.

Heizer, R.F., and A.B. Elsasser. A Bibliography of California Indians. New York: Garland Publishing Co., 1977.

The scientific anthropological series publication of the University of California is titled University of California Publications in American Archaeology and Ethnology. It was published from 1903 (Vol. 1, No. 1) to 1964 (Vol. 50), and is available in many larger libraries. Contained in this series are scores of general monographs on individual California Indian tribes, on mythology, material culture, and linguistics. An easy way to discover whether information of special interest is in this series is to consult the Author and Title Index to the University of California Publications in American Archaeology and Ethnology, Volumes 1-50, 1903-1964, published in the Contributions of the Archaeological Research Facility, No. 32, Berkeley, Calif.: University of California, Department of Anthropology.

Selected references for chapter topics in the present book are listed below; at the end are two groups of selections that relate to several chapters.

Chapter 1

Heizer, R.F., Languages, Territories, and Names of California Indian Tribes. Berkeley and Los Angeles: University of California Press, 1966.

Heizer, R.F., and C. Treanor. Observations on Physical Strength of Some Western Indians and "Old American" Whites. Contributions of the University of California Archaeological Research Facility, No. 22, pp. 47-57. Berkeley: University of California, Department of Anthropology, 1974.

Heizer, R.F., ed. California. Handbook of North American Indians, Vol. 8. Washington, D.C.: Smithsonian Institution, 1978.

Heizer, R.F., and T.K. Whipple, eds. The California Indians: A Source Book. Berkeley and Los Angeles: University of California Press, 1971.

Kroeber, A.L. Handbook of the Indians of California. Bureau of American Ethnology, Bulletin 78. Washington, D.C.: Smithsonian Institution, 1925. Later reprintings.

Powers, S. Tribes of California, 1877. Reprinted 1976 by University of California Press, Berkeley and Los Angeles.

Chapter 2

Kroeber, A.L. Cultural and Natural Areas of Native North America. Berkeley: University of California Press, 1939.

Kroeber, A.L. Culture Element Distributions: III, Area and Climax. University of California Publications in American Archaeology and Ethnology, Vol. 37, pp. 101-116, 1936.

Chapter 3

Beals, R.L., and J. Hester. A New Ecological Typology of the California Indians. In Man and Cultures, ed. A. Wallace. Philadelphia, 1960. Reprinted 1971 in Heizer and Whipple (see chapter 1 entries above).

Durrenberger, R.W. Patterns on the Land. Palo Alto: National Press, 1972.

Hartman, David N. California and Man. Dubuque, Iowa, 1968.

Lewis, H.T. Patterns of Indian Burning in California: Ecology and Ethnohistory. Ballena Press Anthropological Papers, No. 1, pp. 1-101. Ramona, Calif.: Ballena Press, 1973.

Chapter 4

Barbour, M.G., and J. Major. Terrestrial Vegetation of California. New York: John Wiley, 1977.

Baumhoff, M.A. Ecological Determinants of Aboriginal California Populations. University of California Publications in American Archaeology and Ethnology, Vol. 49, No. 2, 1963.

Castetter, E.F., and W.H. Bell. Yuman Indian Agriculture. Albuquerque: University of New Mexico Press, 1951.

Fitch, J.E., and R.J. Lavenberg. Marine Food and Game Fishes of California. California Natural History Guides, No. 28. Berkeley and Los Angeles: University of California Press, 1971.

Grinnell, J., J.S. Dixon, and J.M. Linsdale. Fur-Bearing Mammals of California. 2 vols. Berkeley: University of California Press, 1937.

Mayer, P.J. Miwok Balanophagy: Implications for the Cultural Development of California Acorn Eaters. University of California Archaeological Research Facility, nonserial publication. Berkeley, University of California, Department of Anthropology, 1976.

Merriam, C.H. The Acorn, a Possibly Neglected Source of Food. National Geographic Magazine, Vol. 34, pp. 129-137, 1918.

Ornduff, R. Introduction to California Plant Life. California Natural History Guides, No. 35. Berkeley and Los Angeles: University of California Press, 1974.

White, R.C. Luiseño Social Organization. University of California Publications in American Archaeology and Ethnology, Vol. 48, No. 2, 1963.

Wolf, C.B. California Wild Tree Crops. Claremont, Calif.: Rancho Santa Ana Botanic Garden, 1945.

Chapter 5

Barrett, S.A. Pomo Indian Basketry. University of California Publications in American Archaeology and Ethnology, Vol. 7, No. 3, 1908.

Barrett, S.A. Material Aspects of Pomo Culture. Bulletin of the Public Museum of the City of Milwaukee, Vol. 29, Parts I and II, 1952.

Barrett, S.A., and E.W. Gifford. Miwok Material Culture. Bulletin of the Public Museum of the City of Milwaukee, Vol. 2, No. 4, 1933. Recently reprinted by the Yosemite Natural History Association.

Kroeber, A.L. Basket Designs of the Mission Indians. Ramona, Calif.: Ballena Press, 1973.

Pope, S.T. Yahi Archery. University of California Publications in American Archaeology and Ethnology, Vol. 13, No. 3, 1918.

Rogers, M.J. Yuman Pottery Making. San Diego Museum Papers, No. 2, San Diego, Calif.: San Diego Museum of Man, 1936.

Chapter 6

Balls, E.K. Early Uses of California Plants. California Natural History Guides, No. 10. Berkeley and Los Angeles: University of California Press, 1975.

Heizer, R.F., and A.E. Treganza. Mines and Quarries of the Indians of California. Ramona, Calif.: Ballena Press, 1972.

Merrill, R.E. Plants Used in Basketry by the California Indians. University of California Publications in American Archaeology and Ethnology, Vol. 20, pp. 215-242, 1923.

Chapter 7

Heizer, R.F., ed. California. Handbook of North American Indians, Vol. 8. Washington, D.C.: Smithsonian Institution, 1978. (Articles by A.B. Elsasser, C. King, and W. Wallace on California archaeology.)

Chapter 8

Grant, C. The Rock Paintings of the Chumash. Berkeley and Los Angeles: University of California Press, 1965.

Grant, C., J.W. Baird, and J.K. Pringle. Rock Drawings of the Coso Range, Inyo County. Maturango Museum Publications, No. 4. China Lake, Calif.: Maturango Museum, 1968.

Heizer, R.F., and C.W. Clewlow. Prehistoric Rock Art of California. 2 vols. Ramona, Calif.: Ballena Press, 1973.

Chapter 9

Demetrocopoulou [Lee], D. Wintu Songs, Anthropos, Vol. 30, pp. 383-394, 1935.

Densmore, F. Music of the Maidu. Los Angeles: Southwest Museum, 1958.

Gifford, E.W., and G. Block. California Indian Nights Entertainment. Glendale, Calif.: A.H. Clark, 1930. (Myths.)

Kroeber, A.L. Yurok Myths. Berkeley and Los Angeles: University of California Press, 1976.

Lee, D. Demetrocopoulou. Linguistic Reflection of Wintu Thought. International Journal of American Linguistics, Vol. 10, pp. 181-187, 1944.

Chapter 10

Cook, S.F. The Conflict Between the California Indians and White Civilization. Berkeley and Los Angeles: University of California Press, 1976.

Cook, S.F. The Population of the California Indians, 1769-1970. Berkeley and Los Angeles: University of California Press, 1976.

Dasmann, R.F. The Destruction of California. New York: Macmillan, 1965.

Dillon, R. Burnt-Out Fires: California's Modoc Indian War. Englewood Cliffs, N.J.: Prentice-Hall, 1973.

Heizer, R.F., and A.J. Almquist. The Other Californians: Prejudice and Discrimination under Spain, Mexico, and the United States to 1920. Berkeley and Los Angeles: University of California Press, 1977.

Kroeber, T., A.B. Elsasser, and R.F. Heizer. Drawn from Life: California Indians in Pen and Brush. Ramona, Calif.: Ballena Press, 1977.

FOR FURTHER READING
Ecological Studies of California Indians

Baumhoff, M.A. Ecological Determinants of Aboriginal California Populations. University of California Publications in American Archaeology and Ethnology, Vol. 49, pp. 155-236, 1963.

California. Berkeley and Los Angeles: University of California Press, 1974.

Coombs, G., and F. Plog. The Conversion of the Chumash Indians: An Ecological Interpretation. Human Ecology, Vol. 5, pp. 309-328, 1977.

Gayton, A.H. Culture-Environment Integration: References in Yokuts Life. Southwestern Journal of Anthropology, Vol. 2, pp. 252-268, 1946.

Gould, R.A. Ecology and Adaptive Response Among the Tolowa Indians of Northwestern California. Journal of California Anthropology, Vol. 2, pp. 148-170, 1975.

Hicks, F. Ecological Aspects of Aboriginal Culture in the Western Yuma Area. Unpublished Ph.D. dissertation, University of California, Los Angeles.

Jones, S. Some Regional Aspects of Native California. Scottish Geographical Magazine, Vol. 67, pp. 19-30, 1951. Reprinted 1971 in Heizer and Whipple (see chapter 1 entries above).

Kniffen, F.B. Achomawi Geography. University of California Publications in American Archaeology and Ethnology, Vol. 23, pp. 297-332, 1928.

Kniffen, F.B. Pomo Geography. University of California Publications in American Archaeology and Ethnology, Vol. 36, pp. 353-400, 1939.

Meighan, C.W. The Little Harbor Site, Catalina Island: An Example of Ecological Interpretation in Archaeology. American Antiquity, Vol. 24, pp. 383-405, 1959.

Meighan, C.W., et al. Ecological Interpretation in Archaeology. American Antiquity, Vol. 24, pp. 1-23, 131-150, 1958.

Merriam, C.H. Distribution of Indian Tribes in the Southern Sierra and Adjacent Parts of the San Joaquin Valley, California. Science, Vol. 19, pp. 912-917, 1904.

Stewart, O.C. Notes on Pomo Ethnogeography. University of California Publications in American Archaeology and Ethnology, Vol. 40, pp. 29-62, 1943.

Swezey, S. The Energetics of Subsistence: Assurance Ritual in Native California. Contributions of the University of California Archaeological Research Facility, No. 3, pp. 1-46. Berkeley: University of California, Department of Anthropology.

Swezey, S., and R.F. Heizer. Ritual Management of Fish Resources in California. Journal of California Anthropology, Vol. 4, pp. 6-29, 1977.

Warren, C.N. Cultural Tradition and Ecological Adaptation on the Southern California Coast. *In* Archaic Prehistory in the Western United States, ed. C. Irwin-Williams, Portales, N.M.: Eastern New Mexico University, Paleo-Indian Institute, 1968.

The California Indians in Continental Perspective

Dale, E.E. The Indians of the Southwest: A Century of Development Under the United States. Norman, Okla.: University of Oklahoma Press, 1949.

Hallowell, A. The Impact of the American Indian on American Culture. *In* Contributions to Anthropology: Selected Papers of A. Irving Hallowell. Chicago: University of Chicago Press, 1976.

Jennings, J.D. Prehistory of North America, 2nd ed. New York: McGraw-Hill, 1974.

Sutton, I. Indian Land Tenure: Bibliographical Essays and a Guide to the Literature. New York: Clearwater Publishing, 1975.

Washburn, W.E. Red Man's Land/White Man's Law: A Study of the Past and Present Status of the American Indians. New York: Scribners, 1971.

Index

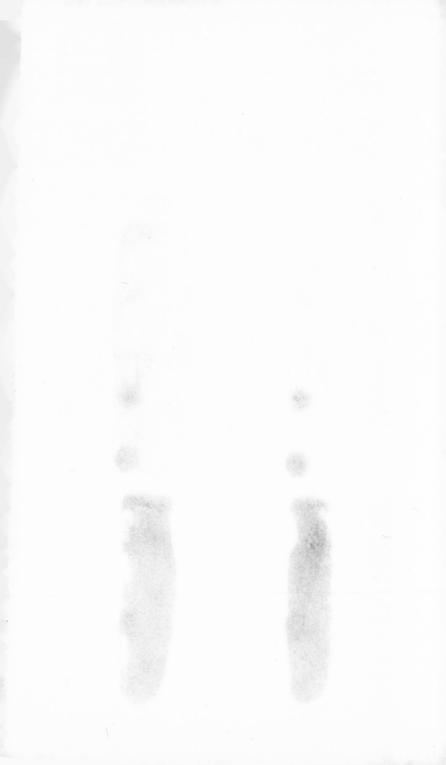